The
WINGMEN

The
WINGMEN

The Unlikely, Unusual,
Unbreakable Friendship Between
JOHN GLENN and
TED WILLIAMS

Adam Lazarus

CITADEL PRESS
Kensington Publishing Corp.
www.kensingtonbooks.com

CITADEL PRESS BOOKS are published by

Kensington Publishing Corp.
119 West 40th Street
New York, NY 10018

All Kensington titles, imprints, and distributed lines are available at special quantity discounts for bulk purchases for sales promotions, premiums, fund-raising, educational, or institutional use. Special book excerpts or customized printings can also be created to fit specific needs. For details, write or phone the office of the Kensington sales manager: Kensington Publishing Corp., 119 West 40th Street, New York, NY 10018, attn: Sales Department; phone 1-800-221-2647.

CITADEL PRESS and the Citadel logo are Reg. U.S. Pat. & TM Off.

ISBN: 978-0-8065-4250-8
First Hardcover Edition: September 2023

10 9 8 7 6 5 4 3 2

Printed in the United States of America

Library of Congress Control Number: 2023936121

First electronic edition: September 2023
ISBN: 978-0-8065-4252-2 (ebook)

For Lieutenant Commander Leonard P. Siegelman,
USNR (1916–2001),

Technical Sergeant Arnold H. Lazarus,
USA (1921–2013),

Staff Sergeant Darrell H. "Buddy" Lazarus,
USA (1924–2017),

and all those who have served this country.

And for Hannah, who was my Slugger.

wingman noun

wing·man | \ ˈwiŋ-mən

a : a pilot who flies behind and outside the leader of a flying formation

b *informal* : a male friend or partner who accompanies and supports a man in some activity

—*Merriam-Webster Dictionary*

"Fighter formation flying takes its basis in the rule that the wingman under all circumstances sticks with his section leader. The large squadron formation may break down to flights, divisions, and sections in combat, but the section is never broken up. The wingman's first and primary duty ahead of everything else is to stick with his section leader."

—*First Lieutenant J. H. Glenn, Jr.,*
Marine Fighting Squadron 218
Squadron Doctrine, Circa 1948

Author's Note

"The word is particularly objectionable to Koreans. They don't like it. So don't acquire a bad habit that can do more harm than all our good intentions could ever accomplish. Treat the Korean as you would your neighbor back home and you will find that courtesy and respect for the other fellow has its compensations in Korea as it does in Kalamazoo."

—*Armed Forces Pocket Guide: Korea,*
September 1, 1950

A few of the quotations in this book include deeply offensive words relative to the United States of America's enemies during both World War II and the Korean War. I have chosen to utilize the complete quotations—some spoken directly to me during the course of interviews, others from published memoirs, newspaper accounts, or other archives—and not alter the terminology. Exact citations of these quotations are available, along with every quotation appearing in this book, beginning on page 241.

I fully denounce these types of racial slurs, but as an author and historian I believe it is important to preserve the language as it was stated. For whatever reasons—ignorance, fear, malice, or just an attempt to isolate and dehumanize their enemies—some soldiers, sailors, and pilots from this time period employed these words. As did many citizens back home in the United States. I do not condone their use or make excuses for the people who said them, but I also will not pretend such racism and hate speech did not exist.

To anyone offended by the very sight of these words, I apologize and hope you will understand my reasoning. And to all readers of this book, it is my hope that you will agree that while such language may have been accepted in 1953 it should not be in 2023.

—Adam Lazarus

Contents

The
WINGMEN

Prologue

Robert Francis "Bob" Conley was a big man on campus at Muskingum College in 1940. The previous fall, as a five-foot, ten-inch, 171-pound right guard, the junior from East Lansing, Michigan, helped power the Fighting Muskies football team to their first Ohio Athletic Conference championship in eight years. Behind Conley and left tackle Dave Evans, the offense averaged 177 rushing yards on their way to an 8-1 record. At the end of a season that included a 55-0 drubbing of rival Heidelberg in the finale of their conference schedule, the *East Liverpool Review* declared the Muskies the "greatest team in 25 years."

Not long after the football season concluded, Conley was voted president of the Stag Club, his fraternity at the New Concord, Ohio, school. So, between weekly fraternity meetings, his studies as an Economics major, the football season—he also kicked the team's extra points— and seeing his sweetheart, sophomore Jane Reed, Conley was very busy during his senior year.

Still, the good-looking upperclassman with dark wavy hair made time to mentor younger classmates, including a fellow offensive lineman and recent Stag Club pledge, sophomore John Glenn. Glenn joined the fraternity as a freshman, but he wasn't a gung-ho member. He felt that initiations "got a little out of line once in a while." At the end of Hell Week the active members blindfolded the pledges, loaded them up in a car, then dropped them off in the middle of nowhere. On a rural campus, that made for a considerable test, but not for Glenn, who had grown up less than two miles down the road.

"I didn't have to peek to know exactly where we were going," he remembered. "When we went across what bridge or whatever, I just knew by the sound where I was, and I think I almost beat them back to town after they had let us out."

Football didn't come as easily for Glenn. He was not in love with the game—he liked basketball more—and failed to earn a varsity letter his first two years at Muskingum. And unlike most of his teammates, he didn't grow or increase his speed following high school. But he learned enough practicing next to the Muskies' star right guard to remain on the team. Glenn would even later succeed Conley as the team's place kicker.

"I enjoyed it," Glenn said about his college football career, "but it wasn't something that I was really that good at either."

Bob Conley, however, was really good. He earned an Honorable Mention All-Conference selection in 1940.

As Conley's playing days came to a close in November, he looked forward to starting a career in business following graduation in early June. But that spring, Conley, Jane, and a group of friends drove north to his home state of Michigan. During a visit to the naval air station in Gross Ile Conley fell in love with airplanes. Right after graduation he returned to Gross Ile, signed up for the naval aviation cadet program, and reported to the naval air station at Corpus Christi, Texas. The brand-new base had yet to receive a single aircraft for training. While new cadets sent to the naval air station in Pensacola, Florida flew right away, Conley spent five months at Corpus Christi picking up cigarette butts on the runway.

Eventually he was airborne. He took his first flight on December 1, 1941, six days before the Japanese bombed Pearl Harbor. Mostly flying a Boeing-Stearman N2S-2 biplane, Conley earned his wings the following spring as a second lieutenant in the United States Marine Corps Reserves. After marrying Jane back in her home state of Pennsylvania, Conley was posted to the naval air station in San Diego, California. By October he had received orders to the South Pacific. From a jeep carrier stationed off the island of New Caledonia, Conley's catapult-launched observation floatplane sprung up in the air then made a perilous landing on a makeshift metal strip at Henderson Field on the island of Guadalcanal. A crew chief popped open the cockpit and shouted, "Welcome to the War!"

Conley served as operations officer for Marine Scout Bomber Squadron-142, a newly formed unit tasked with fending off Japanese naval efforts to retake the island. In rainy, misty, and darkening conditions on the evening of December 3, Conley piloted his SBD Dauntless above Japanese sea vessels, all the while avoiding anti-aircraft fire. He dropped a thousand-pound bomb on the starboard-side of a destroyer, which eventually sank.

Two weeks later, again in nasty weather and limited sunlight, Conley dropped ordnance that demolished an enemy gas dump at Rekata Bay, dealing a significant blow to Japanese vessels throughout the region. For his "daring, skill, and fearless devotion to duty," Conley later received the Distinguished Flying Cross. By the end of the week, he had participated in another major raid, this time at Munda Point. During that mission he was separated from the squadron and suddenly found three Mitsubishi A6M long-range fighters ("Zeros") firing at his tail.

"About then my gunner shot one and the Jap peeled off," he wrote home. "Seconds later he sent another one down in flames. But the third Zero kept making runs as us. Finally, I dodged into some clouds and shook him off."

Conley received a transfer to the First Marine Aircraft Wing (MAW) with Strike Command in February 1943. He also received considerable medical attention: three times he caught malaria, another constant threat to those fighting in the Pacific. Following a brief stopover in the United States—during which time he both trained new pilots at El Toro Marine Air Station in Santa Ana, California, and met his infant son, Robert Jr.—Conley rejoined the fighting as a member of Marine Aircraft Group-14 based in Okinawa. Throughout the summer of 1945 Conley's squadron prepared to invade Japan, which refused to surrender despite Germany having done so several months earlier. Finally, once the United States had deployed nuclear bombs over Hiroshima and Nagasaki, the Empire of Japan formally surrendered to the Allies, bringing peace to the Pacific theater. But not for long.

After the Korean People's Army in the Communist north—backed by Communist leaders Joseph Stalin of the Soviet Union and Mao Zedong of China—invaded the south, the United States entered that conflict on June 25, 1950.

"We are not at war," President Harry S. Truman told the press four days later, while also confirming a reporter's assessment that the United States was merely participating in a "United Nations police action."

By late November 1951 more than 740,000 Americans had been asked to serve in a coalition of United Nations forces. At the same time, UN and Communist negotiators agreed to a thirty-day cease fire and set a December 27 deadline for an armistice agreement. But weeks of peace talks beneath snow-covered, olive-drab "truce tents" in Panmunjom broke down over several issues, including the exchange of prisoners of war and the north's desire to continue building airfields throughout the cease fire.

Statistics released by the Department of Defense that month revealed more than 100,000 casualties to Americans during the eighteen months of war. The Marine Corps alone suffered 16,490, including 2,260 deaths.

Now a career Marine promoted to major in early 1948, Bob Conley awaited orders. Although promised eventual command of his own fighter squadron, Conley was first assigned to an exceedingly dull yet critical administrative role: assistant head of the Aviation Control Unit within the Personnel Department at Marine Corps Headquarters in Quantico, Virginia.

At the outset of the fighting in Korea, Congress approved the Selective Service Extension Act, authorizing the commander in chief to recall any military reservist regardless of desire to serve. One year later, Congress passed further legislation. The Universal Military Training and Services Act required that tours of duty be limited to a predetermined length. Each branch of the military set different parameters, but anyone whose tour of duty began prior to June 20, 1951, would serve between twelve and twenty-four months. Enlisted Marines served no more than sixteen months, officers no more than seventeen.

"The Marine Corps for the most part is releasing both officers and enlisted men before they serve the maximum time provided in the legislation," the Associated Press reported. "Present plans call for release by June, 1952, of all Marine reservists who came on active duty before July, 1951."

In response, the Department of Defense repeatedly increased their monthly recruitment goals. On December 8 the Pentagon announced intentions to bring in fifty-five thousand new bodies, including fourteen thousand for the Marine Corps. As that deadline rapidly approached, Major Conley's department scrambled to find qualified, experienced pilots. And because enlisted Marines did not fly aircraft—some did serve aboard planes as radar operators—he needed officers.

Volunteer Reservists were the optimal candidates. These were considered "individuals that desired affiliation with the Marine Corps but whose personal activities did not permit them to participate in the demanding Organized Reserve program." They possessed years of Marine Corps or Navy training, had in most cases served during World War II, and were an enormous pool from which to draw. Prior to the Korean War there were actually more Volunteer Reserve Marines (87,655) than career, or so-called regular Marines. And nearly a year into the war, 34,043 Volunteer Reservists—many of whom had not put on a uniform since the end of World War II—had still not been recalled to active duty.

"We called up a lot of them who really believed that they had been out of the service since they came home in 1945," Conley remembered years later.

Beginning in the final weeks of 1951, Major Conley processed dozens, if not hundreds, of Volunteer Reserve cases per day. He eliminated some, assigned orders for others. And late into one evening, he reviewed the file of a recall candidate listed as "Williams, Theodore S." The name sounded familiar, but with such a common last name, Conley didn't give it much thought. "Williams, Theodore S." met the criteria for reactivation. The Marine Corps Reserve captain was healthy, received high marks on fitness reports, and had previously served fourteen months as an instructor at the Navy's primary aerial training center in Pensacola, Florida.

On January 7, 1952, Conley's office airmailed a memo with the subject "Assignment to extended active duty involving flying" to the address on file: Fenway Park, Boston, Massachusetts.

Three nights later, while everyone at the Conley home was asleep, the phone rang. An angry Marine general was on the line.

"What are you doing?" the general shouted.

"General, I'm sleeping, it's two o'clock in the morning," Bob Conley answered.

"No, you called up Theodore [S.] Williams. Do you know who that is? That's Ted Williams the baseball player. I've got the press all over me. What are you going to do about it?"

"Yes, I remember assigning a Theodore Williams. He's a Marine pilot still on . . . Reserves. He is going to war."

Conley hung up the phone and went back to sleep.

CHAPTER ONE

From Fenway to Fighter Jets

The 1951 Major League Baseball season proved yet another frustrating one for Ted Williams. Having collapsed down the stretch during the three previous American League pennant races, Williams's Red Sox lost twelve of their final thirteen games to finish a distant third that year. And after Yankees ace Allie Reynolds no-hit Boston in late September, Williams sat out the club's last four games with a bum ankle.

As had been the case during each of his ten seasons in a big-league uniform, Williams had enjoyed a spectacular year at the plate. During a Red Sox ten-game winning streak in late May, Williams hit .537, drove in twenty-two runs, and slammed fourteen extra-base hits. By season's end, he led the ball club in nearly every offensive statistic, including home runs, runs batted in, and batting average. But he did not post the same eye-popping numbers the fans at Fenway Park had come to expect. Even his .318 batting average, fourth in the American League, marked the lowest output during a full season of his career. Injuries coupled with age suggested to some that the thirty-three-year-old's best days were behind him.

If true, fans and the Red Sox front office might no longer tolerate his occasional petulant outbursts. During an exhibition game that spring, Williams had reportedly spat at a crowd who cheered him striking out. The same Tampa Plant Field spectators had thoroughly booed him earlier in the game for not running out a ground ball back to the pitcher. He denied spitting but confirmed to the press "I don't care whether they like me or not."

"Breaking into a tantrum at this early date," one sports columnist noted, "suggests that Ted is in mid-season form."

Once the 1951 season ended, speculation swirled that the team had contemplated trading away the two-time Most Valuable Player in an effort to rebuild a franchise clearly trending in the wrong direction. The selfish, less-than-clutch image often presented by Boston sportswriters only added to the Hot Stove fodder that Red Sox owner Tom Yawkey should trade away Williams.

"[Soon] a few critics began to voice the opinion that 'a team with Williams on it doesn't win,'" *Boston Globe* reporter Roger Birtwell declared that off-season. "But there are some who believe that a team's highest-paid player and highest-hitting star should exude a bit of the old 'come on, gang' spirit and help spark the team . . . The last couple of years some baseball followers have discussed the wisdom of such a move."

A few weeks after the season ended, Boston named their shortstop, thirty-two-year-old Lou Boudreau, the club's manager. Boudreau, who in 1948 had managed the Cleveland Indians to a World Series championship, immediately lent credibility to the trade gossip.

"As far as I'm concerned, there are no untouchables on this ball club," he said in late October. "We'll trade Williams or anyone else if it'll add to the team."

Boudreau's former team reportedly offered star pitcher Bob Lemon and reliable catcher Jim Hegan for Williams, but scoffed at the notion of including all-star center fielder Larry Doby as part of the deal. A blasphemous rumor to Boston fans—sending Williams to their hated New York rivals—began during the World Series and continued well into December. Yankees legend Joe DiMaggio would soon announce his retirement. Williams, rather than a twenty-year-old Oklahoma kid who struck out too much, Mickey Mantle, made perfect sense as a replacement in the lineup. Another alleged deal involved Boston sending Williams to the Washington Senators, who would hold on to him until a favorable trade to the Yankees could be reached.

"We would be a sucker not to take Williams if we could get him," Yankees owner Dan Topping said the day DiMaggio retired. "But I do not believe the Red Sox will ever give him up. I don't think they want to make the kind of deal anyone could afford to make."

Williams told reporters that he would retire from baseball if traded to the Yankees. He then escaped, as he did every off-season, to his sanctuary: alone, on the water, stalking fish.

For several years, he'd spent his winters fishing in Florida. Local newspapers scolded him in January 1948 when a fishing trip in Miami caused him to miss the birth of his first child, daughter Barbara Joyce. He took five days to return to Boston to be with his wife and the newborn, nicknamed Bobby-Jo.

"Fishing is how I relax," he explained. "I go out alone, or with another guy. We don't talk much. Boy, I really relax."

Amid unseasonably cold November weather, Williams moved into his recently built suburban home, which sat on an acre near Route 2 in South Miami. Described as "fashionable" by *Miami Herald* sports editor Jimmy Burns, the house boasted all-new furniture and even an electric heating fan that Williams's wife Doris liked to show off. Williams chose the spot because he was only a few hours' drive from wonderful fishing off the coast of the Florida Keys.

In early December, word came down that Williams wasn't going anywhere. Frustrated with the Yankees' front office—or directed to do so by team owner Tom Yawkey—Boudreau publicly announced that the club was no longer interested in dealing their superstar.

"Having spent my entire major league career with the Red Sox, I naturally would like to play out the string in Boston," he said upon hearing the news. "I have got used to playing that left field wall at Fenway Park, and I now seem to hit better there than anywhere else."

He promptly returned to the peace and solitude of the open waters. On the morning of January 9, 1952, Williams—his tan face still handsome but no longer the boyish one that inspired his nickname "The Kid"—departed one of the Keys in his 10-horsepower outboard. At the end of a long day on the Atlantic he had caught several prizes, including a nine-and-a-quarter-pound bonefish, then returned home to discover an urgent message. His business manager Fred Corcoran, the famed professional golf marketing genius, needed to speak with him right away. The United States Marine Corps had reactivated Williams to duty.

Prior to the United States entering World War II, Williams's Selective Service draft status stood as 3A, meaning he would not be eligible for induction because he was the sole financial supporter for his mother. But after the bombing of Pearl Harbor, the Hennepin County draft board in Minnesota reclassified Williams as 1A, eligible for service. Despite having joined the Red Sox two years earlier, Williams's official residence remained 60 Willow Street in Minneapolis, his address while playing for the minor-league Minnesota Millers in 1938.

The United States Army brought him in for a series of physical exams at Fort Snelling, outside of St. Paul. By late January he appeared destined for service in "the field artillery, the infantry, or the tank corp." Thanks to a lawyer—whom Williams claimed he never actually hired—his case was sent to the President's Board of Appeal. Franklin D. Roosevelt soon issued an order to Director of Selective Services Lewis B. Hershey finalizing Williams's 3A status. The Red Sox, not the Army, could have him for the spring of 1942.

Williams christened the new baseball season with a home run to right-center field in the first inning of Opening Day. The crowd at Fenway Park roared, but throughout that late winter and into the spring columnists razzed him and fans booed him for being a "slacker and draft dodger." Even the Quaker Oats company rescinded a $4,000 endorsement deal rather than attach itself to the controversy.

"I'm no slacker. I'm not yellow. I'm as patriotic as anybody," he told *Liberty* magazine in April. "I'm only human, like anybody else. Despite all you've seen and read, and maybe even have written, I'm sensitive. I'm thin-skinned. The park can be full of people, and they all can be cheering me but one guy, and somehow over it all I can hear that one boo."

The boos—at least for his draft posturing—soon ceased. Encouraged by a young junior-grade lieutenant in the Navy Reserve named Robert P. "Whitey" Fuller, Williams visited the naval air station in Squantum, Massachusetts, on May 6. Fuller, a Dartmouth alum who had just resigned as the Big Green's sports publicist to join the Navy's local Flight Selection Board, convinced Williams to check out the V-5 Naval Aviation Cadet program. For a few hours Fuller and the station's executive officer, Lieutenant Commander William F. Arnold, showed him the base, the planes, and the instruments inside the cockpit. Williams was enthralled and he signed an application on the spot.

Williams did not immediately join the Navy. First, he completed the 1942 season, which ended with him leading the American League in home runs, RBI, and batting average to claim the Triple Crown. He was, however, not presented the league's Most Valuable Player award, which went to Yankees second baseman Joe Gordon. And unlike the previous year, when Joe DiMaggio's remarkable fifty-six-game hitting streak kept Williams from receiving the award, many believed that sportswriters selected someone else for reasons outside of baseball.

From the beginning of his professional career, Williams had famously quarreled with reporters, to whom he was often short-tempered, even "fresh and chesty," as one described. But he also turned off a large swath of the so-called baseball purists who valued grit and tenacity as much as power and speed.

For all his gifts at the plate—an incomparable eye, instantaneous reflexes, upper-body strength that defied his wiry build—Williams earned a reputation as lazy outside of the batter's box. He did not always run out ground or fly balls and appeared disinterested in playing his outfield position. Personal achievements, solely in the form of hits, seemed to overshadow any team goals.

"He did not pull sufficient votes in the balloting because he is not regarded as a good team player, a vital factor that does not show in the averages," one columnist observed in November 1942. "[He] lived for but one thing—base hits. Other departments of the game were just something to be tolerated."

Even Boston manager Joe Cronin—who dressed down, benched, then fined Williams $250 that July for loafing on the basepaths—stated that *his* choice for MVP would have been Red Sox shortstop Johnny Pesky.

"Why, if Ted had only hustled all the time on the field and at bat, and if he had a flair for showmanship, which you can't have unless you hustle forever, he'd be hailed as the greatest player of all time," Cronin said upon learning the results of the voting.

In the eyes of the voting sportswriters, and much of the public, Williams could not be considered the "most valuable" American Leaguer that season because he was selfish, not a "team player." That trait was only magnified by his earlier efforts to escape military service.

"I have to think the reason I didn't get more consideration was because of the trouble I had with the draft," Williams wrote years later.

———

Two weeks after learning of his second-place finish in the 1942 MVP balloting, Williams boarded a train from Minneapolis and headed east. Arriving in Boston at 3 a.m. on a frigid late November New England morning, the twenty-four-year-old slept briefly at a hotel in Kenmore Square. The following morning, a $25 cab ride brought him, albeit a day late, to Amherst College for a civilian pilot training course. Lee Friend was the course's cadet leader and somehow had never heard of Ted Williams. He immediately learned the new cadet was a big deal when the cabbie asked to shake Williams's hand and wished him luck.

For six weeks Williams and twenty-nine other cadets—including the Red Sox' Johnny Pesky and Boston Braves' Johnny Sain and Buddy Gremp—learned to fall in, fall out, salute their superiors, and properly make their bed.

"The ball players go out of their way to do more than the others," Friend noted. "When I told them to clean their room, meaning for them to sweep it, Sain and Gremp got a bucket and mop and washed the floor. Williams is so eager to cooperate that he's like a bird dog."

In addition to physical training—boxing, swimming, calisthenics—and classroom study in math, physics, navigation, and meteorology, Williams and the others studied the basics of aviation. Eventually, the cadets earned time in the air aboard a two-seat Piper J-3 Cub.

"Flying is the last thing I'm worrying about," Williams bragged. "It's a cinch if you just keep thinking and applying yourself. . . . I was fighting the training ship the first few times I was given the controls, but now I am handling them instinctively."

From Amherst, Williams moved on to preflight school at Chapel Hill, North Carolina, then Bunker Hill Naval Air Station in Peru, Indiana. At Bunker Hill, Seaman Second Class Williams soloed a variety of single-engine propeller aircraft, including the Boeing-Stearman N2S-3, a biplane dubbed the "Yellow Peril," partly because of its color, partly because the pilot flying it was usually a cadet.

"You can tell from the way he acts around the training planes that he is a flying enthusiast," said his commanding officer at Bunker Hill, Captain D. D. Gurley. "His flight instruction was completed more than two weeks ahead of schedule, and he was right up with his class in ground school subjects. He has an inquiring mind, and that is a splendid piece of equipment for a flyer."

Next came training at Pensacola Naval Air Station in the Florida Panhandle, where he mainly flew the SNJ-4, an unbearably loud, twenty-nine-foot two-seater that featured a 600-horsepower engine with a range of 750 miles. According to Second Lieutenant Daniel E. Whiteley, who oversaw his first training mission at Pensacola, Williams mastered it immediately. He was not even fazed when the instructor covered the instrument panel with a cloth to increase the difficulty.

"He had a great touch; a good feel for the airplane," Whiteley remembered almost sixty years later. "All he had was an artificial horizon to look into. . . . We had another flight a few days later and he was even better on that flight."

Williams advanced quickly and earned his wings on May 2, 1944, accepting promotion to second lieutenant, but with the United States Marine Corps Reserve, a component of the Department of the Navy.

Given fifteen days on furlough, Williams traveled north to Minnesota, married his girlfriend Doris Soule, then returned to Florida where he remained for the duration of World War II. Although he occasionally played outfield for the Bronson Field Bombers of Escambia County—a team in the Naval Air Training auxiliary bases baseball circuit—his chief task became instructing new pilots, many of whom marveled at his skills during training sessions thousands of feet up in the air.

"Once he came up to my right and caught my eye," remembered John Harris, a cadet at Pensacola in 1944. "It was a very hot day, and he wiped his brow and threw his hands to the side as if to say, 'It's hot up here today.' . . . Before I knew it, he had maneuvered himself atop our formation and was flying upside down and looking straight at us."

Williams also excelled at targeting. While playing minor-league baseball in Minnesota, Williams had become an avid hunter in the Northwoods. Living in Hennepin County during the off-season, he made quite a haul of pheasants in Dayton and foxes in New Brighton. He had first met Doris at the end of a long day hunting ducks near Princeton. After his rookie season, Williams was arrested and fined by a Minnesota game warden for shooting ducks beyond the 4 p.m. cutoff.

His marksmanship with a shotgun translated to manning the artillery aboard the Vought F4U Corsair aircraft. According to legend, while at Jacksonville's naval air station, he set a student gunnery record for accuracy, hitting 196 out of a possible 200 targets with his six wing guns.

"From what I heard," said Johnny Pesky, who served with Williams at several Navy installations, "Ted could make a plane and its six pianos play like a symphony orchestra. From what they said, his reflexes, coordination, and visual reaction made him a built-in part of the machine."

Although the war effectively ended in August 1945, Williams received new orders. He was sent to San Francisco and told he would eventually be attached to a fighter squadron in either Manilla or Japan. But the farthest west he made it was Oahu, Hawaii. Up to nearly 200 pounds, from his 173-pound playing weight, Williams joined several fellow big leaguers in a week's worth of baseball games billed as the Navy's "Little World Series." The two rosters included future Hall of Famers Billy Herman, Bill Dickey, Bob Lemon, and Stan Musial. In the third game, before a crowd of more than sixteen thousand at Furlong Field (tickets were free), Williams belted a home run over the right field fence.

Once the Japanese formally surrendered in September, Williams became eager to return to playing baseball for bigger stakes. Dispatched to the Marine Corps air depot at Miramar in his home town of San Diego, Williams was relieved from duty in late January 1946. But he was not discharged. Like all Marine Corps Reserve officers, he was simply given Volunteer Reserve status, which he chose to accept rather than request a full discharge.

As a Volunteer Reservist assigned to the 11th Marine Corps Reserve District in San Diego (and later transferred to the First Marine Corps Reserve District in Boston) Williams did not have to log flight hours or participate in training exercises and weekend programs to retain his rank. In fact, he was given promotions, to first lieutenant in June 1949 and to captain in October 1951. By accepting these promotions, and their accompanying pay raises, Williams essentially extended his "contract" with the United States Marine Corps, meaning there always remained a chance that he would be recalled.

He was free to resign his commission at any point, but Williams believed that he would never be recalled. But that all changed with the Selective Service Extension Act of 1950, the United Nations failure to reach a truce in Panmunjom, and Major Bob Conley's harried review of candidate files.

"They told me when I was separated after World War II that unless we got into another war, I wouldn't be called back," he wrote decades later, "and I certainly didn't believe that what was going on in Korea would have them call back a thirty-two-year-old pilot."

Upon receiving the news of his client's recall, Fred Corcoran assembled a group of local reporters and photographers to search for Williams at a few of his favorite fishing spots in Key Largo. Outside Bob Perry's Fishing Lodge in Rock Harbor they caught up with Williams, who had just returned with his friend Frank Tiernan. For the press, he put up a brave front.

"As far as Uncle Sam is concerned I'm no different than anyone else," he said while hosing off his outboard. "I wasn't upset about it but I certainly was surprised."

Privately, however, Williams fumed.

"I resented the way they singled me out because I was in the public eye," Williams said a few years later. "I'd have had no squawk if they had called back every reserve officer in the same category. I'll tell you why they called a lot of us back. They wanted an appropriation from the government for airplanes and they needed pilots to fly them. So they recalled 1100 pilots who hadn't flown for 11 years."

Williams's gripe might have been better received had it not been for the bad publicity over his 3A status in 1942. And when chosen again ten years later, he didn't exactly jump back into the service eagerly.

According to Williams, throughout the early months of 1952 men of power fell all over themselves trying to broker a deferment for him. One such person from Ohio promised to speak to United States Senator Robert A. Taft on Williams's behalf. Another, a thirty-five-year-old Massachusetts congressman who was preparing to announce his candidacy for the Senate, told Corcoran that he would pull some strings. But like Taft, John F. Kennedy ultimately did nothing for Williams.

Fans and reporters wrote letters to their local congressional representatives asking for an explanation about the recall. A Wakefield Memorial High School sophomore named Carol Leavitt even wrote to President Truman asking, "if you could tell me how I could help him not get into the Marines."

There was a perception—for those who did not know the story of Major Conley's weary rubber stamping—that the Marine Corps had recalled Williams to drum up support for a war that the public didn't truly understand. The fight over communism in Korea, a tiny peninsula on the other side of the world, did not carry the same weight as World War II, particularly after the bombing of Pearl Harbor. But if star ballplayer Ted Williams was going to serve, then this war must be righteous.

"What earthly use can the Marines make of Ted's War II training?" a high-ranking air officer at the Pentagon told the *Boston Evening American*. "Antiquated ground officers are a dollar-a-dozen. There are thousands of younger, more seasoned air officers still on the inactive list."

Still, Williams's actual return to active duty remained in question.

In July 1950—one week after the city of Inchon fell to the North Korean People's Army—Williams had been in Chicago playing for the American League in the first-ever nationally televised Major League Baseball All-Star Game. In the first inning Pittsburgh Pirates home run specialist Ralph Kiner socked a Vic Raschi pitch deep toward Comiskey Park's left field. Never known for his defensive prowess, Williams tracked down the ball and made a brilliant running catch. With no warning track paved to alert him to the danger, he ran into the twelve-foot-high, unpadded wall, bracing himself for impact with the heel of his left hand.

Clearly in pain, and persistently rubbing his elbow, he remained in the game. Not only did he make another terrific catch of a hard-hit line drive the next time Kiner came to bat, but Williams's single to right field in the fifth inning gave the American League a 3–2 advantage. The next day X-rays revealed an impacted fracture of the head of the left radius: a broken elbow. During seventy-five minutes of surgery at Sancta Maria Hospital in Cambridge, Massachusetts, Dr. Joseph H. Shortell removed seven bone fragments, which he displayed for forlorn young Red Sox fans awaiting news on the procedure.

"With Williams out the Red Sox ain't got a chance," eleven-year-old Jimmy Walker lamented.

Williams missed the next eight weeks—Boston actually won thirty-nine of those fifty-five games—before returning in early September. But for the rest of his playing career his elbow ached, especially in cold or rainy weather. For that very reason, he fully expected to fail his upcoming Navy medical examination, be declared unfit for service, and return for another season in left field.

Two weeks before the start of the 1952 season, Williams and New York Yankees second baseman Jerry Coleman—a Marine dive-bomber who flew fifty-seven combat missions in the Solomon Islands during World War II—traveled to the naval air station in Jacksonville, Florida. Associated Press sportswriter Joe Reichler tagged along to chronicle the day.

Coleman, six years younger than Williams, passed the exam almost immediately. The well-known injury to Williams's elbow prompted X-rays that an officer told the group would take at least a half an hour to develop. Just a few minutes later, a Marine captain entered and announced that Williams had passed the examination, greatly confusing the group.

"With more temper than tact, I questioned aloud the Marines' real purpose in recalling baseball's biggest name," Reichler later wrote.

"The Marines really don't expect a 33-year-old guy with four dependents to fly a plane?" Reichler asked the captain.

"I'm 35, with five dependents and I fly a plane," the captain replied.

Navy physician Captain Julius C. Early observed "no significant limitations to the use of Williams' elbow," and the assisting physician, Commander L. S. Sims, Jr., informed the gaggle outside that the X-rays could not possibly alter their decision. Early approved Williams's return to active service, even replying to reporters' questions about Williams's age by saying "I'm 49, and I'm a pilot."

Prior to the examination, Early had lowered expectations, telling reporters that the medical board deems only a "negligible" percentage of Reserve pilots unfit for duty and that neither Williams's age, nor the stiffness he felt in cold weather would be factors in the determination. Early did not mention that Williams had passed a thorough medical exam the previous September in order to receive his promotion from first lieutenant to captain.

In the years that followed, Joe Reichler told friends, including author David Fisher, that "when they told Williams that they would take him, that he had passed the test, he went berserk, he was screaming and yelling."

Although he received no special treatment from Navy physicians that day, Marine Corps Commandant Lemuel C. Shepherd, Jr. sent a "purely personal" letter to Williams (on USMC stationery) expressing "regret that it was found necessary to recall you to active duty at the height of your baseball career."

Unable to secure a deferment from influential politicians and granted a clean bill of health, Williams accepted orders to report to the Marine Air Reserve Training Command at Willow Grove, Pennsylvania, on May 2, less than a month into the baseball season. The Universal Military Training Act of 1951 meant that he could serve up to seventeen months.

Following his physical in Jacksonville, Williams rejoined the Red Sox on an exhibition tour spanning Texas, Oklahoma, Virginia, North Carolina, and then finally back to Boston. On Opening Day in Washington, D.C., Williams went 1-for-3 as the club topped the Senators 3–0, but he pulled a muscle in his leg that afternoon and could only pinch-hit sparingly over the next two weeks.

The injury healed just in time for the Red Sox game against Detroit on April 30, which also happened to be "Ted Williams Day," as declared by the mayor of Boston, John B. Hynes.

"Naturally I feel greatly honored," Williams said, "but I only wish they had tried to contact me. I would have tried to discourage them."

Following Williams's reactivation, talk about his baseball future was inconsistent. Joe Cronin—now the Red Sox general manager—cast doubt to the press almost immediately. Upon receiving the news, Williams called Cronin who in turn told a reporter the next day that it would take "a miracle" for him to resume playing ball upon his discharge.

"It is hard to visualize Ted coming out of the service and returning as a star at the age of 36, the odds are obviously heavily against him," he said. "You must remember that he has always been a rather determined fellow. Nevertheless, this could be the third strike for him."

During spring training in Florida, Williams said, "If the Marines want me, I'll gladly go, but if I go I'll quit baseball. Heck, in two years I'll be 35." And just prior to his physical at the naval air station he told reporters, "If I pass the examination, I expect my baseball career will come to a sudden conclusion." As he drove back to Jacksonville's airport with Jerry Coleman, reporters continued to beg him for a comment.

"Why don't you write one of those statistical stories after a player has passed away or retired," he said. "Just say Williams is all through. He went to bat 5,096 times during his 10 years with the Red Sox, scored 1,273 runs, made 1,763 hits, 323 home runs, and drove in 1,261 runs."

Still, as Ted Williams Day approached, he held out hope.

"I don't know whether or not I will be able to return to baseball but I hope so," he said on the eve of his final game. "I had only one ambition when I joined the Red Sox in 1939. It was when I'm through I want them to say, 'Gee, that guy was one hell of a hitter.'"

Prior to game time at warm, sun-soaked Fenway Park, both teams lined up along the infield, as did a series of local dignitaries, including Mayor Hynes; the governor of Massachusetts, Paul A. Dever; and the commissioner of the Boston Fire Department, Michael T. Kelleher. Williams stood in the center, gripping teammate Dom DiMaggio's right hand. With his other hand, Williams held that of a young man in a wheelchair named Frederick M. Wolf. Less than six months earlier, the seventeen-year-old medic in the Army's 7th Cavalry was attending to a comrade's severe leg wounds from machine gun fire when a shell hit their position. Everyone in the trench died except Private Wolf, who lost both his legs. Dressed in his Army greens, Wolf thanked Williams for his many visits to nearby hospitals.

"I'm speaking for the guys who can't be here themselves to tell you how much they appreciate what you have done for them," Wolf said.

He continued to hold Williams's hand as the crowd and many on the field sang "Auld Lang Syne." Williams stood motionless, his tearing eyes shut.

Wolf, on behalf of the many veterans of New England, brought Williams a gift, the contents of which he kept private. Others chose to make a far more ostentatious presentation of their offerings. Frederick G. Payne, governor of Maine, sent a smorgasbord of canned local foods as well as a complimentary state fishing license. Mayor Hynes handed Williams a solid silver replica of the Paul Revere Bowl, aka the eighteenth-century Liberty Bowl. Filene's department store hand-delivered gold cuff links engraved with the number "9." Even the local sportswriters gave Williams a baseball they all signed.

"I might let some kids play on the street with it," he joked.

But the brand-new, robin's-egg-blue Cadillac caught everyone's attention as it was driven to home plate. Williams's friends, including his accountant Paul Brophy and local sporting events promotor Sheldon Fairbanks, had purchased the $5,000 Sedan Series 62.

"Some wagon!" Red Sox teammate Vern Stephens exclaimed.

Choked up with emotion, Williams struggled to find words when the program's emcee, Curt Gowdy, prompted him to speak. For a few moments, he sheepishly dug his left foot into the ground as if he were readying the batter's box before hitting.

"It's a day I'll long remember—as long as I live," he told his captive audience. "I never thought it would happen to me. Thank you from the bottom of my heart."

Then, he broke a longstanding vow and one that he had privately reaffirmed to friends that morning. Years earlier, when fans booed him, Williams promised to "never acknowledge their cheers." But spurred on by *Boston Herald* sports editor Ed Costello, Williams waved his cap to the crowd.

Roughly two hours later, the Fenway crowd expected an encore cap-waiving, but this time they would be disappointed.

With one on and one out in the bottom of the seventh inning, Williams came to the plate in a game tied 3–3. He had singled, struck out, and walked in three appearances that day. Ahead in the count 1–0, Tigers reliever Dizzy Trout, a former twenty-seven-game winner now at the tail end of his career, tried to sneak a curveball by him. Unleashing that indelible left-hander's stroke, Williams's six-foot, three-inch frame coiled: United States Poet Laureate Donald Hall once described the swing as "that lanky body twisted around itself almost like a barber's pole revolving." His highly customized thirty-four-ounce, thirty-five-inch bat made perfect contact with the ball, sending it deep over the right field fence for the 324th home run of his career.

The crowd of nearly twenty-five thousand went wild. But not Michael Lopilato, a fruit dealer from the North End. The thirty-six-year-old was too busy scrambling for the ball, which bounced out of one spectator's hands, then ping-ponged around the stands until Lopilato snatched it up.

"Everyone in the stands gave me the business when I got the ball," said Lopilato, who later returned it to the Red Sox clubhouse. "They told me to send it to the cancer fund and a half-dozen other places. But I thought it best to give it to Williams."

While Lopilato scavenged for the historic artifact—Teddy Ballgame's final home run ball—Williams rounded the bases. And although the fans and his teammates wanted him to again acknowledge their cheers, Williams kept his cap firmly on his head as he trotted toward home plate.

The two-run home run gave Boston a 5–3 lead, which rookie right-hander Ike Delock preserved for the Red Sox' tenth win in their first twelve games. In the postgame locker room, teammate Ray Scarborough remarked, "They can talk all they want about other great guys in baseball. Guys pointing to center field and hitting a home run there. Real great players. But did you ever see anybody bow out like Williams did?"

That evening, without any of his teammates or members of the celebrity crowd, Williams enjoyed a small going-away party at Jimmy O'Keefe's Grill on Boylston Street, three blocks from Fenway Park.

"It seems that the fans really wanted me to wave my cap," he told George C. Carens of the *Boston Traveler*. "I thought afterwards they might have liked me to wave after hitting that homer, but that wasn't much of a sock. Boy, if the one I hit in the third had stayed inside fair territory, I'd have tossed the bonnet into the stands."

Although he teased reporters and fans with the suggestion that he might delay his departure to play just one more game, Williams sat out the next day's showdown with the St. Louis Browns. On Friday morning, May 2, he checked out of the Hotel Shelton and climbed into his Ford: Doris kept the new Cadillac, which she drove to Miami with Bobby-Jo. He then picked up two local Marine Reservists who had also been recalled, Captain Raymond W. Sisk of West Somerville and Captain Robert L. Scowcroft of Needham. Williams had served with Sisk at Pensacola. He barely knew Scowcroft; they used the same tailor.

Sisk, who had been stationed at Willow Grove during World War II, knew the best route and drove the several hundred miles. The three men stopped for hamburgers at a Howard Johnson's near the New Jersey Turnpike—Williams signed several autographs for fans—then arrived at the base in late afternoon. A swarm of Philadelphia-area reporters and photographers ambushed them. Eventually Williams signed in, was fingerprinted, given an identification card and flight gear, and headed for the Bachelor Officer Quarters, then dinner.

Although he was now a captain with more than a thousand hours of flight experience, Williams was sent to Willow Grove for a pilot's refresher course: air-and-ground orientation, three to five hours of flight time with an instructor, and twenty hours of solo flying, all in the same Navy SNJ trainer which he had once taught to cadets.

Bill Churchman had also instructed pilots at Pensacola during World War II, and the two men became close. A native of Philadelphia's Chestnut Hill, Churchman had been recalled to service a year earlier than Williams, and following stops at Willow Grove and El Toro in California he was sent to the Pacific in January 1952. He spent three months flying missions for the Marine Corps' VMF-312 squadron. Stationed aboard the USS *Bairoko*, a Navy escort carrier, the "Checkerboards" flew F4U Corsairs to provide air support to Army and Marine troops. When Churchman's squadron was transferred to the USS *Bataan* in April 1952, he returned to the United States. Reassigned to Willow Grove, he became an instructor to, among others, Ted Williams. Over the next month Captain Churchman shared some advice with his famous friend.

"Ted, try to get into jets," he told Williams. "If you go to Korea, and you will, it's plain arithmetic. You'll probably make a lot of bombing raids in support of the ground troops. If you are in a Corsair, you'll go down at 400 miles per hour and come up at about the same time. If you are in a jet, you'll make your run at 500 and come out at 500. The Corsair is a great plane, but the jets will give you more speed when the gooks are firing at you."

"That made a lot of sense to me," Williams recalled. "So I put in for jets."

By the end of four weeks, Williams had completed his retraining. Base commander Lieutenant Colonel Jack R. Moore endorsed his request for a transfer to the Marine Corps air base at Cherry Point, North Carolina. But on his second-to-last day at Willow Grove Williams received a frightening preview of what might await him. That afternoon, Lieutenant Jack L. Welle, a test pilot at the Johnsville Naval Air Development Center in Bucks County, lost control of his jet and plunged from an estimated five thousand feet. At five hundred miles per hour it smashed into the ground, less than a hundred yards from a local man driving his tractor.

Hundreds of Marine and Navy personnel from nearby Willow Grove, including Captain Williams, arrived to the scene. A small crew from the group surrounded the fiery crater in the ground.

"At first they couldn't find the pilot," Williams remembered. "Then a Marine pulled out a foot. It was still in the pilot's boot. That guy was spread all over the place . . . You were going so damn fast that if you got in a jam, it was hard to get out of trouble due to the speed of the plane."

The plane was determined to be an F9F Panther, the exact same jet that Williams would begin to train on at Cherry Point.

———

Williams remained at Cherry Point for much of the next six months. Initially part of a twelve-officer class within VMAT-20 training group, he advanced to VMF-223 by late July. In the fall, he briefly flew to Northern California to attend his father's funeral and also spent six weeks training at Roosevelt Roads Naval Station in Puerto Rico, one of ten thousand Marines training for an amphibious "mock assault" on Onslow Beach, North Carolina. But for the hot Southern summer Williams, Doris, and Bobby-Jo settled into a comfortably air-conditioned, off-base bungalow in Havelock. Most officers at Cherry Point lived in far more modest quarters.

Throughout his stay in coastal North Carolina, local fans and institutions hounded him with requests to appear at their events. He turned down most but posed for a team photo with eleven-year-old ballplayers from New Bern and on a night in July signed baseballs for a group of high-school-aged ballplayers before an American Legion Baseball playoff game at Grainger Stadium in Kinston. Unlike his time at Pensacola, however, Williams did not play any baseball while stationed at Cherry Point. According to a rumor on the base, a high-ranking officer asked Williams to join the station's baseball team. Williams said he would . . . for his standard fee of $10,000 per game.

"Flying right now is taking my time and consideration," he told the press. "I really don't have time to think much about baseball."

As much as he missed the game—the Red Sox were mired in fifth place at the All-Star Break—he welcomed the new challenge posed by jets.

Williams had been incensed at his recall and during his time at Cherry Point often spoke on the phone to a lawyer who pursued legal avenues for his client's discharge based on the considerable money he would lose. His contract with the Red Sox would have paid him $100,000 in 1952—he reportedly received $25,000 for the six games he did play—and in previous years Williams earned several thousands more in endorsements. As a Marine Corps Reserve captain, he would earn $6,500.

But Williams decided that if he had to serve, he wanted a meaningful post that exercised both his physical and mental skills, not a safe desk job.

"I didn't want that," he said. "Maybe I could have got one but I wanted what I got."

"He came to us inadequately trained as were many Reserves," Williams's commanding officer during the war later wrote. "Ted never complained though. He did tell me that he tried everything he could think of to keep from reporting to active duty during the Korean War but when it appeared hopeless, he said, 'Oh, what the hell.'"

At Cherry Point Williams liked to "shoot landings," became skilled at strafing, rocket runs, and close air support maneuvers, and often took the F9F Panther's "navigational computor" home with him for practice. (The "computor" was actually a climb-and-descent tabulator used by pilots in the cockpit to calculate distances and fuel consumption rates). Time in the "Dilbert Dunker," simulation training for planes that crashed in the water, wasn't as thought-provoking.

He also enjoyed the camaraderie with his fellow officers, including Cleveland Indians outfielder Bob Kennedy, who had been recalled to duty at Cherry Point in May. In their light brown flight suits or leather bomber jackets, pilots played checkers and beer-and-Coke dice games in the squadron's Ready Room. Occasionally, Williams and a few others drove off-base together for meals in Morehead City or fishing in Kinston.

"Sure, it was rough having to leave baseball," he told Bob Quincy of the *Charlotte News*. "That was my life—all that I knew until I took up flying in the last war. But I don't feel sorry for myself. In fact I'm lucky in a way. I look at some of these fellows I am associated with. A few of them are in shape, maybe have flown regularly during the past few years. I hadn't, my time being devoted to baseball. But still I'm healthy and have good reflexes and find a number of things about flying that are directly in line with the co-ordination I learned playing ball.

"But how about the fellow who has been sitting behind a desk in a good job, getting fat and lazy and bald. He's the guy to feel sorry for. How do you think he feels returning to this sort of thing? How does he feel when he gets in the air?"

As a professional ballplayer, Williams loathed speaking to sportswriters on a daily basis. During his eleven seasons in the major leagues he went out of his way to avoid the Boston press, who in turn penned negative, often unfair columns, about his performance, his effort, or his selective service status. But he had become used to their probes. So when reporters like Bob Quincy and *The Sporting News'* Bud Johns sought exclusives and profiles, he obliged. Perhaps he thought that repeating the same details about his abrupt career change would gain traction through the newspapers as his lawyers pursued a discharge.

"I'm losing two very important years of my earning power," he often told the press.

Williams learned to fly the Panther with such ease he remarked that Bobby-Jo could maneuver the plane once it was in the air. The absence of a propeller meant far less torque was needed on the controls in order to steer the aircraft, and he explained, "I can handle one with my little finger, actually."

From his superiors, Williams frequently received high, even exceptional assessments, including the top mark of "Outstanding" in the categories "Endurance," "Cooperation," "Force," "Leadership," and "Loyalty." In one Official Fitness Report, VMF-223's commanding officer, Lieutenant Colonel Hoyle R. Barr, deemed Williams "a fine young officer . . . his personality and appearance create a distinctly favorable impression." Both Barr and Williams's previous commanding officer at Cherry Point recommended him for promotion. In July, Williams applied for assignment to the Navy's all-weather flight program in Corpus Christi, Texas, citing 1,450 lifetime flying hours in his written request. But he was denied due to lack of qualifications.

On December 1, 1952, the Department of Defense released weekly statistics to the press: 127,383 total casualties had been reported since the fighting in Korea began two-and-a-half years earlier. The number caused such a public outcry that the Pentagon immediately issued a statement announcing that it would no longer use the term "casualty" to refer to soldiers killed, wounded, or missing. Too many people across the country thought the number of dead American soldiers had surpassed 100,000, instead of the true number, 20,004. An analysis of the D.O.D statistics conducted by the International News Service revealed that military spending had surpassed $50 billion annually (more than half the rate spent during World War II in less than half the time), and that "compared with the First World War, the Korean fighting—and its related U.S. military buildup throughout the world—already has put more men in uniform, cost more money, and resulted in more than one-third as many casualties."

That same week, Lieutenant Colonel Barr recommended Williams be transferred to the First Marine Aircraft Wing, meaning his deployment to the battlefront was now imminent. Based at El Toro Marine Air Station in Santa Ana, California, the First MAW was comprised of thousands of men divided into dozens of squadrons, all under a new commanding officer, Major General Vernon E. Megee.

Given a few weeks' leave before reporting to El Toro, Williams drove down to his home in Miami. There he relaxed in the sun, attended a party on the eve of the Orange Bowl, and signed the paperwork to purchase 25 percent interest in Southern Tackle Distributors, the fifth-largest fishing tackle distributor in the nation. On New Year's Day 1953 he flew west to California with Fred Corcoran then slept comfortably at the luxurious Town House Hotel on Wilshire Boulevard. The next day, Corcoran, the promotional director for the Professional Golfers' Association, brought Williams to the opening round of the Los Angeles Open at the Riviera Country Club. Walking the course in a wide-lapel blazer and cabana shirt Williams talked fishing with former U.S. Open champion Cary Middlecoff. The sportswriters outside the ropes pestered him with questions about his baseball future.

"I think I could play baseball till I'm 40," he said. "Anytime I can't hit .300 I'll quit. I'm in good shape and if I feel this great next spring I'll take a whack at baseball for another two years."

He snuck away from the cameramen and reporters long enough to catch up with a friend for dinner one night in Southern California. Ironically enough, the friend was famed syndicated sports columnist Grantland Rice. Although Williams hated most of the local Boston press, the national reporters did not bother him as much.

Over wine the two chatted about Williams' love for hunting and fishing, his poor play during the 1946 World Series, and especially his return to the Marines. At one point in the meal, he confided in his friend.

Ted Williams never lacked confidence in anything he did: talking to women, fishing, hunting, and of course playing baseball. In speaking of his skills at the plate, he often told reporters and fans that "no one can throw a fastball past me. God could come down from Heaven, and He couldn't throw it past me."

Even in his second career as an aviator Williams seemed sure of himself. Chatting with fellow Marine jet pilots, he confidently troubleshooted hypothetical power failure hazards at takeoff ("I'd jettison my tanks first, then raise my wheels") and taught reservists at nearby Camp Lejeune the aptly named technique for landing a plane that has been damaged: "sliding in."

And true to that nature, for nearly a year Williams publicly spoke with confidence and verve about his recall. Although furious behind closed doors, and privately hopeful that he would be considered ineligible for service, he accepted his duty and approached the training with complete dedication.

"I really enjoy it," he said. "At least I'm getting a chance to fly a jet, which I think is about the wish of every service pilot."

But on this one particular night, at dinner with Rice, a few weeks before departing for the Far East, Ted Williams was not so optimistic.

"Then he said—and this is what I can't get out of my mind," Rice told fellow New York sportswriter Frank Graham, "'I expect to be killed, of course.' He wasn't being maudlin about it. He said it very calmly. He simply had accepted what he was bound to think was his destiny."

CHAPTER TWO

My Life's Work

One hundred and fifty miles east of the bicycle shop where Orville and Wilbur Wright constructed the first airplane, John Hershel Glenn, Jr., was born in Cambridge, Ohio, on July 18, 1921.

Flying captured his imagination from a very early age. Not yet six years old, the redhead nicknamed "Bud" cheered the news of Charles Lindbergh's aerial journey from New York to Paris aboard the *Spirit of St. Louis*. Throughout childhood, he built, crashed, then rebuilt model airplanes made from balsa wood. And after John Sr. paid five dollars to a local pilot for a quick father-son flight above Cambridge in a Waco biplane, the boy yearned to fly.

"You could hear 'Bud' and one of his friends in the back yard pretending they were flying," John Sr. remembered decades later. "They'd spread their arms out like wings and go 'zzzooommm' as they ran around, dipping their arms as they banked for a turn."

As he grew up, John developed plenty of additional interests. His second grade teacher, Lota Ford, remembered him as "the most curious little fellow I ever did see." That curiosity developed into passions for sports, camping with a group he helped form called the Ohio Rangers, and the civics class taught by his high school principal. And starting in eighth grade, he went steady with Annie Castor, a shy high school freshman whom he'd known since they were toddlers. They would spend the next eighty-two years together.

But apart from Annie nothing interested John Glenn more than airplanes. He graduated from New Concord High School in 1939, then followed Annie to nearby Muskingum College, where football and the Stag Club brought him varying degrees of joy. As a sophomore, he earned a physics credit by completing a government-sponsored Civil Aeronautics

Authority training program. Three times a week, Glenn and a few other classmates borrowed the college's station wagon and drove an hour north to New Philadelphia, where they learned navigation, thermodynamics, heat transfer, and most importantly to fly a 65-horsepower Taylorcraft.

On July 1, 1941, while his friend Bob Conley was in Gross Ile, Michigan, joining the Navy, Glenn passed the certification exam at New Philadelphia Municipal Airport to earn his private pilot's license. Five months later, he was driving Annie—a music major at Muskingum—to her organ recital at Brown Chapel when a radio news bulletin informed them of the bombing at Pearl Harbor. He left school when the fall semester ended, drove to Zanesville, and enlisted in the Army Air Forces. No orders came, so a few weeks later he drove back to Zanesville, and enlisted in the Navy Reserve's V-5 program, the same aviation cadet training program that Ted Williams would sign on to two months later.

In late May he was sent to the University of Iowa for three months of grueling physical preflight training. Transferred to the Naval Reserve base in Olathe, Kansas, Glenn flew the Stearman Yellow Peril, then moved on to the naval air training center in Corpus Christi, Texas. Among other planes, he flew the noisy and bumpy SNV trainer (the "Vultee Vibrator") and the Consolidated PBY Catalina, a "flying boat" mainly used for bombing and cargo transport.

Neither plane was particularly agile or advanced. After nearly two years of civilian and military training in the cockpit of heavy, sputtering single-engine planes, Glenn wanted to soar. A rumor that he and fellow cadet Tom Miller heard gave him hope. Pilots in the Marine Corps would soon be flying the Lockheed P-38 Lightning, a twin-boom, twin-engine fighter plane. The two friends applied to the Marines and both were accepted. Glenn earned his commission as a second lieutenant on March 31, 1943, then married Annie a week later back home in Ohio.

As a wedding present, John Sr. gave his son a 1934 Chevrolet Coupe to use on the newlyweds' long drive from Ohio to John Jr.'s post at the naval air station in Cherry Point, North Carolina. Not only did the car turn out to be a lemon—flat tires, blown tubes—but nine days after their arrival, Glenn's superiors informed him of a transfer to the naval auxiliary station at Kearny Mesa, outside San Diego, California.

Glenn was assigned to VMJ-353, a transport squadron, not a fighter squadron. That meant he would not be flying the P-38, but rather the

C-47, the Navy's version of the DC-3, a passenger plane. In his mind, the C-47 required far less skill to fly. Pilots called it "The Placid Plodder . . . Old Fatso . . . Gooney Bird." And, as he soon learned, several other pilots in the squadron already had vast experience in the DC-3 from commercial airline training at Fort Worth, Texas.

"They had a very decided head start on the rest of us and in all probability they would become the first pilots with the rest of us stringing along as co-pilots," Glenn wrote in his war journal.

He did not want to fly as co-pilot on transport missions in the Gooney Bird. He wanted to be a fighter pilot, commanding, as he said, "a small, fast ship that really gives you a feeling of being part of the ship." The Grumman F4F Wildcat was that ship, and it taunted Glenn from the other side of his airfield.

Stationed alongside VMJ-353 at Kearny Mesa, VMO-155 flew the F4F-3P Wildcat under the command of Major J. P. "Pete" Haines. Featuring an air-cooled engine with a two-speed supercharger as well as six .50-caliber machine guns, the Wildcat gave American pilots a chance against the fabled Japanese Zero. On wings that folded in to save space when stored, the Wildcat could reach 350 miles per hour and 35,000 feet with a range of 1,000 miles. Just before Vought introduced its new F4U Corsair, the Office of War Information publicly called the Wildcat "unquestionably the best carrier fighter now in battle service."

Glenn, a twenty-two-year-old second lieutenant, brazenly hatched a plan for new orders. He and Tom Miller would cozy up to Major Haines in the mess hall and win his favor. Over time, Haines agreed to let the two join his unit under one condition: they obtain the necessary permission from their two superiors—the commanding officer of the transport squadron, Major Edmund Zonne, and the group commander, Colonel Deane C. Roberts. Miller followed the proper chain of command. Glenn did not. He went directly to Colonel Roberts's aide.

"Anytime John gets his sights set on something, it's Katy-bar-the-door," Miller later recalled. "But there was a certain bit of military protocol that had to be observed. I knew this but I'm not sure John ever did get it, or really cared about it."

Before long, Major Zonne discovered Glenn's insolence and threatened to destroy both men's careers before they had begun.

"I've never been dressed down like that before or since," Glenn wrote half a century later. "But I wasn't ready to give up. I apologized profusely and did everything I could to smooth things over. [Zonne] finally relented."

Both men ultimately received their transfer to 155, and Glenn learned a valuable lesson that had nothing to do with the proper chain of command.

"Sniveling, among pilots, means to work yourself into a program, whether it happens to be your job or not," recalled Glenn's fellow first lieutenant, Richard Rainforth. "Sniveling is perfectly legitimate, and Johnny is a great hand at it."

It was the first, but not the last case of Glenn's sniveling paying off.

Glenn and Miller joined 155, which immediately moved to the Marine air base in the boiling hot desert of El Centro, California. During cooler times of the day—when the sun wouldn't melt his tires—Glenn learned aerial and gunnery tactics from instructors who had recently returned from combat in the Pacific. The "Ready Teddy" squadron, as it became known, progressed enough to fly the Vought F4U Corsair.

Aided by inverted gull wings, the Corsair carried the same firepower as the Wildcat but vastly outperformed it in the air. The 2,000-horse-power Pratt & Whitney R-2800 Double Wasp radial engine drove a Hamilton Standard Hydromatic three-blade propeller that pulled the plane through the air at four hundred miles per hour. It could reach thirty-five thousand feet and had a fifteen-hundred-mile range. Vought publicists spread the unfounded claim that Japanese pilots referred to the Corsair as "Whistling Death."

"It is one of the finest feelings anyone could imagine," Glenn wrote about the Corsair in his war journal, "to take off, point the nose up and just climb for the clouds. There is nothing any more fun than to play around 'upstairs' in a powerful, fast lightning plane that will really get up and go places when the pilot pushes the throttle forward. It is an incredible feeling, but a very good feeling, sort of [as] though you were sitting on top of everything in the world."

Apart from the heat, the Glenns enjoyed their stay in Southern California. Annie found work as the organist at a Methodist church. They hiked Mount Laguna, frequently crossed the nearby boarder into Mexico, and visited a few famous Los Angeles nightclubs and restaurants. On November 10, the Marine Corps birthday, Annie and John went to Grauman's Chinese Theater to attend the world premiere of a film starring, among others, a young Anthony Quinn. Based on war correspondent Richard Tregaskis's celebrated book of the same name, *Guadalcanal Diary* told the story of the First Marine Division's battle for control of the Solomon Islands.

The gala event proved prophetic for Glenn. Not only did he meet Marine major Joe Foss—the future governor of South Dakota who shot down twenty-six Japanese fighters over Guadalcanal—but the unabashedly patriotic film concluded with Marine aircraft rescuing the heroes. Within a few months, Glenn would be one of those Marine fighter pilots securing the Pacific.

Ordered to ship out, he kissed Annie goodbye on February 5, 1944, took a Navy bus to San Diego, and boarded the USS *Santa Monica.* Overcoming terrible and unexpected seasickness—"[I] fed the fishes twice"—Glenn settled in for the six-day voyage to Hawaii. He spent a week at the Marine air station at Ewa then crammed into a Curtiss C-46 Commando with twenty-two other Marines for a twelve-hundred-mile flight to Midway Atoll.

Nearly two years had passed since the critical Allied victory in the Battle of Midway, so Glenn's squadron spent much of the early weeks there training for their eventual orders at the Marshall Islands. They also chauffeured crewmen from Navy submarines, such as the USS *Barb,* back and forth to sea. Glenn enjoyed the tropical setting, especially the coral reefs and seeing the beautiful but awkward black-footed albatross fly through the air.

By the summer, VMO-155 was sent to the bridge of the USS *Makin Island*, a carrier with an extremely short flight deck that made landing their Corsairs treacherous. The very light ship belonged to the class later known as "Kaiser's Coffins," because the Kaiser Shipyard–built vessels developed a reputation for sinking.

From the *Makin Island,* Glenn's squadron landed at a repurposed Imperial Japanese naval airfield on the Majuro Atoll and joined the Fourth Marine Aircraft Wing. On four nearby atolls, Jaluit, Maloelap, Mili, and Wotje, hundreds of stranded Japanese soldiers remained. With no enemy aircraft in the region, 155's mission became protecting dive-bombers from heavy anti-aircraft fire down below. The Corsairs were soon fitted with pylons underneath the wings and fuselage so they could carry napalm or three one-thousand-pound bombs.

"On strafing runs we generally go in ahead of the SBDs and rake the target area with our wing guns," Glenn explained to Marine Corps combat correspondent Sergeant Peter B. Germano. "This keeps down Jap [anti-aircraft] fire and helps our dive bombers unload their eggs right on the nose."

On July 10, 1944, Glenn set out on his first mission for 155, his first-ever combat mission. His wingman on the four-plane attack along Taroa, an island in the Maloelap Atoll, was a jovial twenty-two-year-old named Miles Franklin Goodman, Jr.

Monte, as he was known, had been a top-notch golfer, winning the club championship at Blue Ridge Country Club in his hometown of Harrisburg, Pennsylvania. After his sophomore year at Penn State University, he reached the championship flight of his district's tournament. Considered "a rising young star" by his local newspaper, Goodman withdrew from college following Pearl Harbor and enlisted in the Navy. He trained in Athens, Georgia, and Anacostia, D.C., then earned his wings at Corpus Christi, two months after John Glenn.

At El Centro, the two became good friends and were bunkmates on the *Santa Monica*. The entire squadron at Midway loved watching the freckled Jewish kid's Frank Sinatra impression.

Their Corsairs cruising at speeds well over four hundred miles per hour, First Lieutenant Glenn and First Lieutenant Goodman finished a run along the coral perimeter then pulled straight up to rendezvous with the rest of the squadron above the clouds, safe from return fire. Goodman's plane didn't show. Glenn called repeatedly to his friend, "Red 2, are you aboard? Red 2—where are you?" But there was no response. Glenn and the other three pilots, including Tom Miller, flew back to the atoll to search for his plane. Over the course of several hours, all they found was an oil slick along the surface. When they returned to base, Glenn openly cried in front of his squadron mates.

"I don't know if I've ever seen anything that touched him more," Miller remembered. "I guess John felt a certain amount of responsibility for his own wingman. Of course, there wasn't anything John could have done about it, but it really hit John hard."

The entire squadron, not just Glenn, took Goodman's death hard. But the war persisted. Over the next eight months Glenn flew fifty-six more missions throughout the Central Pacific, including a few with his boyhood hero. Charles Lindbergh, a consultant for the company that made the Corsair, visited the Marshall Islands to demonstrate bombing tactics.

Other missions required Glenn to push the limits of the Corsair further than ever before. On November 4, 1944, he and a select team were charged with attacking the island of Nauru, a critical resource to the enemy. Due to limited farmland, the Japanese depended greatly on fertilizer to grow crops, and approximately 80 percent of the phosphates needed for that fertilizer came from Nauru.

Following a guide plane, Glenn flew roughly four hundred nautical miles from Majuro to the tiny island, "a long, long flight for a Corsair." Given that range, a terrain composed of many caves and hills, and ceaseless anti-aircraft fire, the mission took precise planning, timing, and execution. It proved a complete success with no casualties.

Over time, Glenn worked his way up the ladder. Beginning as a section leader, he commanded two planes, his own and his wingman's. As a division leader, he commanded two two-plane formations. Finally, as a flight leader, he was responsible for two four-plane formations on a single attack. By the summer, when sidetracked by administrative tasks, commanding officer Major Pete Haines periodically chose Glenn to fill in as leader in the air.

For one such mission, on November 12, 1944, Glenn commanded the entire squadron, twenty-two planes, as they joined an eighty-eight-plane attack on a Japanese base on the Jaluit Atoll. Diving to eight hundred feet, Glenn deployed several napalm tanks, then pulled up less than five hundred feet from a nearby lagoon. The Corsairs trailing behind followed his lead, and together they destroyed or damaged all sixty military buildings in Jabor Town. For that mission Glenn earned his first Air Medal.

As much as his superiors, those pilots under his direction greatly respected Glenn, in addition to being awed by his skills in the air.

"John was always stable—never reckless," recalled Captain Julian Craigmiles, who flew several missions with Glenn as a member of the Fourth Marine Aircraft Wing's VMF-441. "He never tried to set records against the enemy or took unnecessary chances. . . . He used to say to the other pilots: 'It's better that we all stick together and get there, even if we have to take the long way, than to scatter in every direction with some getting there and some not.'"

Set to last the standard twelve months, Glenn's tour in the Pacific ended in early February 1945. Awarded two Distinguished Flying Crosses and ten Air Medals, Glenn received a promotion to captain and orders to report to Patuxent River Naval Air Station in Maryland. Serving a ninety-day stint at the fairly new base, Glenn tested experimental planes developed during the war, including Grumman's F7F Tigercat and F8F Bearcat and the Ryan FR Fireball, a propeller plane outfitted with a jet engine.

"I really got a kick out of that, in feeling that I had contributed to maybe making that a better airplane for everybody to fly later on," he remembered. "It was increasing the combat capability of this country, and I was proud of that."

His next few posts did not fill him with the same sense of purpose.

Although the war in Europe had ended, the Japanese refused to surrender well into the summer of 1945. In preparation for invasion of the mainland, squadrons were being formed and Glenn was assigned to one at Cherry Point Marine Air Station in North Carolina. But in early August, with the deployment of atomic bombs over Hiroshima and Nagasaki, World War II came to an end. Suddenly Cherry Point now had an influx of pilots while maintenance personnel mustered out and planes stopped coming in.

"So it was a time when there wasn't a whole lot of flying," Glenn recalled. "And yet we were trying to keep the squadrons together and keep them as well trained as you possibly could, but that was a hard job back then."

While he waited to fly, he also waited to learn his future in the military.

Repeatedly during their time together in the Marshall Islands, Major Pete Haines encouraged Glenn to become a career Marine. Every Marine who completed flight training was assigned to the Reserves. Those who wanted to remain in the Corps, after the war, could apply for a transfer to the regular Marines. Glenn completed all the necessary steps when he came home from the Pacific, but the approval process dragged on for months.

Twenty-four years old, a new father (Annie gave birth to son David that winter), and at something of a crossroads in his career, Glenn considered backup plans.

For years, John Sr. had hoped that his son would take over the family plumbing business in New Concord. During summers in high school, Glenn had assisted his dad by cutting, reaming, and threading pipes. But as an adult, a future in drains and clogs didn't appeal to him. Neither did his father-in-law's dentistry practice.

Given five years of advanced flying on a variety of planes, he flirted with the idea of becoming a commercial airline pilot. He and another Marine at Patuxent River also dreamed up a business venture. The Army and Navy held a postwar surplus of small transport planes, such as the Beechcraft 18, and they considered building a fleet to deliver fresh seafood from the Atlantic coast to the Midwest.

But he quickly recognized, as did everyone—Annie, his parents, his fellow veterans—that there was only one possible destiny.

"It was obvious that Glenn would stay in the Marines," recalled Captain Clyde W. Coats, a fellow pilot in 155. "It seemed like he was made for it."

On March 6, 1946, Glenn received commission as a regular Marine, beginning a five-year nomadic postwar military lifestyle.

From Cherry Point, the family headed to Southern California, where Captain Glenn served in VMF-323 (the "Death Rattlers") and bounced between El Centro and El Toro Marine Air Station. Seeing an opportunity to fulfill the regular Marine requirement of an overseas peacetime tour, he volunteered for assignment to VMF-218 based at Nan Yuan Field, just south of China's capital, Peiping. Glenn dropped David and a pregnant Annie off with her parents in New Concord for the next twenty-eight months.

In heavily armed Corsairs, the "Hellions" patrolled the skies over north China in search of the Communist armies that threatened the peace General George S. Marshall attempted to negotiate during the Chinese Civil War. Lyn Glenn was born while her father waited in Okinawa, Japan, for a transport home. He briefly met his week-old daughter, flew back to the Hellions, now stationed at Orote Point in Guam, then returned stateside in late 1948 to collect his growing family and move south to Corpus Christi, Texas.

A homecoming to the place he had first earned his wings was not a happy one. Denied assignment to a flying squadron, Glenn served as a glorified security guard, overseeing the Navy's downtown headquarters. His staff monitored the streets for rowdy customers on shore leave, corralled drunks, and broke up knife and razor-blade fights, locking the perpetrators up in small jail cells. Even when transferred to an instructor's position at

Cabaniss Field, Glenn wasn't doing what he loved. In time, his role as an instructor became instructing instructors on how to instruct.

"I didn't much want that," he said decades later. "That was something that most active fighter pilots saw as sort of a way station taking them out of more active or squadron-type flying for a while."

In the summer of 1951, he returned east, to Quantico, Virginia, for six months of study at the Amphibious Warfare School, "another assignment I didn't particular want." Once he completed the course, he was added to the general staff of the Commandant for the Marine Corps School (MCS).

The post came with several fringe benefits. At each of his previous stops the family had lived in dingy, overpopulated off-base apartments or cramped, two-family Quonset huts with paper-thin, fiberboard walls. At Quantico, for the first time in his military career, Glenn received base housing.

The large, three-bedroom apartment coupled with a promotion to major, clearance to handle sensitive and secret material, and free tuition to classes at the University of Maryland made his new stay at Quantico seem ideal. In July 1952 alone, an opinion piece he wrote (including a headshot and byline) was published in *Marine Corps Gazette* and he flew to New York City to represent the Marine Corps at a National Air Transportation Coordinating Committee conference. He particularly enjoyed the glitzy setup at Idlewild Airport.

"It was the epitome of a Hollywood version conference room," he explained in a report for his speech class at the University of Maryland. "The room was air conditioned, soundproofed, indirectly lighted, water containers on the table, deep carpeting, large leather armchairs, around a mahogany table approximately twenty feet long shaped like a diamond with the points cut off. If atmosphere and surroundings make for deep thought and correct decisions, this conference room should be utilized by the United Nations."

But Glenn wanted to fly, not supervise live-fire training exercises, monitor safety precautions regarding roadblocks, and study two dozen pages of tables depicting the difference in airspeed between water-filled bombs and wet-sand-filled bombs. The only pilot on the commandant's staff, Glenn was permitted just four hours of flight time per month, usually in the dreaded Gooney Bird.

Worse yet, Glenn believed that his exceptional skills could have been put to better use.

That summer—around the same time that the Associated Press reported "The Korean war is two years old . . . and peace never seemed farther away"—Glenn began writing monthly letters to the operations officer at Quantico, Colonel Richard E. Thompson. As politely as possible, he requested assignment to the war.

"All the materials we had studied in school there involved the Korean War. The talk was about the Korean War. You had people coming back from the Korean War," he said years later. "So I thought this was my vocation, this was my life's work, and to not go to Korea was something that I couldn't contemplate."

Although his boss at the Marine Corps School reprimanded Glenn for the attempts to snivel his way into combat, orders for Korea arrived in November. While Captain Ted Williams participated in a mock assault off the nearby coast of Onslow Beach, Glenn reported to Cherry Point.

Following the completion of a brief jet refresher course with VMAT-20 training squadron, he loaded the family up in their 1950 Buick Roadmaster Convertible. Singing songs the entire way, Glenn drove them back to Central Ohio. For a third time in nine years, Annie—now with two children—would stay with her parents while her husband left for the Pacific. Before leaving, Glenn and seven-year-old David together built several plastic models of the United States military airplanes in action above North Korea.

On the chilly, rainy runway of the airport that would one day bear his name, Major Glenn, dressed in his Marine Service Alphas and garrison cap, carried out a longstanding family tradition. Every time he left for the dangers of a distant assignment—be it Midway Atoll, Peiping, Korea, or later on, a far more uncertain destination—Glenn handed each member of the family a stick of Doublemint gum. "Here," he said. "I'm going to the store to buy another pack. I'll be back."

His mementos delivered, Glenn prepared to board a twenty-four-hour-long Trans World Airlines flight to Los Angeles, which included layovers in Indianapolis, St. Louis, Kansas City, Dallas, El Paso, and Albuquerque. There were tears—David remembered his mother sobbing in the car that morning—but at no point did they discuss the obvious.

"We didn't talk about how much we would miss each other or the chance I might not return," Glenn remembered. "Death never entered our conversations."

CHAPTER THREE

The Blow and Go Group

By way of California, Ted Williams landed at Oahu in Hawaii on January 29, 1953. Dressed in officer's service khakis, he checked into the Bachelor Officer Quarters "B" at Barbers Point Naval Air Station, signed autographs and took photos with fans around the island, then relaxed at one of Honolulu's many gorgeous beaches.

The following day he and a few dozen fellow Marine and Navy personnel boarded a Martin JRM Mars flying boat. The transport stopped briefly for fuel at the naval air station in Guam, then at the naval air station in Atsugi, Japan, and again at the naval air station in Itami. On February 3 one last transport finally brought Williams to Korea.

As part of the First MAW, Williams was attached to Marine Aircraft Group-33 (MAG-33), stationed at Yongil-man Airfield in the lower half of the south Korean city Pohang. Imperial Japan had built the airstrip during its occupation of the region prior to World War II.

At the start of the United States' intervention in Korea, the Air Force assumed responsibility for many of these airfields and ports. By 1953, there were fifty-seven, and rather than using Japanese or Korean names, each was given its own unique designation, starting with "King" followed by a number. Yongil-man Airfield became King-3 or K-3 for short.

MAG-33 was composed of seven subordinate units. Three were staff and aircraft maintenance, and four were operational squadrons flying missions. VMF(N)-513, VMF-115, and VMF-311 were the fighter squadrons. ("V" stood for "heavier than air," i.e. an aviation unit, "M" stood for Marine, "F" stood for "Fighter.") VMJ-1 also flew missions over North Korea, collecting "tactical aerial photographic reconnaissance." Each month, this photographic squadron of a dozen pilots snapped tens of thousands of pictures of enemy supply lines, barracks, and ammunitions warehouses, both before and after Allied attacks.

VMF(N)-513 was stationed at K-8, near Kunsan, 150 miles west of K-3. But VMJ-1, VMF-115, and VMF-311, to which Williams was assigned, were all stationed at K-3. Carrying out the exact same type of missions, 311 and 115 were considered "sister squadrons."

In addition to pilots, maintenance workers, communications specialists, radar officers, as well as multiple doctors, dentists, and chaplains—roughly fifteen hundred enlisted men and officers in all—fell under the command of Colonel Louis "Ben" Robertshaw. A third-team all-American center and captain for the 1935 Navy Midshipman football team, the Philadelphia native had made a name for himself during World War II. Piloting a Douglas SBD-1 Dauntless as a dive-bomber for Marine Scout Bombing Squadron-132, Robertshaw sank a Japanese troop carrier during the Battle of Guadalcanal. A month later, after the squadron's commanding officer, Major Joseph Sailer, Jr., was killed, Robertshaw took command and led an attack of a Japanese base on Munda Point.

Ten years later, in August 1952, the forty-one-year-old became commanding officer of MAG-33.

"Robertshaw impressed me so much," Ted Williams later said. "I saw him as a young kid play when he was an All-American out of Navy. And here I am under his command in Korea. He led flights as a colonel, he had a lot of guts, he was a great leader, tremendous guy. I always told him after I resigned from the Marine Corps, 'If they ever make you Commandant, I'll rejoin the outfit!'"

Another senior officer impressed Williams during his first few weeks in Korea.

"So I get into K-3, which was our base over there, and we're having a big squadron meeting, you know," Williams remembered forty-five years later. "And there's two guys standing over there, maybe 60 to 70 feet. And I look and say, 'That looks like the right stuff to me. . . . One of them was John Glenn."

Major Glenn arrived at K-3 twelve days after Williams. Given his yearning to serve and an impressive résumé—two Distinguished Flying Crosses, a spot on the commandant's staff at MCS, test pilot work at Patuxent River—Glenn became a valuable asset to the squadron. Immediately assigned to the post of assistant operations officer, he soon took over as operations officer, a vital job that he had previously performed with the Hellions in Guam and the Death Rattlers at El Toro. After 311's commanding officer, Lieutenant Colonel Francis "Ken" Coss, and executive officer, Lieutenant Colonel Art Moran, Glenn considered the role "sort of third in command, although there may be other senior people."

The operations officer occasionally planned missions and briefed the entire squadron, but by far his most challenging task was assigning flights, or "hops." Per Marine regulations during the war, when a pilot reached one hundred combat missions, they were either reassigned to a desk job or sent home. Some officers hoped to cram in as many flights as possible.

"All the fellows are really hot to go and get griped when anyone gets ahead in missions," Glenn wrote Annie in February. "Of course, some of them may have this '100 missions to relief' in their heads and want to get them in for that reason, but it's so unusual to see a whole squadron so eager. Guess the jets have a lot to do with it. If we were all pushing throttles on the 'bent-wings,' some of the eagerness would probably dwindle.

"Any guy who is always around trying to get a hop is a 'sniveler,' so with a whole squadron like this, it makes it rough on 'snivelers' like myself because we have so much competition."

But even John Glenn did not care for one particular duty assigned to all pilots within 311. Two-hour combat air patrol (CAP) shifts were scheduled half an hour before sunrise or half an hour after sunset, and pilots sat in the cockpit of their aircraft, on the runway ready to take off at any moment. Oftentimes, the plane never left the ground: "Hate these weeks where we have this blasted CAP. Sit in the plane and sit and sit," he wrote Annie. The transistor radio on which he listened to orchestra music helped Glenn pass the time. He also brought his Kodachrome camera aboard; during missions, he snapped photographs from thousands of feet in the air.

Despite the CAPs, as Glenn told Annie that spring, he was having "the time of my life. May even pass up my first R&R."

Ted Williams was not a sniveler, and certainly not having the time of his life. Beginning with his arrival at Willow Grove to begin retraining—"I'm still praying for a truce in Korea," he told reporters that day—to his departure from California, Williams had resented his recall. And once he arrived at K-3, he was more focused on the food in the mess hall and where he might get a haircut than fulfilling his one hundred missions.

"Looks like I'll beat the 15th of Feb. deadline for my first missions as the day after tomorrow should be 'it,'" he wrote to a friend in the U.S. "You can say that again about me being in any more outfits. This is the last."

By the middle of February, the reluctant, fatalistic Reservist and the eager, optimistic active-duty regular Marine had each settled into the same spot for the foreseeable future. And from the outset neither knew what to make of the other.

"When Glenn joined the squadron I didn't know who he was," Williams remembered. "None of us knew much about him."

"I didn't know what to expect from him," Glenn said. "I didn't know whether he would be a guy who only talked about baseball."

Both men's initial assessments were wrong: Williams avoided the topic of baseball, and several members of 311 knew quite a bit about Glenn.

Upon hearing of Glenn's arrival to K-3, a pair of second lieutenants approached Lieutenant Colonel Art Moran. They urged the squadron's executive officer to ensure that Glenn was assigned to 311, not 115. Moran asked why.

"He is the greatest guy and the best instructor ever to have been seen in the Navy's flight school," replied one of the two young lieutenants who had likely earned their wings at the naval air station in Corpus Christi, where Glenn instructed pilots from 1949 to 1951.

A few of the more seasoned officers already flying missions for 311 knew Glenn as well. Majors James G. Fox and Robert Sabot had served alongside him in China after World War II.

And Major Julian Craigmiles, a pilot in the photo squadron, had served with Glenn in the Marshall Islands as part of VMO-155. While at K-3, Craigmiles told others of Glenn's leadership and abilities in the cockpit, but also his subtle humor.

"When we were going overseas on an aircraft carrier, we were sunbathing on the deck," Craigmiles remembered about their time together in World War II. "Glenn remarked that the voyage reminded him of the fellow who fell off the Empire State Building; and as he was passing each window, called out 'Everything is all right so far!'"

Not everyone knew Glenn's reputation when he first arrived. Many of the Reserve pilots at K-3, like Ted Williams, had been inactive for several years before war broke out. Aside from brief refresher courses and retraining stops, they had not been near a Navy or Marine air base since World

War II. To Reserve pilot Robert "Woody" Woodbury, Jr., a first lieutenant in VMF-115, Glenn "was just a nonentity; just another Marine pilot."

No one would say the same about Captain Williams. The tall baseball star and national pitchman for Chesterfield cigarettes, Thom McAn dress shoes, and Johnson's Car-Plate Auto Wax stood out like a sore thumb.

Several officers playfully chided Williams when he arrived. Every pilot, including John Glenn, took to calling the lifetime .347 hitter "Bush," short for "bush leaguer" or well below acceptable standards.

"Let's see now, Bush, in 1948 you batted .269, didn't you?" one might say.

"No, no, you're cheating ole Bush," added another. "He hit .270 that year."

Williams would laugh, and reply, "Look it up, fellows, it's in the book."

Even Lieutenant Colonel Moran, teased him, saying Williams was safer flying jets over Communist North Korea than he was "dodging all those pop-bottles" at Fenway Park.

And a fake memo that circulated among 311 pilots, written in response to the CO's real memo, joked about whether or not Williams "could get to first base with Marilyn Monroe. . . . DiMaggio didn't." The starlet had recently told a Hollywood reporter that she and Joltin' Joe were "just good friends."

Still, there was no denying that K-3's newest resident was a bona fide national celebrity. Marines who wrote home to their wives and children mentioned just seeing Williams around the base. On the day he joined 311, Glenn wrote a letter to Annie. Among the many details about the base, his quarters, and familiar officers, Glenn told her, "Ted Williams is in outfit. Lives in next hut. Met him—seems OK."

Both enlisted men and officers encouraged Williams to join the base's occasional softball game. The public information officer of the First MAW read through weekly requests from the Associated Press, the International News Service, *Pacific Stars and Stripes*, *Colliers*, and *Sport* magazine for interviews with Williams. Six weeks before the start of spring training, Williams was answering reporters' questions about the Yankees, the Indians, and the Red Sox' wacky young outfielder Jimmy Piersall.

Williams preferred not to talk about the Red Sox, other major-league stars, his homer one afternoon in Chicago that defeated a fellow pilot's local club, or anything of the sort.

Second Lieutenant Harold Breece, an electronics officer at K-3, did not care much about baseball. He had no idea who patrolled left field for Boston. Someone introduced him to Williams at the Officers' Club and the two made pleasantries. Eventually Breece, born and raised in Yakima, Washington, mentioned his interest in fishing. Williams perked up, and they talked at length about their favorite spots all over North America.

"Well, lieutenant colonels and colonels would come by and interrupt our conversation and talk baseball," Breece recalled. "A few days later I bumped into him. We met on the flight line or someplace, just going our different ways. I go up to him and apologize for not knowing who he was. He said 'I didn't mind. I'm up to here with baseball. I go to the club and that's all they want to talk about! . . . I'm full of it. That's my occupation. I love fishing.'"

New arrivals to K-3 in late 1952 and early 1953 immediately endured two overwhelming blows to the senses.

"Pohang had a terrible smell, especially when the wind would blow," remembered Sergeant Fred Miser, a member of the Air Maintenance Squadron. "Human waste was their main fertilizer used in growing rice."

John Glenn noticed it too, although the scent of a traditional Korean food fermenting outside the neighboring homes bothered him nearly as much.

"He didn't care for kimchi," David Glenn remembered. "Something about that really put him off, I think maybe it was the strong garlic smell or something or his New Concord palate back then in the early 1950s."

But it was the intense cold of, not the smell carried by, the wind that made a deeper impression on Glenn and every member of Marine Aircraft Group-33.

K-3 sat below Yongil-man, a six-mile-wide bay cut out from the Sea of Japan. With temperatures twenty degrees Fahrenheit or lower, winters so close to the water were brutal.

Aware of the frigid conditions on the peninsula, the Marine Corps sent personnel slated for deployment to cold weather battalion training at Camp Pickel Meadows in the Sierra Nevada's Toiyabe National Forest. Chosen for the high altitude, craggy terrain, and thick snow, the spot twenty miles north of Bridgeport, California, closely resembled the landscape of Korea, making it an ideal location for fifteen-mile training courses and mock battles in the snow.

"Nobody can fight in bitter cold, but those Commies never got the word," *Marine Corps Gazette* explained. "As long as they do it, we'll just have to learn."

For several days, both enlisted men and officers slept in sleeping bags and ate C rations out of a rucksack. Eventually they moved on to cozier quarters inside Quonset huts and dined at a makeshift mess hall. During his week-and-a-half training in January, Ted Williams caught a virus that stayed with him for months. On the route to K-3, his Navy transport stopped for a few days in Tokyo, where "everybody went out on the town except me. I stayed in bed for two days feeling lousy."

The accommodations at K-3 didn't cheer Williams up any.

Officers at K-3 were housed in long rows of small square huts. During World War II, the Army used these canvas-lined huts in the tropical climates of the Central and South Pacific. In Korea, during the winter, Marines practically froze in the poorly insulated quarters. "These huts are like a screen," one officer at K-3 wrote from underneath four blankets.

"Korea is the coldest hole I have ever even imagined and here we are in these damn tropical huts," recalled First Lieutenant Rylen B. Rudy, who arrived at K-3 in December 1952. "You got strings going across that you can hang your clean laundry on and you'd sit there and watch the socks or skivvies or whatever wave in the breeze 'cause the wind was going through that darn tropical hut."

Each hut housed three men, who slept inside mountain sleeping bags atop cots far too short for the six-foot, three-inch Williams. With no indoor plumbing, pilots relieved themselves in the squadron's outdoor latrine or one of the upright pipes ("piss tubes") located around the base. Shaving and teeth-brushing were done standing over a small tin basin using a compact mirror and jerry cans of water. Bathing was available at the nearby "shower hut."

In the middle of each individual hut sat the most important equipment, a potbelly stove that burned kerosene when there was enough and jet propellant (JP) when there wasn't.

"The Army was the one that controlled the oil for the potbellied stoves that we had," said First Lieutenant Rudy. "Well, they gave us about four hours per day of oil and that's all. The thing that they didn't realize, we're flying jet airplanes. JP-3 is coal oil so what we'd do is we'd take an airplane refueler down through the hut area into these fifty-gallon drums that we had sitting outside and we'd fill those damn drums with JP and we had a hot stove twenty-four hours a day. . . . If you were more than about four feet away from the potbellied stove that sat in the middle, it was cold."

Fresh off a rough night's sleep, pilots within 311 carried out daily flights, or sorties, from within F9F Panthers. Introduced by the Grumman Engineering Aircraft Corporation in the late 1940s, the Panther became the highest-performing fighter of both the Navy and the Marines during the Korean War. By the time Ted Williams and John Glenn reported to K-3 in February, 311 flew three different versions of the single-seat plane: the F9F-2, the F9F-4, and the F9F-5. By late April, 311 would use the F9F-5 model exclusively.

Spanning 38 feet and powered by a 6,280-pound-thrust Pratt & Whitney J48 turbojet engine, the F9F-5 could attain 543 miles per hour (Mach 0.82) in level flight at 35,000 feet. At the end of each wing was a fuel tip-tank, which could be jettisoned if necessary. Combined with the internal fuel, the two tip-tanks gave the Panther a range of approximately 1,000 miles.

"[The Panther] wouldn't go as fast as a lot of other jets," Glenn recalled, "but it was a very tough airplane and would take a lot of hits, which I found out later was to my advantage."

Both the F9F-4 and F9F-5 models reflected improvements that strengthened the wings to carry up to four thousand pounds of weaponry affixed to multiple pylons on the underside of each wing. The pylons were designed to accommodate general purpose (GP) bombs of several different weights up to a thousand pounds, napalm incendiary bombs, and two types of fin-stabilized rockets.

Sporting a five-inch diameter warhead, the steel-encased high velocity aircraft rocket (HVAR) streaked toward its target at more than one thousand feet per second. The HVAR was highly effective against most enemy ground transports and targets, but not the Soviet-built T-34 tank that both North Korea and China utilized. To combat the T-34, the Navy air weapons station at China Lake, California, modified the HVAR with a six-and-a-half-inch, shaped-charge warhead. This improved weapon was called the anti-tank aircraft rocket (ATAR).

Depending on weather conditions, MAG-33 Panthers flew north every day from Pohang into Communist-held territory above the 38th Parallel. GPs, HVARs, ATARs, and napalm tanks, dropped from a few hundred feet above, pounded enemy supply lines, ammunition depots, and troop shelters. In early 1953 targets in the North resided in places such as Sinanju, Wonsan, and Songchon. Occasionally 311 and 115 teamed up for larger strikes featuring as many as thirty-six planes.

Flying strictly air-to-ground sorties, pilots rarely encountered or engaged enemy aircraft during these strikes. Although on July 21, 1951, a Soviet-made MiG-15 shot down Richard Bell, a first lieutenant with 311, who survived two torturous years as a prisoner of war. In addition to interdictions (i.e. attacking enemy resources), some missions, known as close air support (CAS) sorties provided aerial cover for Marines and United Nations ground forces. Deploying GPs and dropping napalm tanks ("nape scrapes") required flying hazardous, low-level pinpoint attacks within range of rifle and anti-aircraft cannon fire from enemy ground troops below.

"Our job was to support the ground-pounders on the front lines," Ted Williams remembered. "We'd dive down on the Chinese, drop our load, and get the hell out of there as fast as we could."

After a while, MAG-33 became known as the "Blow and Go Group," a moniker posted on the official sign that hung outside K-3.

Before joining the Blow and Go Group on daily sorties, new pilots underwent additional training by way of lectures, briefings, and review of procedures listed in the exhaustively detailed "VMF-311 S.O.P for Tactical Flight Operations" handout. The fifty-one-page document outlined everything from cruising speeds, landing procedures, bombing tactics, and flight patterns to emergency protocols such as ejecting from the cockpit, parachute deployment, and survival gear. In addition to a first aid kit, pilots carried flares, a life vest (referred to as a "Mae West"), and shark repellent in preparation for a crash-landing in the freezing Sea of Japan or the Yellow Sea. For encounters with friendly or unfriendly locals, each also carried a blood chit, cerise (friend or foe) panel, barter kit, knife, and revolver.

"What the hell good that peashooter was going to be, only God knows," Williams recalled. "Mine was never loaded. I'd decided that if I was forced to parachute out behind Chinese lines, I was going to float down with my hands up in that air. 'I'm Captain T.S. Williams,' I was going to tell the gooks, 'and I don't know a fuckin' thing.'"

In addition to operational study, "familiarization" or "fam" flights, also known as "cream puff hops," were required. The cold weather, winds, and physical terrain differed greatly from Cherry Point, El Toro, and Roosevelt Roads in Puerto Rico. And as the new assistant operations officer, John Glenn became fixated on studying the detailed maps posted around the S-3 Operations Office.

The peninsula was vastly different from the atolls and islands that he had navigated while in the Pacific during World War II. Glenn became especially focused on the mountain ranges throughout Korea.

"This is a really rough area to fly over," he wrote Annie, "but I guess it would be worse to walk over. . . . Mountains, mountains, all over the place."

Five fam hops, each roughly an hour, offered new pilots a chance to get the lay of the land as well as learn the important code words for particular hot spots and situations.

Communist territory, north of the Main Line of Resistance (MLR), was considered "Indian Country," and anyone hit by anti-aircraft fire caught an "arrow." Pilots flying at the end of a formation, known as "flak back," were most vulnerable to arrows. On-again, off-again peace talks took place in "The Holy Land," a location in between Panmunjom and Kaesong. Flying near there was strictly forbidden. Colloquialisms also applied to the terrain. Bodies of water were dubbed the "Boot," and the "Nutcracker Lake." Key spots along the Rimjin River, near the Main Line of Resistance, were known as "Double Bend" and the "M in the Rimjin" (because it resembled the letter). And a noteworthy twin-peaked mountain range became "Marilyn Monroe."

On Saturday, February 14, Jack W. Campbell, Jr., who had also served as an instructor at Pensacola during World War II, led Williams on his final fam. The hop doubled as a reconnaissance mission, with the two captains surveying the MLR and reporting back to K-3.

The next afternoon, Williams joined Mission Number 3333, a routine interdiction (ID) of enemy supply lines. He executed a preflight checklist and inspected the Panther assigned to him as well as its accompanying ordnance. Back in the squadron's Ready Room he observed a briefing from the mission leader, Major Lloyd Dochterman. Twenty-five minutes before takeoff Williams trotted out to the runway. The fifth and final strike conducted that day would be comparatively small, just five pilots: Dochterman,

Williams, Captain Joseph Carruthers, Captain Charles Street, and Captain William B. "Bill" Clem.

Born in Louisville, Kentucky, Clem had attended the University of Louisville before World War II interrupted his business administration studies. The twenty-year-old sophomore joined the Navy aviation cadet program and earned his wings at the naval air station in Livermore, California. Stateside throughout the fighting, Clem was attached after World War II to the Volunteer Reserve out of the Fifth Marine Corps Reserve District.

A real estate salesman in his hometown, he was recalled to active duty the same week as Ted Williams. Following retraining stops at Cherry Point and Roosevelt Roads—in North Carolina he went to a few restaurants and a ballgame with Williams—Clem left his wife, Marian, and young daughter, Barbara, for California in January 1953. During cold weather battalion training at Camp Pickel Meadows, he reconnected with Williams, and the two journeyed to Japan and then Korea aboard the same Navy transports.

By the time both men joined 311, Clem considered Williams one of "the guys" with whom he regularly socialized. In letters home to Marian and Barbara, he often spoke of "Ted."

Five minutes before the scheduled liftoff at 1430 hours, Williams, Clem, and the rest of the strike team "lit up" their airplanes; then they taxied along the runway, accelerated to 110 knots IAS (indicated air speed), and climbed. At twenty thousand feet in the air, the planes rendezvoused, checked in with the flight leader via radio, and headed northwest to an area fifteen miles outside of Sariwon.

Williams, Clem, and Carruthers—each on their first-ever combat mission—knew that fighters in 311 had encountered meager to intense automatic weapon anti-aircraft fire on similar bombing missions during the previous few days. Clem remembered feeling "nervous, but not too scared."

"Boy I really had my eyes open for anything that looked like flak or MiGs," Ted Williams wrote that evening. "But the trip was uneventful except we blew a bridge out and a rail cut."

At 1534 hours, the planes reached their primary target, the rail line, and deployed thirty GPs. One confirmed cut was observed, and two more were considered probable. The mission having been deemed successful, the team swung around to make the 250-mile flight back to K-3. Forty minutes later the planes arrived and initiated landing procedures, beginning with the leader, Dochterman.

Clem attained a seventy-degree bank, reduced his engine's revolutions per minute (RPM) to 70 percent, extended the landing gear and flaps, checked that the wheel indicators and hydraulic gauge read ninety degrees, and laconically reported on his radio: "One-Four, turning base. Wheels indication down and locked. Pressure up." But as he neared Runway 09, he completely missed his mark and smashed the hull. According to one report, the munitions on an adjacent aircraft caught fire as a result.

Medical and fire personnel hurried to the runway to discover an unsalvageable airplane and an unharmed pilot. Nevertheless, Clem went to the hospital, where the only medicine prescribed was a shot of brandy.

"Luck was with me and I haven't a scratch," he wrote home.

That night pilots on the successful railroad cut, as well as others from MAG-33, relaxed and visited the Officers' Club. Released from the hospital, Clem joined them, but did not stay long. The afternoon's crash continued to bother him.

"I'm real mad at myself because it was all my fault," Clem wrote to Marian and Barbara. "I had to see that all the guys got their free drinks at the bar tonight. I left early cause I don't feel too glad about the whole thing."

Clem worried about being grounded, perhaps permanently, as punishment for the crash.

"There is a big strike planned for tomorrow, I hope I can fly," he continued. "I've got to redeem myself."

Clem would indeed redeem himself. The following morning, he participated in the large-scale attack below the North Korean capital of Pyongyang. With exact precision he deployed all eight of his 250-pound GPs at once, triggering a secondary blast that shredded a Communist storage warehouse. And just for good measure, upon his return to K-3, he executed a textbook, easy landing, leaving the plane in pristine condition.

His friend Ted Williams, a part of that very same mission, could not say the same.

CHAPTER FOUR

Three Runs, Three Hits, Three Errors

Major John Glenn was not part of the enormous raid that Bill Clem helped successfully execute. Even the highly decorated and thoroughly trained pilot needed five cream puff hops, familiarization with his issued equipment—"I have never seen so much survival gear," he told Annie—and review of the squadron handbooks before jetting out on missions. He spent his first several days inside the S-2 Intelligence Office studying and refining the small maps that he would carry with him inside the cockpit.

"One week since my arrival in this beautiful land and [I] still have yet to cross the bomb line," he wrote to Annie. "I'm a little more than somewhat disgruntled."

But he had already settled into his bitterly cold quarters and learned the names of the Korean waitresses inside the officer mess hall ("Ingrid," "Hedy," and "Lara") as chaos began to encircle K-3.

"Hey, they got the Bush Leaguer! Ted Williams!" a radio operator shouted to anyone within earshot. "He's on fire and going down near Kyomipo!"

"What!" responded Martin Loski, a freelance reporter visiting K-3 to interview Williams. "Anybody with him?"

"No one."

"Now someone is telling him to ditch!" the radio operator continued to narrate.

"Looks like the Boston Red Sox will need a new outfielder," Loski replied.

———

On the morning of February 16, two hundred Allied planes began to converge over the North Korean town of Kyomipo, twenty-five miles south of Pyongyang. While F-86 Sabre jets from the United States Air Force engaged Soviet-made MiGs, four additional Air Force wings and two

Marine aircraft groups (MAG-12 and MAG-33) were to bomb dozens of Communist supply buildings and troop shelters. Nineteen pilots from VMF-311 and sixteen from VMF-115 flew for MAG-33. From K-6, near the western city of Pyeongtaek, pilots in MAG-12 would join with MAG-33 in the air above Kyomipo.

Prior to takeoff, Major Marvin "Pinky" Hollenbeck pulled aside Captain Ted Williams. The thirty-one-year-old Hollenbeck had been made leader of a four-plane division on the mission and was assigned Williams as his wingman. Well aware of the Reservist/ballplayer's lack of combat experience, Hollenbeck told him, "Ted, I don't care whether you hit the target or not, I just want you to get home safe."

The thirty-five MAG-33 pilots left K-3 starting at 0935 hours and arrived at the target eighty minutes later. Just as Bill Clem did, Hollenbeck unloaded his eight 250-pound GPs, pulled up, and headed for the rendezvous far away from the target: Blow and Go. Hollenbeck's wingman Williams trailed right behind and unloaded his GPs on a target he believed to be a tank and infantry training school. On his way out of the drop, small arms fire from Communist troops below missed Hollenbeck soaring by at several hundred miles per hour but was perfectly aligned with Williams. Multiple hits perforated the plane, which caught on fire.

Williams had learned at Cherry Point the previous summer that his Panther's controls were very sensitive: "I can handle one with my little finger, actually." The controls, also known as "the stick," governed pitch (nose up and nose down) and roll (left and right wing up and down). But after his plane was hit over Kyomipo, Williams noticed a drastic change as he pulled up.

"I felt the plane mush up on me for an instant but I didn't even know I was hit," he said. "The first warning I had was a tightening of the controls. The stick got stiffer on me and I knew I had lost my hydraulic system. Then the electrical system went out on me. No radio, no fuel or speed gauges. No nothing."

With the plane now difficult to control and leaking fuel, Williams followed standard procedure. He turned off the leaking hydraulics system, meaning the brakes and assisted control of the throttle no longer functioned. Several warning lights appeared on the cockpit's console, including one which indicated that the engine was on fire. Despite flying a smoking, leaking, instrument-less, bullet-riddled aircraft, Williams was actually fortunate.

"John Glenn told me later that I was lucky the whole plane didn't blow up on me," he said.

With his plane still intact, Williams barked the standard "Mayday" call into his radio, which no longer worked. He could, however, see comrades in the air through his canopy. Several urged him, via hand signals, to eject from the plane and parachute to safety.

Williams, who had now removed his oxygen mask, foresaw two major problems with their suggestion. First, given how close to the target he had been hit, he remained in enemy airspace. Kyomipo was at minimum sixty miles from Allied-held territory. His barter kit, unloaded revolver, and salty demeanor—"I'm Captain T.S. Williams . . . and I don't know a fuckin' thing"—would not do him much good that deep into Communist territory.

Bailing out posed another concern for the thirty-four-year-old who hoped to one day return to baseball. Because he was much taller than most combat pilots, just squeezing into the cockpit had become a challenge for Williams and the ground crew at K-3.

"We actually had to physically jam Capt. Williams down with our feet to get his shoulder harness straps fastened," one of the crewmen recalled. "We really had to cram him into the cockpit. We often thought 'Boy, if he ever has to crash-land, he'll come out of the cockpit like a spring.'"

The tight confines didn't really bother Williams. The SNJ-4 that he had flown for two years at Pensacola was by no means spacious. But a rumor circulating among jet pilots terrified him.

"Ted told me later the reason he didn't want to get out," John Glenn said. "He'd heard about some Navy pilot a short time before that [who] ejected and his feet had hit the canopy and cut his feet off as he was being ejected. And Ted said he didn't want to take a chance on that and so he'd rather ride this thing in."

Refusing to bail out left Williams with just one option: climb as high as possible. This served two purposes. At that altitude the atmosphere contained less oxygen, which meant the engine fire that was indicated by the cockpit warning light could not burn as fiercely. Although the plane was rapidly leaking fuel, if Williams could reach roughly twenty thousand feet he would benefit from the thin air by flying with less drag. And if the engine did fail, he could then coast without fuel for miles, hopefully finding a safe place to land. Pilots referred to this method as flying "dead stick."

Jerry Coleman—the New York Yankees second baseman who had

joined Williams for a Navy physical examination the year before—served on the mission near Kyomipo. A pilot in VMA-323, which flew Corsairs, not jets, Coleman was attached to MAG-12. Around the time that Williams's plane came under fire, Coleman unloaded his two thousand-pound bombs on his target. Suddenly, he heard over the radio great commotion, pilots yelling out "Mayday, Mayday." Coleman had no idea that the pilot was his teammate on the 1950 American League all-star roster.

"You listen and here comes another young pilot, 'I've got you, I've got you, you're burning, I'll take you to [K-13]' and so off they go," Coleman recalled. "And so whether you realize it or not that's your brother, that's you, when you listen. . . . Finally, the next morning we found out that that was Ted Williams, had an angel on his shoulder."

The angel was twenty-two-year-old First Lieutenant Larry Hawkins.

Hawkins had enlisted in the Marines as a high school student in Pine Grove, Pennsylvania, outside Harrisburg. While Ted Williams was winning his third and fourth American League batting titles in 1947 and 1948, Hawkins served as the Pine Grove High basketball team's manager and sports editor for the school yearbook. ("Would like to be a test pilot" accompanied his senior year photograph.) Just to be accepted for basic training at Parris Island in South Carolina, Hawkins needed his parents to sign a waiver.

After preflight school in Pensacola, Hawkins earned his wings as a second lieutenant in November 1951. Again, because he was still a minor, his parents had to formally approve the commission via telegram. Less than a year later, he was assigned to K-3, and he had already flown forty missions for VMF-311 by the time he witnessed Ted Williams's plane spewing white smoke from the engine and leaking fluid along the fuselage. By now the fuselage was on fire, not just the engine, something which Williams later said that he was unaware of.

"If I had known then that my ship was on fire, I damn well would have shot my canopy and jumped," Williams soon wrote in the *Saturday Evening Post*.

Meanwhile, Hawkins continued to tail Williams, who without knowing it continued to head north, farther into Communist territory. Hawkins pulled alongside, and the two began exchanging hand signals: Hawkins tried in vain to coax Williams into ejecting.

Following Hawkins and his rudimentary instructions (tapping his chest to indicate "follow me") Williams slowly turned south, continuing to climb, toward Allied territory. Realizing that Williams had no chance of reaching K-3, Hawkins radioed Major Hollenbeck, asking for instructions. The division leader, now also trailing Williams, told Hawkins to guide the plane to the nearest Air Force base, K-13. Hawkins radioed the tower at K-13, located roughly twenty-five miles south of Seoul, where the field had become crowded. Not only were Air Force F-86s returning back to base from the mission, but twenty-five pilots from VMF-311 and VMF-115 were now following or escorting Williams to K-13, each running low on fuel. As pilots scrambled to clear planes off the runway, fire and medical personnel prepared for Williams's arrival. Meanwhile, First Lieutenant Hawkins continued to monitor the damaged bird in the air.

From thirty-five hundred feet Hawkins gave Williams the "gear down" signal to ready a landing. Without a functioning electrical system, Williams prepared to "blow" his gear down, in other words ignite a cartridge that would manually open the wheel well doors so that the landing gear dropped.

"The minute he hit the gear handle down, the wheel well doors came down, and immediately the fire erupted right underneath the fuselage," Hawkins said. "So I called out over the radio 'Eject! Eject! Eject!'"

Sitting atop billowing smoke and fire and unable to hear through his inoperable radio, Williams continued to descend and target the ground. Fortunately the runway at K-13 stretched ten thousand feet long, twice the length at K-3. At roughly 225 miles per hour—more than double the normal speed of a conventional landing—Williams brought the plane in. With the hydraulics system turned off, his dive brakes—essentially air flaps that increased drag on the plane, thus slowing it down—no longer worked. And with only one wheel barely protruding down from its well door, there was another problem. With the wheel well open, leaking fuel might collect beneath the fuselage, where fire had already broken out. Williams wisely pulled the lone wheel back into the well and closed the door.

From that point on, he would have to "belly" the plane in, sliding on the fuselage along the runway and relying on time, distance, and friction to stop the Panther.

As sparks flew, a piece of the plane, possibly the metal panel covering the wheel well, ripped off, smashing into the K-13 mess hall. Coasting for more than a thousand yards prompted Williams to do something unusual.

"If I ever prayed in my life, the only goddamn thing I said was 'If there's a goddamn Christ this is the time old Teddy Ballgame needs ya,'" he remembered. "I had to lean that way. . . . I have to feel that Christ is responsible, somebody's responsible for this. Somebody's gotta be in charge."

Dozens of Air Force crew and pilots surrounded the runway to watch the speedy wreck, still unaware that the pilot inside had famously once ended the 1941 All-Star Game with a towering three-run home run. The spectators hit the ground as the Panther, and its 20 mm cannons, skidded by: they knew heat from the fire might set off the ammunition. While the plane started to slow down and the fire crew covered the hull in flame-retardant foam, two members of the K-13 rescue team helped Williams open the canopy and exit the cockpit. He climbed onto one of the wings, jumped down to the runway, then, according to First Lieutenant Rylen Rudy "took off for high cotton; he ran the 880 in absolutely world record time."

Finally, the plane veered slightly off the runway into a dirt road, then came to a stop, twenty feet from a fire truck that the ground crew couldn't get started.

For precautionary measures, the medical staff rushed Williams to the base's infirmary. Major Hollenbeck made sure to check in on his wingman and noted he was "a bit pale but calm." Other than a twisted ankle from instinctively slamming his feet repeatedly on the useless rudder and brake pedals, Williams was unscathed. But not undisturbed.

Eventually Air Force, as well as Army personnel who happened to be there that day, learned the identity of the pilot. Inside K-13's weather station and the mess hall hit by a piece of his plane that afternoon, Williams signed autographs and posed for pictures in his freshly singed flight suit.

Airman Joseph V. Giaimo, Jr., was working at K-13's weather station when Williams's scorching plane fell from the sky. About an hour later, Williams walked by his desk. Out of pure instinct and excitement the twenty-one-year-old Giaimo rose to his feet, grabbed Williams's hand, and said, "Glad to meet you, Ted!" Airman Second Class Dan Moody, the starting quarterback at Centre College when drafted into the Air Force two years earlier, also jumped at the chance to meet the ballplayer who had appeared on the cover of *Life* magazine at the age of twenty-three.

"We were ready to haul out a dead pilot but he jumped clear before the plane stopped sliding," Moody, a would-be college senior, wrote home.

"We watched the plane burn and then had chow with Ted. . . . He seemed like a good guy and must be as good a pilot as he is a ball player."

For a pair of young enlisted men such as Giaimo and Moody to be so starstruck was understandable. A senior Air Force officer was a bit more surprising.

First Lieutenant Woody Woodbury, a member of VMF-115, flew on that morning's mission to Kyomipo. Like Hawkins and Hollenbeck, Woodbury noticed Williams's plane in distress and joined the convoy escorting him to the nearest airfield. Running low on fuel, Woodbury landed safely at K-13 and saw Williams's "wheels up" landing. From the runway, Woodbury witnessed an even stranger scene than the fiery crash landing. As Ted Williams ran from the wreck, a green Plymouth, a staff car, approached him. A colonel leapt out. Williams saluted his superior, who saluted right back, then handed him a piece of paper.

A few days later, Woodbury asked Williams, "Why'd the colonel hand you the paper?"

"I just got my ass blown off," he answered. "I'm fucken lucky to be here. And this guy asked me for my fucken autograph!"

Half-a-world removed from Boston and caked in smoke, Ted Williams still could not escape his fans.

American newspapers from coast to coast carried the story of Williams's crash. Letters from pilots to their families back in the States, albeit days if not weeks later, did as well. Hours after Williams returned to K-3, John Glenn wrote to Annie, "Ted Williams had a deal today. . . . Guys with him seem to think he was more than somewhat lucky. Not a scratch but plane was a total strike. He's back here tonight. May as well tell you because you'll read it all, undoubtedly in a few days."

In some cities, television reports beat the morning editions: Doris Williams first learned of her husband's near-death experience when Bobby-Jo ran to her yelling, "Mommy, Mommy, there's something about Daddy on TV!"

At K-13, not long after the crash, Williams and his fellow officers sat for a debriefing of the events that occurred on Mission Number 3301. He then hopped aboard a R4D transport plane for a return to K-3—the other MAG-33 pilots refueled their Panthers and flew back—where he endured another lengthy debriefing with the executive and commanding officers until dark.

Certainly, Williams had been fortunate his plane didn't break in half or explode, either when first hit, when fire erupted near the compressed air inside his engine, or when he slammed into then steamed across the K-13 runway for more than a mile. But his own mistake, the result of his combat inexperience, had caused his Panther to take on fire in the first place.

Over the years, both Williams and lionizing journalists would offer several different justifications for flying too closely to Major Hollenbeck and too close to the ground. Author Glenn Infield attributed the error to disorientation and pain in his head caused by the intense physical pressure inside the cockpit. In his autobiography, Williams explained that he simply "lost visual reference" with Hollenbeck. Years later, Williams even suggested that Hollenbeck was to blame, saying "as we were going down, I was startled to see the guy ahead of me starting to jinx [zigzag]. You weren't supposed to do that until you were coming out of your dive. I'm going straight for the target so naturally I'm closing in on him. So I have to start jinxing while I'm looking for a feasible target. We were told to drop our bombs from 2,000 feet, but we never did. We'd usually go lower than that, and this time I'd gone a lot lower."

Whatever the reason, Williams, his superiors, and his fellow pilots recognized that Williams had been at fault. Immediately upon exiting the plane, Williams was livid, mostly at himself, and smashed his helmet on the ground.

"I followed the guy in front of me too closely going in on the run," he admitted that summer.

Still, other members of 311 didn't blame Williams. Pinky Hollenbeck told a reporter the very next day that "for a comparatively green pilot over here, Williams must have done everything right. . . . He made the greatest play of his career."

The higher-ups at K-3 didn't hold the crash against him either.

MAG-33's official Type-B Report (or Command Diary) for the month of February 1953 detailed some of the fun the group had at Williams's expense. Designed by the Intelligence Section and reproduced by VMJ-1 photo squadron, paper cards were printed as proof of membership in the newest fraternity at K-3, the "Hole in One Club." The day after his Panther survived dozens of enemy shells, in addition to a flaming, wheels-up landing, "Captain Ted Williams became the charter member" of the Hole in One Club.

The card that he received featured a cartoon golfer striking a ball that pierced the wing of a nearby jet then clunked the pilot (wearing a tam-o'-shanter rather than a helmet) on the head. Above a putting green labeled "K-3," the card read:

> THIS IS TO CERTIFY THAT *Capt. T.S. Williams* WHILE PLAYING ON A STRANGE COURSE, THE NORTH KOREAN COUNTRY CLUB, SCORED A "HOLE-IN-ONE" ON *16 February 1953* BY PICKING UP A 'SUKOSHI HOLE' FROM . . . ? FROM ENEMY GROUND FIRE!
>
> SIGNED *LB Robertshaw*
> COL. USMC

But Williams's Hole in One Club card had been just the first in a batch printed and held in reserve for the next pilot to be shot up. In time, several hung for all to see on the wall of one of the Quonset huts frequently populated by officers in 115 and 311. Within a few weeks, John Glenn's Hole in One Club card would be posted near Williams's.

———

As the chaos surrounding Williams's crash began to die down Major Glenn completed the first of his five fam hops. Toward the end of February, the assistant operations officer assigned himself to his first combat mission, a successful bombing of railroad tracks near the Haeju Peninsula.

"Pretty easy hop," he told Annie. "Dropped 2 1000-pounders each, which leaves a rather neat hole in the area. I suppose it's considered unethical in the better circles to enjoy such things, but I had a fine time. As you know, this combat stuff appeals to me more than just somewhat, so I guess I'm either overboard on the Marine Corps attitude or something, anyway, I'm enjoying myself thoroughly."

Four days later, on another railroad bridge cut twenty-five miles south of Pyongyang, Glenn flew on the wing of Major Thomas Cushman. Following Cushman's lead, Glenn unloaded two thousand-pound GPs precisely on target.

"Just want to keep my batting average now and I'll be OK," he told Annie.

Over the next month, Glenn carried out more than three dozen combat missions. Several of them were assisting ground forces on close air support missions, which provided Glenn a sense of achievement but also tremendous purpose. During a CAS on the evening of March 13, Glenn delivered a direct hit to a series of caves sheltering enemy troops in direct combat with First MAW troops on the ground.

"It gives me the biggest thrill in the world to have a hop that really helps out the Marines on the lines," he told Annie.

But the bulk of Glenn's hops over this time were IDs, Blow and Gos of roads, bridges, and enemy weapons facilities. The bombings he completed with near perfection; the exits, on several of the missions, he completed with near disaster.

On Glenn's tenth mission, 311 and 115 joined up for another large-scale interdiction, similar to the attack on Kyomipo. From K-3, twenty-four planes crossed the resistance line to a spot north of Pyongyang. Over an array of targets, including bunkers, troop shelters, and a possible command post, MAG-33 dropped a total of 172 GPs. During the mission, Glenn's horizontal stabilizer was struck by small arms fire. At no point did he lose control of the Panther, or struggle to return to base, but "my first genuine People's Communist Army-type flak" earned Glenn a Hole in One Club membership, one that he would renew multiple times over the next month.

Taking on flak was common even for battle-hardened combat pilots. Weeks earlier, twenty-nine-year-old Captain William Armagost, who had already flown thirty-three combat missions for 311, suffered considerable injuries when small arms hit the underside of his Panther, igniting a fire in the cockpit.

But Glenn's small arms encounter was different, and not simply because he had spent eight months dive-bombing Japanese-held atolls during World War II then become a career Marine who monitored the skies over a fledgling Communist revolution in China.

Major Julian Craigmiles, who served beside Glenn in the Marshall Islands then reconnected with his friend as part of MAG-33, noticed he had become "more willing to take chances." Rather than blow and go, Glenn developed the habit of dropping his GPs or napalm, pulling off the target, and circling back around to assess the damage, locate additional targets, or pick off enemy combatants on the ground with his 20 mm cannons.

This exasperated whichever 311 pilot Glenn assigned as his wingman on such missions.

"You didn't want to be on Glenn's wing," Lieutenant Rudy said. "You had to follow your leader on the bombing runs and the whole bit. Normally what you did was you peeled off at twenty-eight thousand feet or whatever and came whistling down to drop your thousand-pounders and five-hundred-pound bombs or whatever you were carrying, or you ran in low right on the ground practically if you had napalm.

"But if you were with John Glenn . . . he goes in and drops his bombs and you were behind him and you dropped your bombs on the same basic target. And then you've got to stay with him. All the other leaders would be headed for as high as they can get to get out of the range of the guns. And he's down there running around through the trash cans trying to find something else to shoot at. So he's skidding around, not very far off the ground and you've got to stay with him. . . . I didn't fly his wing very often and I tried not to fly it at all."

The squadron's commanding officer, Lieutenant Colonel Ken Coss, discouraged Glenn from taking unnecessary risks. Coss told his pilots that destroying an enemy target was not more important than the life of an American pilot or his aircraft. This wasn't about sentimentality. He stressed that if the pilot and his aircraft survived, they could be employed on more missions and attack countless targets throughout the war; if the pilot and his aircraft didn't survive, they could not.

But the man who wrote letters to his superiors practically begging to serve in Korea "was rather intent on war-making when I went out there. I had trained for so many years for combat. I won't say I was trying to win the war all by myself, but I took it all very, very seriously, and things such as making a second run on an anti-aircraft position, which wasn't exactly—well, I won't say it was foolhardy, but you put yourself in a lot of danger and you knew it."

Even Glenn's oldest friend in the service couldn't get through to him.

Tom Miller, who had served by his side at Corpus Christi, El Centro, Midway, the Marshall Islands, and Quantico, was sent to Korea two months before Glenn. In December 1952, Miller was assigned to VMF-323, a squadron within MAG-12. Much to his chagrin, 323 flew Corsairs, not jets, out of K-6 near Pyeongtaek. Experienced senior officers with Corsair training had become hard to find, and Miller grudgingly accepted his post with 323. Glenn breathed a great sigh of relief when he escaped the same type of assignment.

As part of MAG-12, Miller's squadron had flown dozens of attack missions over North Korea, including the bombing near Kyomipo that Ted Williams barely survived. That winter, Miller visited Glenn at K-3. Apart from exchanging news about their wives and young children, the two discussed business. Miller provided some advice to his friend.

"I told John that the Koreans were a hell of a lot more serious than the Japanese were in the Marshalls," he recalled. "I know your enthusiasm. Just be careful. Don't make two runs if you don't have to, because you can be sure the guys on the ground are watching you and will be able to shoot more accurately at you the second time."

Glenn didn't listen.

On the morning of March 22, he took off from K-3, heading northwest. While Air Force B-29 Superfortresses slaughtered a network of bridges in the Sunan district of Pyongyang, Glenn and nine other pilots would target a railroad bridge about thirty-five miles to the north in the Sinanju region. Despite the fairly simple objective, the mission was a bit unusual. Colonel Robertshaw, MAG-33's commanding officer, joined the formation as the mission's tactical air coordinator, or "pathfinder." Another high-ranking officer within the group, Lieutenant Colonel Harold G. Schlendering, flew on Robertshaw's wing.

Although Colonel Robertshaw, Lieutenant Colonel Schlendering, Major Glenn, and Major Tom Ross each outranked him, Captain Jerry Hendershot led the mission. The twenty-five-year-old Hendershot had been flying missions for nearly five months. A captain leading multiple superior officers into battle was not uncommon. As far back as his time in the Marshall Islands, under the command of Major Pete Haines, Glenn had actually become accustomed to "this no-rank-in-the-air stuff."

"The flight leader always had full authority, regardless of rank," Tom Miller said years later. "But there are damn few captains who are going to object when a major says he's going to do something."

Unleashing a total of seventeen thousand pounds of GPs, the team blew a gaping hole in the targeted bridge as well as the road leading to it from the south. But Glenn wasn't finished.

"I see that son of a bitch and I'm going after him," he declared over radio.

Neither Hendershot, nor Schlendering, nor Robertshaw replied as Glenn swung around and returned to the area to tangle with a Korean People's Army anti-aircraft cannon. Fifty feet off the ground, he took out the enemy with his 20 mm cannons but, just as Tom Miller had warned, not before a 37 mm shell struck his plane.

"Boy, those anti-aircraft guys," Glenn said years later. "I hated those bastards. They're the natural enemies of fighter pilots, just like pitchers were Ted's natural enemies."

The explosive shell mushroomed out the metal in his tail's horizontal stabilizer, damaging the plane's elevator tab and making it difficult to ascend. At four hundred knots, the Panther nosed over and nearly crashed into a rice paddy embankment. But Glenn remained calm, announcing over radio, "I'm going to ease out of here." (To his fellow 311 pilots he admitted that was the closest he had yet come to "buying the farm.") Without the aid of hydraulics, Glenn used all his strength and yanked on the stick with enough force to pull the plane up and out of danger.

"Took two hands to manhandle that beauty most of the time," he wrote to Annie. "Could hold it with one arm but the arm sure got tired. Got to about 6000 feet and then the fun really started."

Seeing Glenn's damaged Panther, Communist troops on the ground opened fire with additional anti-aircraft cannon, nicking the fuselage, nose, and his windshield with more shrapnel. In low visibility he was unable to rendezvous with the rest of the squadron but managed to reach a safe altitude for the 260-mile flight back to base.

"That's a small sweat until you're back over friendlies," he wrote. "Keep wondering just how long that thing is going to run and what you'll do when she stops."

A crowd at K-3 gathered near the runway to watch Glenn descend from thirty-two thousand feet and land with far less drama than Ted Williams had a few weeks earlier at K-13. The ground crew helped him out of the Panther then surveyed the damage to his plane. With a cantaloupe-sized hole, and several other piercings, the entire tail would need to be replaced.

That night, at the desk inside his windy, chilly tropical hut, Glenn sat down to write up his recollection of the events in metered rhyme:

'Twas up Sinanju way one day,
In Indian Country, deep
To cut a bridge was our desire
Then rendezvous we'd keep

The sky was blue, no flak in sight
As we began our run,
High speed approach, all in good form
Then peeled off one by one.

The run began, the bridge loomed big
With mil lead fifty-five
A perfect day, and easy flight
'Twas great to be alive

Then off to one side of the tail
A tracer stream did pass,
A thought ran flashing through my mind
"They're shooting at my (censored)"

I'll note that wily devil's spot,
To him I will return,
The nerve of him to shoot at me,
Just cause his bridge I'd burn,

So sweeping wide at end of run,
And noting landmarks clear,
I held the Panther Jet on the deck,
To sneak up on his rear,

About this time, right on the deck,
And throttle open wide,
I gathered something wasn't right,
With AA on either side,

With his position in the sight,
And twenties flowing free,
The run continued to the spot,
Where "Break" it had to be,

Just at the spot over his head,
The AA still did pound,
A shudder swept the Panther's frame
It headed for the ground

Four hundred plus, things happened fast
With inches yet to spare
Full hard max. upon the stick
So low, but in the air . . .

The elevator tab was out,
Which caused the nose to drop
With pressure full and toward the rear,
She struggled toward the top,

The nineties pounded right behind,
Their fire, it was intense,
And when they ceased at me to shoot,
Relief it was immense,

The journey home from there on out,
Was uneventful, true,
Post-flight inspection showed a hole
That you could lean into . . .

Was on the tail and was quite large,
Down by the tailpipe low,
With pieces sprinkled all about,
And holes both to and fro . . .

Now the saga of the skies
A moral I'll draw for you,
When up Sinanju way some day,
Don't test their aim, it's true,

If you must buy your chunk of ground,
Don't pick a foreign spot,
Go back to Uncle Sugar's shores
Let old age name your spot,

Jousting with the Red AA
Is lots of fun 'tis true,
But he may have a buddy,
Who is waiting there for you,

If you would bold and older be,
Be "Tigers" all, 'tis true,
But on a bombing run just make,
One run, just one, not two . . .

Sergeant Curt Giese, a roving Marine Corps photographer/journalist stationed temporarily at K-3, typed up the poem for Glenn and submitted it for publication in the *Naval Aviation News* magazine.

Prior to his deployment, Glenn and Annie had reached an agreement. In correspondence home he would not discuss any flying accidents and the dangers of past or upcoming missions. But he did not stick to his word for very long. In a letter just a few days earlier, Glenn had told Annie of the mission that earned his Hole in One card.

"Lovely subject—know how you enjoy it, but I've told you I couldn't see being so 'everyday, in every way, everything is fine.' That's a bunch of hooey. You know it isn't always that easy and so do I, so I might as well mention such happenings. Not gruesome, just fact."

And between hoping to see his poem in *Naval Aviation News*, the First MAW's public information officer sending a photograph of his shot-up Panther to newspaper outlets, and Ted Williams's crash-landing experience a few weeks earlier, Glenn no longer withheld any details.

"I've come to the conclusion that it's rather silly to take the 'no-tell' attitude," he wrote to Annie on April 6, 1953, coincidently the date of their tenth wedding anniversary. "I'm sure you realize that people shoot at each other in such 'police-actions.' I shoot and they shoot. According to the law of averages, I've had my share for a while so 'no sweat' as they say. Guess I'm a fatalist."

The self-proclaimed fatalist poet resumed his destiny the following afternoon. Twenty-five-year-old First Lieutenant John M. Verdi drew the perilous honor of flying as Glenn's wingman. During a four-man mission near the westward Ongjin Peninsula, Glenn unloaded a few of his five-hundred-pound GPs on his first run, came around for a second run to unload the rest, then returned a third and fourth time to strafe the area with his 20 mm cannons. As Glenn's wingman, Verdi had to follow him each time.

"I went under him to strafe the ridgeline on one side, then over him in a barrel-roll to strafe the other side, keeping him in sight the whole time," Verdi wrote. "Then he did it again! So I had to do the whole set of maneuvers again too, fully expecting to see him take a hit. He didn't and I breathed several very deep breaths of relief when we at last headed outbound."

Back at K-3, in the Operations Office, Verdi approached Captain Marshall S. Austin, the leader of the mission.

"Tell me, does John always drag a target like that?" Verdi asked. "I mean, hooray for the college try and all that—but he's going to lose his ass."

"John likes to get a good look at the target," Austin replied, opening the drawer of a nearby desk to reveal a photograph of the mammoth hole in a Panther tail. "Look, here's one he picked up getting a good look at a target. He got that coasting over a target at 250 knots, 500 feet off the deck."

Just three days later, Glenn—now the full-time operations officer—assigned himself, as well as First Lieutenant Verdi, to Mission Number Intake 01. At 1006 hours all twenty-four pilots reached Sariwon. Dropping an arsenal—fragmentation bombs (essentially grenades), five-hundred-pound GPs, napalm tanks—they leveled two enemy supply buildings. Glenn, upon finishing his run, declared over radio that he would swoop to the left, rather than climb for the sky, because, "he had seen something there."

Along with the squadron's CO, Ken Coss, 311's executive officer, Lieutenant Colonel Art Moran, served on the mission. "I told him to be careful," Moran wrote. "He seemed to have a habit of getting hit." Within seconds Glenn responded that his plane had taken multiple shells. Moran told him he hadn't seen anything.

"You normally don't," Glenn replied. "You go in first and shoot them all up and then they give the rest of us hell."

"John, that's not fair," Moran replied. "I fly tail-end charlie in this squadron as much as you."

During this seemingly casual conversation, the port side of Glenn's Panther continued to take on fire from two anti-aircraft cannons. An explosion within one of the napalm tanks he carried sent dozens of metal fragments ripping through the canopy, wing panel, outboard flap, wing stub butt, and fuselage. Flying through the flames and smoke, First Lieutenant Verdi, who took a shell in his own right horizontal stabilizer from small arms fire, witnessed Glenn perform an ingenious recovery.

"I thought instantly he had had it, but no," Verdi said. "He rolled through *to the right*—that is, *with* the impact instead of against it. As the airplane rolled level again, he cleaned the stores off the right wing and broke left."

With his electrical, hydraulics, and (somehow) fuel systems still intact, Glenn jettisoned his remaining napalm tanks, escaped further ground fire, and climbed to thirty-five thousand feet. Escorted by Verdi, Moran, and two other 311 pilots, Glenn flew more than 250 miles back to K-3.

"You know, I sometimes think this racket could get dangerous," he wrote Annie. "Oh, well, you step up and take your chances. I know it's screwy, but I'm having a fine time. Can't seem to get scared about it all."

Marines on the runway were amazed at the contrasting image of the uninjured pilot exiting the battered aircraft. The MAG-33 ground crew counted the new gouges in Glenn's Panther. In the coming decades, the tally increased, seemingly in proportion with Glenn's growing celebrity, but the official VMF-311 report noted somewhere between 150 and 200 holes.

Lieutenant Colonel Moran carried out a lengthy debriefing with Glenn that afternoon.

"[Glenn was] another of those hard-headed individuals of whom it was accurate to say: 'You can tell a fighter pilot—but you can't tell him much,'" John Verdi wrote. "He would listen without argument, then go ahead and do things his own way. But once a lesson had been taught, it stayed learned."

For the third time in less than a month Glenn's Panther had returned from a routine mission with still-smoking bullet holes of varying sizes. But he had survived each debacle. And while his CO and XO weren't happy about the damage—or the risk he'd taken with his far less experienced wingmen—fellow pilots were impressed by Glenn and his skills. And in the same spirit of playful ribbing that inspired Ted Williams's nickname "Bush," MAG-33 officers bestowed upon Glenn his own pejorative but good-natured moniker.

"He seemed to draw 'flak' like a magnet," Major Jonathan Mendes recalled, "so we called him 'Old Magnet Ass.'"

CHAPTER FIVE

Hospitality

"Everyone just counts the days till R&R in Japan"
—Captain Bill Clem,
letter home, February 13, 1953

Crash-landing a five-ton fireball at two hundred miles per hour took a lot out of Captain Ted Williams. Emotionally drained from nearly dying, physically drained from smashing around in a cramped, smoking cockpit and banging his feet on the useless pedals, and mentally drained from hours of debriefings, Williams just wanted something to eat when he returned to K-3.

"I remember Ted Williams coming out of the debriefing saying, 'I AM STARVING!'" Woody Woodbury said. "They told him there was nothing to eat. He could get a candy bar."

Hungry, but not gun-shy, Williams impressed 311's executive officer Art Moran by saying he would like to fly again as soon as possible.

"That is the right attitude when one has had a narrow one: Get back in the air and don't think about it," Moran believed.

Twenty hours after bellying the plane in at K-13, Williams launched on an interdiction thirty miles northwest of Pyongyang. With 104 GPs and 1,995 rounds of ammunition Williams and the other nineteen pilots on Mission Number 3301 destroyed a Communist tank and infantry school then escaped to safety. Low on fuel, Williams again landed at K-13, refueled, and arrived at K-3. During a phone call with the United Press's in-country war correspondent Victor Kendrick, Williams described the mission as, "all right, I guess, I couldn't see very much up there."

Two days later, he completed a run-of-the-mill bombing near the

Taedong River, off the Kangso ward of Nampo. Immediately after Williams took off, Moran received a phone call. Major General Vernon Megee, the commanding officer of the entire First MAW, was irate.

"Moran, what in the hell are you doing down there?"

"Just trying to run a fighter squadron, General," he answered.

"Did you launch Ted Williams again?"

"Yes sir."

"Well for Christ's sake, what if he gets shot down again? Think of the publicity."

"Down here, General, he is just another fighter pilot."

Moran—as well as 311's CO, Ken Coss, and MAG-33's CO, Ben Robertshaw, both of whom flew with Williams on these two post-crash missions—seemed to have forgotten a Marine Corps policy stating that pilots who crashed were temporarily restricted from flying. When General Megee returned from K-8, he ordered Williams grounded for three days. But nearly six weeks would pass before he again squeezed his oversized frame into a Panther.

Williams had never shaken the virus he caught while training at Camp Pickel Meadows. In his first few weeks at K-3, he made frequent trips to the base's infirmary for headaches, fever, clogged and congested ears, fluid leaking from his ears, and difficulty hearing. VMF-311 flight surgeon and Navy doctor Lieutenant (JG) George F. Catlett, Jr. diagnosed Williams as having bilateral aerotitis. Catlett explained that flying fam hops and bombing missions in compressed air at twenty-five thousand feet—particularly his crash-landing at K-13—had only exacerbated his ailments.

Catlett prescribed nasal decongestants, a prophylactic antibiotic (terramycin), and eventually a shot of penicillin. He also grounded Williams for a minimum of five days: regardless of his discomfort, a pilot unable to hear over radio was a liability to everyone in the air.

"I was really sick, the sickest I've been in my life," he later wrote.

More than two weeks of rest didn't show much improvement, and on March 12, Catlett ordered Williams to the naval hospital ship, the USS *Consolation*. Two days later a Marine helicopter transferred him to the USS *Haven*, which was docked near Inchon off the Yellow Sea. Upon his arrival, Williams was quartered with Nicholas A. Gandolfo, a ground infantry troop serving on the front lines with Company I of the Third Battalion for the First Marine Regiment. Sergeant Gandolfo had caught pneumonia while in the trenches atop the frigid Korean mountains. At one point his temperature reached 105 degrees.

"He wasn't very happy because he didn't want to be with the enlisted personnel," recalled Gandolfo. "He wanted to move to better quarters. Well, he made such a stink they finally did move him to other quarters."

Once transferred to an officer's quarters, Williams enjoyed several amenities not offered to men like Sergeant Gandolfo. Enlisted personnel were housed three or four decks below, in crowded rooms with bunk beds, and had to wait in line for food at the ship's mess hall. Officers enjoyed their own room with stewards who brought them far better quality meals.

Private First Class John Breske, a rifleman in Company E of the Second Battalion for the First Marine Regiment, also spent time aboard the *Haven*. Recuperating from severe grenade shrapnel wounds Breske heard the ship's doctor refer to Williams as "the arrogant son of a . . ." during his daily rounds with patients.

Others aboard the ship found him charming. During Williams's brief stay aboard the *Consolation*, both crew and patients clamored to catch a glimpse of the baseball star. Tony Ybarra, a 23-year-old Navy corpsman from Southern California, stopped by Williams's bedside several times to keep him company.

"We were all interested, here we had a celebrity aboard the ship and we all wanted to go down and see him, and when we got a chance we did," Ybarra remembered nearly seventy years later. "We talked mainly about why he was aboard the ship, what happened and all that. Not much about his career in baseball."

While on the *Haven*, a Navy nurse named Nancy "Bing" Crosby monitored Williams's ward and called him "the most gracious fellow . . . a neat guy." He even agreed to pose for a few photographs with Crosby and the ship's personnel.

Williams even granted an interview with Dick Hill, a radio correspondent for *The Marine Corps Show* which aired Friday nights on NBC. He initially refused, but Hill, who had flown in a helicopter then boarded a dinghy to reach the *Haven*, would not give up that easily. "Capt. Williams, I used to watch you play for the Minneapolis Millers," he blurted out. Intrigued, Williams vetted Hill with an impromptu baseball trivia quiz about Teddy Ballgame's minor-league playing career. Fortunately for him,

Hill had grown up in Minnesota and seen Williams play at the Millers' Nicollet Park.

Wearing a hospital-issue robe, Williams chatted with Hill on the record in the ship's social hall. Nasal, with a scratchy, weary voice, he talked of his illness, the recent crash-landing, and his fondness for catching up on baseball news via issues of *Stars and Stripes*. He accurately picked the New York Yankees and Brooklyn Dodgers to repeat as American and National League champions, respectively. Williams bristled at Hill's question about his own baseball future.

"Well, I really don't know, I have a tour of duty to perform over here before I think too much about what I'm going to do when I get out. However, I'm supposed to get out sometime in September/October and one of my first thoughts of course will be to get back to Florida. . . . It all depends how I feel."

Although at first Williams had been constantly nauseated from a new antibiotic (aureomycin) prescribed by the *Consolation*'s physician, Lieutenant Harold W. Jayne, several weeks into his convalescence his symptoms subsided. He no longer felt "weak as a cat" and began walking around the ship, taking trips to the top deck to view Inchon Harbor. On one such tour through the often crowded, chaotic lower decks where loudspeakers frequently called out triage updates, Williams witnessed doctors operating on a young soldier hit in the face by shrapnel.

"They took a piece about the size of three-eighths of an inch thick out of this fellow's head behind the eyes," he wrote during his stay aboard the *Haven*. "I got a little woozy when they started using a drill to get into his brain. They did a beautiful job and today he's not too bad."

He took to visiting other sick patients—particularly enlisted men—and signed autographs. And he wrote so many letters that he joked about needing to have his arm put in a cast. A few went to Bill Churchman, his friend from Pensacola and Willow Grove. Once they arrived (often weeks later) back in the United States, Churchman casually mentioned the letters to the *Boston Record*'s Joe Cashman. He told Cashman that in addition to the pneumonia, Williams had become concerned about hearing loss as a result of his ears being clogged. Suddenly Churchman had become the press's source for all news on Ted Williams's health. Nearly every newspaper in the country soon reported that the hearing loss might lead to his relief from duty. Churchman told each reporter that Williams did not want a discharge, explaining that he "always wanted to finish first in everything."

"It may be because of Ted's desire to become an ace that he may cover up his ear trouble," Churchman said. "Ted may not complain about it. He has great pride in what he wants to do and he may not say anything about his hearing difficulties."

Pleased with the results of X-rays revealing clear lungs, Navy doctors deemed Williams fit for service again. Just as the fierce Korean winter started to tame, he returned to K-3 on April 1, and within three days was back in a Panther flying bombing missions across the MLR near Pyongyang.

After seven IDs in ten days Williams earned his first week of rest and recreation (R&R). Per the routine, a dozen or so officers went on leave in a rotation roughly every four weeks. Williams had been due for R&R in mid-March but missed his opportunity while aboard the *Haven*. Like all MAG-33 pilots, especially his friend Captain Bill Clem, Williams looked forward to several days in Japan, the designated R&R location for Marines serving in Korea.

On Tuesday, April 14, Williams, Clem, and a few other officers boarded a C-119, known as a "flying boxcar," and flew 350 miles east to the Air Force base in Itami, located in the Osaka prefecture. Younger, unmarried officers and enlisted men on R&R—also known as "I&I, which is Intercourse and Intoxication"—enjoyed late nights in crowded bars or geisha houses. Williams chose more conventional tourist spots in the larger cities. He visited the Nishimura Lacquer factory, the Amita Damascene factory, and the Tatsumura Silk Mansion. Along the way he remembered his upcoming ninth wedding anniversary and purchased a gold-and-jade bracelet with matching earrings for Doris.

Near Osaka, Williams stopped by a cablegram office. Since leaving for Willow Grove the previous May, he claimed not to know much about the daily exploits of Major League Baseball, although he kept a copy of the latest sports almanac in his quarters at K-3. But by reading *Stars and Stripes* aboard the *Haven*, Williams had learned that on April 16 the Red Sox would open their 1953 season on the road against Philadelphia. To manager Lou Boudreau, Williams wired "Good luck in opener and best wishes to all—Ted Williams." Prior to Boston's 11–6 victory over the A's, the cable was posted in the visitors' clubhouse beneath Connie Mack Stadium.

While dazzled by the bright lights of the larger cities' downtowns at night, Williams preferred quieter sites, such as Hirohito's Hayama Imperial Villa overlooking Sagami Bay. He took dozens of Kodachrome and black-and-white photographs of the idyllic gardens and traditional Japanese architecture where General Douglas MacArthur had drafted Japan's unconditional surrender of World War II. In Kyoto, for a few thousand yen—the conversion rate was roughly 360 yen to one U.S. dollar—he rented a room at the hillside Miyako Hotel, which overlooked the ancient city of roughly one million people. Known as the "shrine city" for its 1,429 Buddhist temples and 405 Shinto shrines, Kyoto offered Williams countless opportunities to snap more photographs.

More so than anything, he enjoyed the food, particularly the fresh shrimp and seafood. In Osaka he dined on "damn good steaks." Something about the presentation of sukiyaki, a one-pot dish consisting of beef, vegetables, and noodles, turned him off and he refused to try it.

Six weeks later, Williams returned to Japan for his second leave. He dropped by a casino in Kobe that was populated with beautiful women and, in his words, "an Indian prince or something," then visited towering Buddhist monuments in Nara.

John Glenn was on leave that week as well.

"I went on R&R to Japan with him once for a week and we had a great time. No comment on that," Glenn teased a crowd, grinning as he said it, during a lecture at the Smithsonian National Air and Space Museum in 2012.

Earlier in the spring, Glenn had also visited Japan. He stopped at several tourist spots, picked up silk samples and glassware brochures for Annie, but decided against purchasing a ninety-six-piece custom hand-painted Noritake china set that came with guaranteed shipping to the United States. He was thoroughly impressed by the country's cleanliness and burgeoning industries—"[a] 100% change from China . . . tremendous progress"—as well as the efficiency of a train system that allowed him to see Itami, Tokyo, Yokosuka, Kyoto, Osaka, and Tokorozawa, all within a few days. But it was Ted Williams that impressed him the most.

For the most part during his stay in Japan, Williams avoided being recognized by fans and reporters, an impossibility if he visited restaurants, nightclubs, and tourist attractions in America. But Japan had become baseball-crazy beginning in 1934. That November a team of barnstorming major leaguers led by Babe Ruth and Lou Gehrig had played a series of games against local all-stars in front of huge crowds at the Koshien Stadium in Nishinomiya and Meiji Shrine Stadium in Tokyo.

A few days into his R&R, Williams's anonymity ran out.

On the streets of Kyoto several MAG-33 officers, including Glenn and Williams, were touring the city. Along the way, they stopped to admire the scenery and take a few photographs. Dressed in green Service Alphas and garrison caps, the Americans already stood out. But Williams in particular caught the attention of a group of children gathered nearby. Whispering and pointing from afar, they thought they had spied the unmistakable physique and rugged face of a baseball legend. The children did not speak English, and neither Williams nor any of his Marine buddies spoke Japanese, but the two parties communicated.

The boldest child among the group stepped forward, fixed himself into a baseball batting stance, swung for the fences, then pointed directly at Williams, who let loose a distinctively loud, deep laugh. He nodded, acknowledging his identity.

Delighted by his discovery, the young Japanese boy swung again, but this time Williams furrowed his brow. He trotted over, spread the batter's feet farther apart, bent him more at the waste, aligned his head properly, and cocked his arms back. Now satisfied with the boy's stance, Williams walked sixty or so feet in the opposite direction. Toeing the mock pitching rubber, he arched into a windup, and threw the boy shadow batting practice.

"[The boy] swung with all his might," John Glenn remembered. "Ted ducked, let out a whooshing, whooping big yell, swung around 180 degrees as though that non-existent baseball was headed for the center field bleachers. The kids were jumping up and down and no one was more surprised than the batter, and I'm sure he was an instant hero, but Ted got a bigger kick out of that than the kids did."

For years John Glenn had known *of* Ted Williams the peerless baseball star. And during those early weeks of 1953, while they served together in VMF-311, Glenn knew Ted Williams the inexperienced, if not unlucky, Marine Corps fighter pilot. But on that day John Glenn, for the first time, saw Ted Williams the man: reclusive yet gregarious, a perfectionist yet accommodating.

Over the next five decades Glenn and Williams would share many similarly brief, yet memorable episodes together. Some born out of achievement or celebration, others out of relief or sheer luck, still others out of disappointment or even anger. But perhaps more than any other, the playful scene on the streets of Kyoto remained with Glenn. And with Williams as well.

"Nothing gave him more pleasure than talking in that inimitable booming voice of his about those Marine days in Korea," Glenn recalled nearly fifty years later. "And he still remembered those kids in Kyoto."

CHAPTER SIX

Bush and Old Magnet Ass

"They had a policy that the regular Marine pilot, which I was, would be teamed up with a recall Reservist to sort of make a pair."
—JOHN GLENN, 2012

In the wee hours of an early spring morning, John Glenn awoke in his tiny, half-open tropical hut. Although the weather at K-3 had become far more pleasant than the seemingly arctic conditions of the weeks before, winds off the Sea of Japan still blew harshly. Glenn dressed in his flight suit and loaded up a plethora of supplies, including his pistol, knife, first aid kit, and escape and evasion equipment. He then hurried to the squadron Ready Room. As flight leader, Glenn was responsible for briefing the officers chosen to fly the day's first hop, Mission Number Acme 33. In a mission known as a "road recce," short for "road reconnaissance," a small group of planes would take off before dawn—pilots referred to this type of assignment as an "early-early"—in an attempt to catch Communist trucks moving supplies and troops along roads and bridges.

With his briefing prepared, Glenn turned his attention to the simpler task of executing the standard preflight combat protocols that each officer carried out before going into combat. Although clearly outlined in Chapter II, Section 200, Paragraph 2 of the *VMF-311 Standard Operating Procedure for Tactical Flight Operation* manual, by now every pilot already knew to:

    a.   Check the bombline on their maps.
    b.   Check the condition of various alternate fields.
    c.   Procure an authenticator and shackle code sheet.

    d.   Procure the password.

    e.   Mission Number

Perhaps he was in a daze from waking up so early or operating on a mostly empty stomach. Maybe something or someone waylaid him. Maybe he just plain forgot. But in his haste to deliver the briefing and meet the mission's 0525 hours start time, Glenn bypassed the very first step: Check the bombline on the small map he used inside the cockpit.

During each preflight briefing pilots received coordinates from the Joint Operations Command (JOC). Based near Seoul, JOC ensured that multiple squadrons, groups, divisions, and branches of the military communicated to operate in unison. Still, air strikes on or near Allied soldiers did occur in the Korean War. In February 1953, three members of the Army's Seventh Infantry Division's 17th Regiment were killed, and several others wounded, when an Allied plane bombed its own troops. A similar incident weeks earlier had killed fourteen American soldiers and wounded nine more. The results of a Marine board of investigation were submitted to the First MAW's commanding officer, General Megee, but never made public.

"Some of our troops had recently taken casualties from friendly fire," Glenn remembered. "Our group commander [Colonel Robertshaw] had put out orders saying that the next time it happened the flight leader was going to be held responsible and court-martialed."

But the six-digit coordinates, aligning with Military Grid Reference System (MGRS), handed out to each pilot only corresponded to the general vicinity of their target. To assist pilots thousands of feet high in the air, Marines or other ground personnel marked the intended location.

"We worked closer into the front lines to our people on the ground than any of us had ever done before, any flying we had done," Glenn said decades later. "The usual procedure was that they would either use a grenade or a mortar round that was white phosphorous—Willy Peter it was called, WP—and they'd fire it out and try and hit the spot that they wanted us to hit with the airplanes right on the enemy lines. . . . So you knew exactly where you're to hit. It wasn't left up to a grid pattern or reading a map, you had something there on the ground."

Well before sunrise on April 22, Glenn's three-man team climbed into their individual F9F-5 Panthers, were strapped in by enlisted crew members, and launched on time. Not long after pulling away from K-3 and heading northwest, Captain Lenhrew "Ed" Lovette began rocking his plane's wings back and forth, the visual signal for "I have an emergency and must land this pass." His entire communications (radio) system had malfunctioned. Protocol dictated Lovette return to base.

Now Glenn was flying into Communist North Korea with just one comrade: Captain Ted Williams.

Despite arriving at K-3 only twelve days apart, Glenn and Williams had not flown a single mission together. Between Williams's procedural and medical groundings, the subsequent stay aboard the *Haven*, and his first R&R in Japan, he'd missed more than four weeks of active duty. During that time Glenn flew twenty-five missions. Even when Williams finally returned to duty and both men were regularly flying missions (nine for Glenn, six for Williams), none overlapped. Until Mission Number Acme 33.

"We got up before light and we took off in the dark," Williams remembered. "And we tried to get over the 38th Parallel just at light . . . and we were there to greet 'em and say, 'Good Morning.'"

Glenn and Williams delivered their first wakeup call at 0607 hours. Alternating altitudes—Glenn flying low, Williams about a thousand feet above, then switching—they reached an area not more than ten miles from the bombline, in the county of Pyonggang. The duo each dropped one of their two five-hundred-pound GPs on a road bridge, returned some cursory anti-aircraft fire with 20 mm cannon-fire of their own, then exited the smoking scene in a hurry. By all indications it had been an effective strike, but the mission was not yet over.

Over the decades, Glenn frequently told the story of his first combat mission alongside the baseball hero. Although he recalled carrying HVARs, separate, official command diaries for MAG-33 and VMF-311 indicate that on Mission Number Acme 33 the two Panthers carried a total of twelve ATARs, not HVARs. Glenn also mentioned an important nuance, fuses, to the weaponry both Panthers carried.

As opposed to the contact fuse—which detonates upon impact—the proximity fuse detonates when it reaches a specific distance from the target. A radar sensor on the bomb triggers the explosion *before* impact. A different type of fuse delayed detonation a few seconds, until *after* impact. This delay fuse gave the bomb a chance to collide with and embed into a target, then explode, greatly increasing the weapon's destructive capability.

More importantly, the delay fuses gave pilots a few precious extra moments to escape the blast radius.

"If dropping those with instantaneous fusing, you must drop high and be level by a minimum of 1000 feet or you get caught in your own bomb blast," Glenn explained. "With delays you can really carry the mail right on in there and only worry about dropping with enough altitude to get out of your dive above the terrain."

The official MAG-33 Command Diary for Glenn and Williams's early-early explicitly states that the weapons they employed carried delayed fuses, not proximity fuses. So rather than HVARs with proximity fuses, as Glenn remembered, each pilot was hauling ATARs and two five-hundred-pound GPs with delay fuses, particularly fuses with a "4 to 5 second delay tail."

Regardless of the distinction, pilots operating aircraft with these radar- and delay-fuse weapons were instructed not to bring them back to base.

"There had been some problem with proximity fuses," Glenn recalled, "so the orders were that you never landed with proximity fuses, for fear one of them might give some problem after landing. So if you didn't use those HVARs, why, you unloaded them either out over the water, just shoot them into the ocean, or shoot them at a target of any kind you just happened to pick in North Korea just to get rid of them."

Heading west from their strike in Pyonggang County but still very close to the bombline, Glenn searched for a good spot for the pair to unload the rest of their armament, two more delay-fuse five-hundred-pound GPs and all twelve ATARs. Along the Rimjin River, Glenn discovered the perfect target, a bridge. Both pilots unloaded their half of their ATARs but not yet their remaining single GP. Glenn swooped around, made another run at the same area, and deployed his last GP on the already-destroyed bridge's abutment.

Williams followed behind, and along the same run he attempted to dump his last delay-fuse GP as well. But the GP didn't launch. Williams had forgotten to turn on the master arming switch before engaging the bomb. He swerved and headed back around—*toward* Allied territory— armed the system, and fired. Glenn watched in horror as the ordnance, unexpectedly to him, jolted from beneath Williams's wing. In a magnificent hail of fire and smoke the GP destroyed a small troop assembly.

"On my chart I thought he had hit in our own lines," Glenn said, "and I could just see my court-martial coming up."

Glenn promptly headed back to base, Williams trailing behind him. At 0705 hours they reached K-3. Sweating, pale, and irate, the seemingly unflappable "Clean Marine" dressed down Williams.

"I was calling him everything but good," Glenn remembered.

Desperate to report the incident as soon as possible, Glenn sprinted to the Operations Office adjacent to the airstrip. Williams followed, listening to Glenn's reprimands the entire way.

"You made that 180, you were shooting south, towards our troops!" Glenn said.

Inside the Operations Office, Glenn pulled out the paper map that he'd brought with him on the mission. While still in the air, he had marked on it the exact location that Williams's GP hit. Comparing the small map to the mural-sized map pinned to the back wall of the Quonset hut gave Glenn both great surprise and great relief.

Glenn's failure to complete objective "a" of Chapter II, Section 200, Paragraph 2 of the squadron manual meant that he did not have the most up-to-date geographical information. In recent days, the bombline had moved several hundred yards south. North Korean personnel, not Allied personnel, occupied the area Williams had blasted. Still, rather than catalogue the mission's blunder, the official unit diary recorded that "two (2) 500 GPs were jettisoned in the K-3 jettison area and six (6) ATARS were returned to base."

"I never took off on another mission without closely checking the ops office chart against my flight chart," Glenn later wrote. "I made that part of the squadron briefing from then on."

Williams, nationally known as a high-strung, temperamental ballplayer, remained unmoved.

"I knew where I was shooting and let 'em go," he told a fellow Marine in 1999. "But I could see the headlines, 'Major Glenn and Ted Williams fire on American line.' But we didn't and everything turned out all right."

———

By default, Captain Williams had served as the wingman to Major Glenn on Mission Number Acme 33. With only two MAG-33 pilots in the air, Williams deferred to the flight leader. But the majority of combat missions flown by VMF-311 included between four and twelve planes, all of which followed a specific formation.

"You fly as a two-person element," Glenn explained. "We call it a section. That means two planes, and then your next flight formation is four planes. You put those two sections into a division as it's called, and then build on up to a squadron from there. Your two people stick together and if you're going into combat, why, they fly together and if there's air-to-air combat, then you watch out for each other and you fly back and forth together. . . . And if somebody got hit then you stuck with him, you stuck with that guy, and you made every effort to get him back."

Despite the near catastrophe on their first hop together, Glenn wanted to continue flying with Williams on his wing.

Glenn, who had already flown in combat with his childhood hero Charles Lindbergh, did not choose Williams for his celebrity.

And as the squadron's operations officer, he could choose his wingman. Marine Corps policy during this period mandated that the career or regular Marine pilots, such as Glenn, fly with Reserve pilots, such as Williams, on their wing.

"We were just better trained," said Glenn, a regular Marine beginning in 1946. "So they always tried to match up a Reserve pilot with a regular pilot. You didn't fly every mission with that person, but if you were assigned to the same flight, well, you flew together. So I guess probably half the missions that Ted flew in Korea, he flew as my wingman, so I got to know him very well."

Marine Corps records do not quite mesh with Glenn's memory. According to VMF-311 Command Diaries, Glenn and Williams only flew on eight pre-briefed combat missions together. By the time Williams was discharged from active duty, he had flown a total of thirty-nine (official) missions. Although it does remain possible that both men flew together on several additional missions, the dreaded combat air patrol missions that Glenn hated. Because these missions often resulted in just sitting on the runway for two hours, the pilots who actually carried out CAPs were not logged by name in unit diaries.

Nevertheless, Williams served as Glenn's wingmen at least eight times, perhaps more. The first instance, which Glenn had thought would result in his court-martial, was memorable. And in each successive hop together Glenn made sure to keep an eye on Williams.

On May 16, Glenn, Williams, and twenty-four-year-old First Lieutenant Francis L. Keck, Jr., joined flight leader Captain Ed Lovette on an afternoon close air support mission. To assist Republic of Korea (South Korea) infantrymen the four Panthers crossed over the bombline carrying two 1,000-pound and two 250-pound GPs. In a quick, low-level strike the four planes damaged or destroyed six buildings, two bunkers, and a seventy-five-yard-long trench sheltering Communist ground personnel. On his way out, however, Captain Williams ran into some trouble.

Glenn recognized that Williams had exceptional instincts as a pilot: his famous hand-eye coordination as a world-class athlete certainly helped him in the skies. But he had arrived in Korea with no experience as a combat pilot. A seven-year, post–World War II layoff coupled with less than a year of jet training made Williams a bit insecure in the air. He often crowded the other pilot in his section so that he would not veer too far off course. Flying too close to Major Hollenbeck on his second combat mission may well have caused Williams to be hit by enemy fire, which led to his crash-landing at K-13.

"He didn't like to fly on instruments," Glenn said sixty years later. "It was natural because the Reserves at that time had not had as much instrument flight training as the regulars had. When we'd get flying on instruments, he'd tuck it in tight enough that it was affecting the air flow around my airplane and I'd move out a little bit."

Over North Korea, in choppy wind, bad weather, or air filled with debris from a nearby ground explosion, pilots had to rely on their aircraft's instruments, such as radio navigation, artificial horizon, and a turn-and-bank indicator. Glenn tried to teach Williams the finer points of flying on instruments, but the lessons didn't always get through.

"Been working some on Ted," he wrote home. "Yesterday he hit the top of a built up trench area on CAS and darn near tore the top of the hill off. Like a kid with a new toy. You'd have thought it was a home run in the All-Star game. All tickled. As Ed Lovette said, Hill 468 is now Hill 460."

The next week Glenn saw his prize pupil again celebrate a group effort. On the morning of May 21, Glenn led a ten-plane ID targeting North Korean troops holed up in a series of small buildings within a mountain range twenty-nine miles west of Wonsan. Amid tremendous anti-aircraft fire, eight Panthers unloaded four five-hundred-pound incendiary bombs equipped with time fuses in the nose of the casing. The spectacular blast obliterated the troop shelters, leaving a smoking crater in the mountain. MAG-33 executive officer Lieutenant Colonel James K. Dill, observing the mission as the tactical air controller, endorsed Glenn's team's efforts as a rousing success. Glenn eagerly awaited photographs from VMJ-1 assessing the damage, while his wingman enjoyed himself as well.

"Ted flew my wing this morning and was all bubbling-over when we got back," Glenn wrote home. "What a character!"

But the most harrowing mission the two flew together took place five days after their first, the near court-martial episode and confusion near the bombline.

Throughout that day, April 27, the Allies carried out large-scale attacks across North Korea. Air Force, Navy, and Marine planes along both the eastern and western coasts of the peninsula flew a total of eleven hundred sorties, blowing up military installations on the ground and enemy MiGs in the air.

MAG-33's role in the coordinated effort was to destroy a Communist ammunition factory in Nampo, where the Taedong River flows into Korea Bay. Twenty-five miles southwest of Pyongyang, Nampo—known as Chinnampo during the Japanese occupation earlier that century—fell to the Communists in October 1950. As a port city close to the capital, Nampo became a frequent target for the Allies throughout the war.

Major Carroll Bernard, VMF-115's executive officer, served as the MAG-33 flight leader for this attack, Mission Number Acme 03. Twenty-two pilots in all began departing K-3 at 1340 hours, with Major Glenn and his wingman Captain Williams forming one section. Within an hour they reached the target along the north shore of the Taedong. Right away, the team started to dispense their GPs while dodging both moderate anti-aircraft fire and the unexpected threat posed by weather conditions.

"Heavy winds made bombing difficult," said Colonel Robertshaw, who joined that mission as pathfinder.

Not only could they alter the trajectory of 250- and 500-pound bombs, but heavy winds blew smoke, fire, and flak in unpredictable directions.

Following Glenn, Williams was the fourth pilot to make his run.

"I watched the first three and I thought, 'This is easy,'" he said.

Williams dove to the target and dropped his GPs. Pulling up he witnessed a blanket of flames rise up from the ground below. He must have felt the sensation that his friend, New York Yankees catcher Yogi Berra, allegedly called "Déjà vu all over again."

"I knew I was hit, I had to be," he said. "I looked out and there was this big damned hole in my right tank. Big as your fist."

Unlike the small arms hit he'd endured over Kyomipo in February, this time his hydraulics, electrical, and radio systems remained functional. Even more fortunate for Williams, Nampo was at least 280 miles from K-3. His Panther's right tip-tank was close enough to empty that it did not explode and the plane with it. Nevertheless, a fire broke out. Over the radio he informed the squadron of the situation. Pulling beside him, Glenn gave his wingman some advice: bail out.

Historically opposed to that option, Williams felt confident he could handle the aircraft. So Glenn calmly offered new instructions: follow me.

Sixty-three years later, just days after Glenn passed away at the age of ninety-five, retired four-star General Jack R. Dailey told the tale of Mission Number Acme 03 to a crowd of a few thousand mourners gathered at the Mershon Auditorium on the Ohio State University campus.

"His wingman in Korea, the great baseball player Ted Williams, once called him 'one of the calmest men I have ever met, no matter how perilous the situation,'" Dailey began. "He might have been referring to an occasion where Williams was hit and his plane was ablaze. John pulled alongside, pointed up, and they climbed to higher altitude. And with the lack of oxygen the flames were actually extinguished, and Williams made it back to base.

"Of all the war stories, this one perhaps best illustrates what John meant to us. He invited us up to his level, where we discovered what an American could do."

Flying southeast, Glenn and Williams rose to well above ten thousand feet. Williams was likely low on fuel, but by climbing so high he could reach still reach base by flying dead-stick if necessary. At 1535 hours the two landed at K-3 safely. Once again, Williams was blasé about the event, and he told reporters, "It wasn't that important."

Glenn was a bit more curious. While flying above, underneath, and beside his wingman's plane to inspect the damage, he noticed the six-inch hole in the right tip-tank, but nothing else. To Glenn, "this was a little bit screwy." If anti-aircraft or small arms fire had punctured the tank, then a shell almost certainly would have blown through the opposite side.

On the ground, the enlisted crew of MAG-33's Maintenance Squadron inspected the tip-tank. No exit wound was discovered, nor was a shell or any other enemy ammunition. All they found inside the tank was a rock, "a big damn rock."

During that afternoon's mission, Marine pilots had launched a total of fifty-six 500-pound GPs, thirty-six 250-pound GPs, four 500-pound incendiary bombs, and returned fire with 1,335 shells of 20 mm ammunition, all within a matter of seconds and over an area with a diameter of less than five hundred feet. The Far East Air Force's operational summary officially described the mission as "pouring 100,000 pounds of bombs into an ammunition factory near Chinnampo." Years later Williams recalled the target more specifically as a factory that manufactured hand grenades. The detonation of all those GPs and incendiary bombs probably ignited the highly combustible materials inside that factory, increasing the range and force of the blast. The ensuing "secondary explosion" chewed up the entire region, and black smoke could be seen for miles.

"They tell me rocks bounce 2,500 feet if they hit right," Williams said. "But I had to see it to believe it."

Word around the base spread quickly. First small arms fire, now rocks had brought down the Bush Leaguer. Some member of the squadron even presented Williams with the rock "all done up" as a souvenir that night at the O Club.

"We always kidded him about the *Williams* anti-aircraft fire," Glenn remembered.

CHAPTER SEVEN

Liberty

The son of a Baptist pastor and his wife Sarah, Joe Dean Bailes was born in Greer, South Carolina, on November 25, 1922. At the age of five, Bailes moved with his family to Tyler, Texas, where he would become a star end for the Tyler Lions High School football team. Following a year at Tyler Junior College, then a year at Baylor University, Bailes enlisted in the Navy Reserve in December 1942. Immediately after World War II, the upperclassman was sent to Midway, where he flew Corsairs as a second lieutenant in VMA-322.

When Bailes returned home to his wife Jane, he completed his business administration degree then took a job as sales manager of his father-in-law's wholesale business, Kirkpatrick Sales Company. "Dimmitt's only complete fuel dealer," Kirkpatrick sold Phillips 66 gasoline, motor oil, and tractor fuel throughout North Texas.

In 1952, the Marine Corps recalled Bailes to active duty, retrained him to fly jets at El Toro, then sent the thirty-year-old captain to Korea the following spring. He joined VMF-311 at K-3 on March 20, 1953, and participated in his first combat mission ten days later.

"He worked for Phillips 66," Ted Williams remembered. "So he had his helmet all painted up in those colors."

During his first five weeks, Bailes flew twenty-two hops and enjoyed a long R&R in Japan the same week in April as Williams. Lieutenant Colonel Art Moran observed that he was "greatly loved and respected by his comrades."

On May 6, Bailes joined Captains Armagost, Clem, and Carruthers on an early morning close air support mission. To provide cover for the Republic of Korea's 20th Infantry Division, the four pilots dropped eight 1,000-pound and eight 250-pound GPs just a few hundred yards across the bombline then turned back for base. But as it neared Pohang, the squadron encountered dense fog rolling in off Yongil-man. Clem and Armagost landed safely at K-3, but Carruthers and Bailes struggled to find the airfield. They both circled the area in search of landmarks.

Running out of fuel, Carruthers managed to guide his Panther to a spot two miles into the bay. He exited the cockpit, inflated an emergency life raft, and began paddling. A "Dumbo," an Air Force SA-16 rescue seaplane, dispatched to the area dropped down and picked him up. Unharmed but freezing from nearly an hour in the water, Carruthers checked in to sick bay, where he was prescribed several doses of medicine (brandy). Per squadron regulations for any pilot forced to ditch, the CO gave Carruthers four days of special leave in Japan.

Bailes, however, could not find the base or the bay. While Carruthers floated on his life raft, Bailes's plane ran out of fuel. He lost control of his Panther and crashed into the countryside roughly seven miles southeast of K-3. The following morning, a member of the civilian South Korean police department reported the wreckage to the commanding officer of the nearby Third Marine Ground Control Intercept Squadron. Scattered human remains were also found, so several MAG-33 pilots, including Ted Williams, were dispatched to the scene.

"And, God, there's his helmet, lying on the side of the hill," Williams said forty-four years later. "I'll never forget that."

Bailes's parents and widow received telegrams immediately. On the following Sunday, Navy chaplain Lieutenant (JG) Ernest R. Lineberger presided over a well-attended memorial service in the Wing Chapel.

"It's the first guy we've lost since I've been here," Williams wrote. "God, we have been lucky. I can think of at least 15 different cases where it could have been the other way but luck was with us. Guys coming back with wings, tails all shot up, burning engines running rough, no hydraulics or [brakes] and they've all come out OK. Everyone is just sick about our friend. This place is really gloomy today."

Marines at K-3 had several outlets for their grief.

A few nights per week, General Megee's Mess and Wing Hall—dubbed the "Rice Paddie Bijou Theatre"—offered movie screenings. Every month the wing's Special Services Office obtained dozens of new releases and classics from the Navy Motion Picture Exchange at K-13. Marines at K-3 were treated to a range of films, from John Wayne's *The Quiet Man* and Gary

Cooper's *Springfield Rifle*, to Bob Hope and Bing Crosby's adventure-comedy *The Road to Bali*, to a pair of swashbuckling films, Errol Flynn in *Against All Flags* and Burt Lancaster in *The Crimson Pirate*. Navy Lieutenant (JG) John I. Hense, the Second Marine Aircraft Control Group's dental officer, left the theater thinking both pirate films were "stinkers."

"Meteor," one of the Armed Forces Korean Network's nine radio stations, broadcast at 250 watts around the base Jack Benny, *The Adventures of Ozzie and Harriet*, and the popular *Your Hit Parade* program. The station even took three requests per day. During the *Mail from Home* program, a host read letters from Marines' loved ones that asked for specific songs. The most popular request in February (i.e. Valentine's Day) was Teresa Brewer's hit "Till I Waltz Again with You."

K-3 also boasted an updated library that included new arrivals such as Thomas Costain's *The Silver Chalice*, John Steinbeck's *East of Eden*, as well as Ernest Hemingway's *The Old Man and the Sea*. Ted Williams, who at some point read the famed tribute to his rival Joe DiMaggio, focused mostly on the fishing: "I never could've sat in that boat as long as that old man did. . . . It wouldn't take me that long to catch that fish." As for current events, the latest issues of *Life*, the *Sporting News*, *Colliers*, the *Saturday Evening Post*, and *Stars and Stripes* were brought in each week from Japan.

Along with all the other squadrons and maintenance units that comprised the First MAW, pilots in VMF-311 participated in bridge, poker, and acey-deucy (a version of backgammon) tournaments. Some gambled on sports they never saw. Given twelve-to-five odds, Ted Williams still lost $50 betting on Jersey Joe Walcott to win his rematch with reigning heavyweight champion Rocky Marciano.

Those interested in more physical activities played basketball, volleyball, and softball. One afternoon, when bad weather in North Korea grounded the entire wing, John Glenn pitched during a pickup softball game.

Even when he was healthy and at K-3 Ted Williams reportedly did not participate in these softball games. Cincinnati Reds reserve outfielder Lloyd Merriman did. A first lieutenant in VMF-115, the 28-year-old had arrived at K-3 three weeks after Williams. The former Stanford University fullback socked plenty of softballs out over K-3's Seabee wall.

Although he chose not to show off his own hitting skills, Williams did join Merriman one afternoon to give their fellow Marines an informal baseball clinic . . . so ordered by General Megee. They cut the event short upon realizing that the base's scant inventory of balls would not survive the grounders hit across the hard, rock-covered infield.

Some recall seeing Williams swing a baseball bat at a nearby stationary tire or hitting fly balls to enlisted men with a fungo bat. (Employing the same wrist action with a fishing rod, he also practiced casting by dropping a lure into a bucket that he placed at various points around the base.) And on one occasion, as a group of pilots walked by the playing field on their way to the Ready Room, an errant ball rolled across Williams's path. He bent down, picked it up, and threw it back onto the field.

"A flip of the wrist was all that it took out of him," First Lieutenant Rylen Rudy remembered. "And that ball was at eye level like a bullet all the way back to where these [Marines] were playing ball. I never saw a ball thrown that way."

Despite the camaraderie that these games and activities bred, a degree of tribalism developed among the different subsets of those men stationed at K-3. And perhaps the fiercest rivalry emerged between VMF-115 and VMF-311. Not only did the two squadrons routinely fly joint missions together, but their quarters were adjacent, sitting on the edge of the bay.

Much of that rivalry centered around pranks. 311 nailed down the lids to the toilets in 115's wooden latrines. 115 responded by "kidnapping" 311's recently promoted CO, Art Moran, and enchaining him in the Officers Club but with plenty of beer to drink. That was followed by a latrine being burned down: decades later pilots from both squadrons couldn't remember who claimed responsibility.

By far the greatest catalyst for one squadron pranking the other was "kroindyking." Purportedly named after an ancient Korean game, kroin-dyking (or krondyking) meant throwing nearby chunks from the ground at the opposing squadron's tropical hut. Made out of tin, the roof of the hut rang loudly and the walls vibrated when struck by the projectile. Night kroindyking interrupted many pilots' sleep.

Eventually kroindyking evolved into pelting the opposing squadron's pilots. First Lieutenant John Verdi of 311 once kroindyked Major Bob Rickles—who actually was not a member of 115, but rather head legal officer for the First MAW—so forcefully between the eyes that K-3's provost marshal thought Rickles was dead.

"Rivalry was intense, with Art [Moran] leading the charge," John Glenn wrote years later. "For Art, 311 was the 'heavy haulers' while [115] was disdained as 'that light observation unit next door.' Maintenance figures were posted daily with in-commission/out-of-commission rates a matter of prime importance.

"The competition didn't end in his mind even after hours. I still remember Art 'egging-on' Ted Williams to 'Go ahead and 'krondyke-em, Ted,' while walking past the [115] huts late at night, returning from the 'O' Club. . . . As a 'krondyker' Ted Williams had few peers. While his fame as a baseball player came from his hitting, he also had hands like catcher's mitts. In other words, he was a high-volume 'krondyker,' able to place a larger load of pebbles on-target per pitch than anyone in the squadron. Ted usually obliged Art's entreaties."

Not long into his tenure as CO, Lieutenant Colonel Ken Coss issued an order stating that "use of KROINDYKES weighing more than three pounds is absolutely forbidden—the Buildings and Grounds Officer is overworked already."

Rather than team sports, kroindyking, pranks, and card games, some of the more solitary individuals preferred quieter leisure activities. The base's Hobbycraft Sales Store offered stamps for collecting, model airplanes, and train sets. Along with Captains Bill Clem, Jack Campbell, and his new hut mate Jim Scott, Ted Williams returned to an old hobby: photography.

Years earlier, Williams had shown an interest in cameras to connect with his absentee father, Sam, a professional photographer in Southern California. While in the Far East, Williams used his German Leica to snap hundreds of photographs of his fellow pilots, as well as landscapes and villagers. He was particularly fond of a shot featuring a "Pappa-San" (an elderly Korean man) wearing an elaborate hat made out of horsehair. In addition to identifying the Pappa-San as a landowner, when wind blew through the hat it was "supposed to spread his knowledge to the rest of Korea," Williams explained.

Sergeant Curt Giese was not attached to VMF-311, or even the First MAW. A photographer and reporter, the twenty-one-year-old from Milwaukee traveled from base to base profiling Marines. In the fall of 1952 Giese was stationed with VMA-212 at K-6. While there he snapped a famous photo of six enlisted Marines all huddled around a pop culture magazine. The walls of the Quonset hut in which they sat were papered with thousands of photos of pinup girls, including more than two hundred of Marilyn Monroe.

That summer, First Lieutenant Forest A. Nelson was carrying out a mission for 212 when his AU-1 Corsair was shot down by anti-aircraft fire northwest of Kaesong. Although a pilot on the formation saw him parachute to safety and run for cover in a rice paddy, Nelson was never recovered. Back home in California, his three-year-old daughter, Penny—recently paralyzed with polio—stopped receiving weekly letters from her father. Members of 212, as well as Curt Giese, took up writing letters to Penny, signing them "Daddy." One included a check from the Marines at K-6 for $1,301.30. When his tour in Korea ended, before returning to his own family, Giese visited Penny and brought gifts for her and Nelson's widow.

In January 1953 Giese moved to K-3, where he met Ted Williams and John Glenn, whose post-mission poetry Giese typed up for publication. Williams and Giese quickly became friends, chatting about cameras, shots, and lighting. Giese showed Williams how to develop film inside the shack converted into the squadron's darkroom.

"Ted and I have shot quite a few pictures of Korean kids in the village near the base," Giese said. "He always does his own developing and printing and he does very good work."

Still, Williams's greatest passion during his off-hours was shooting ducks, not photographs.

Just as he befriended Sergeant Giese over one hobby, Williams befriended Major Edmund "Edro" Buchser, Jr., over another. During World War II, Buchser flew 101 combat missions in the South Pacific for VMF-115, then returned to active service with the same squadron in Korea toward the end of 1952. By early January he had completed eighty-seven missions, earning a Bronze Star, his third Distinguished Flying Cross, and a transfer from combat pilot to the cushy post of K-3's provost marshal.

"Making me provost marshal was like making one of those guys on *M*A*S*H* provost marshal," he said. "We had a lot of fun."

An affable Kentuckian, Buchser patrolled the base for kroindykers and trespassers while on duty and patrolled the nearby rice paddies for ducks while off. A sergeant serving on his staff would alert Buchser via radio when he noticed a particularly promising spot.

Williams heard about Buchser's large hauls and asked to join him.

"He could shoot a shotgun better than anybody I ever saw," recalled Buchser, a competitive skeet shooter himself.

Using 12-gauge shotguns, they routinely bagged a hundred mallards together—Williams refused to shoot pintails—which was enough to have a big feast for all the pilots. Duck was a nice change of pace from the routine meals such as chicken pot pie, cold mashed potatoes, and even colder green beans.

Eventually, Major General Megee learned of Williams's recreation and asked to join the hunting party. Williams eventually warmed to the idea. Megee and his aide-de-camp drove out to meet him and Buchser.

"We weren't there 10 minutes, and here come the ducks," Buchser remembered. "The aide, this Ivy Leaguer, he stood up and said, 'There they are, General!' Well the ducks all haul ass. And I can hear from Ted's blind, 'Grrrrr, grrrr, grrrrr.'

"About five minutes later, this aide stands up again and says, 'There they are again, General!' And the ducks go flying away. Ted stood up in the blind, he jacked in a shell and he said, 'You son of a bitch, if you do that one more time I'm going to shoot you.' And he sat down. The General had enough sense to tell the aide to go sit in the jeep. And that's what the guy did the whole afternoon, was sit in the jeep. And we had a good duck hunt."

———

John Glenn does not seem to have participated in many of the base's extracurricular activities. Between flying fifty-eight missions during a twelve-week span, routinely briefing the squadron, carrying out his critical duties as operations officer, and writing post-mission poetry, Glenn's days were full.

But he did stop by and socialize with fellow pilots at the Officers' Club, the large Quonset hut next to the Officers' Mess. In late February, he attended a "hill-billy band" concert by "The Pohang Wranglers," a group of Marine musicians celebrating their pending release from active duty. Sometimes Glenn came carrying a metal tin of treats that his sister-in-law Jane sent from Ohio. Ted Williams consumed large quantities of her homemade fudge.

Williams contributed his own recipe to the atmosphere at the O Club. Early one evening in April, he returned from a twenty-four-plane interdiction in Nampo, near the Taedong River. After expending napalm tanks, GPs, ATARs, and hundreds of rounds of 20 mm ammunition, Williams and several pilots stopped by the O Club to unwind. He introduced a few of them to one of his favorite drinks, a mix of two jiggers of rum, half a glass of orange juice (canned was all he could find), and half a glass of pineapple juice. Within a week, Williams bragged that "they don't drink anything else now."

Williams very well might have fixed one for the man who first set him on the path to Korea.

With his task of identifying and contacting Reserve recalls completed, Bob Conley—now a lieutenant colonel—finally earned his next combat assignment. In September 1952 he joined VMF(N)-513, the all-weather night fighter squadron known as the Flying Nightmares.

Within a few months Conley assumed command of the squadron and, alongside an enlisted radar operator in a two-seat Douglas F3D Skyknight, often provided protection from enemy MiG planes for Air Force bombers. Missions frequently took place in the dead of night.

"It'll be done with radar," Conley told reporters at a press briefing. "The Red fighter pilots, they still can't make it out. They figure they're up there alone, waiting to shoot down a big fat bird at leisure and—whammo— someone clobbers them. It'll be our toughest mission. If there's any kind of moon, it could be a fiasco. We don't need moonlight to see them, but they need it to find us."

In his second week as CO, Conley and radar operator Master Sergeant James N. Scott escorted an Air Force B-29 Superfortress bomber into the South Hamgyong province. With Scott's assistance Conley spotted a bandit late into a moonless night. Firing his Skyknight's 20 mm cannons, Conley blew the enemy MiG-15 out of the sky, marking 513's eighth kill in sixteen months. In addition to his fourth Distinguished Flying Cross, Conley was awarded the Legion of Merit with the Combat Valor distinguished device.

Although part of Marine Aircraft Group-33, Conley's squadron of forty-some pilots was stationed at K-8, outside Kunsan, on the western side of the Korean peninsula. But as CO of one of the group's three fighter squadrons, Conley visited K-3 often. When time permitted, he stopped by the O Club. On the day that John Glenn first arrived at K-3 in mid-February Conley saw his fellow Muskie offensive lineman there and the two chatted at length about the MiG Conley had recently nabbed. On another visit to the O Club Conley spotted Ted Williams.

"So he goes up to Ted," said Captain Bob Massaro, an aide to Conley years later at Cherry Point.

"Ted, do you know who I am?" Conley asked.

"Yea, you're the commanding officer of the night fighter squadron."

"Well, that's true. But I'm also the fellow who . . . called you up for your second tour of duty."

Williams simply laughed then sat down with Conley for a drink.

The hard liquor and beer, supplemented by Williams's tropical concoction, only livened up an already boisterous environment at the O Club.

Before his recall to the Marines in early 1952, VMF-115 First Lieutenant Woody Woodbury had been a popular comedian and pianist at resorts and night clubs in Miami and Las Vegas. He had been on stage performing at the famed Clover Club in Miami when he learned that the Communists had invaded South Korea.

In the years following the Korean War, Woodbury ran his own nightclub in Fort Lauderdale, released eight comedy albums (two of which went gold) from 1959 to 1964, and hosted or guest hosted several talk shows during the 1960s. When Johnny Carson left *Who Do You Trust?*, the ABC game show that brought him to the attention of the *Tonight Show* producers, Woodbury took over.

A master of one-liners and puns, Woodbury also played zany music for his fellow pilots. Unfortunately the piano inside the Officers' Club was not up to his standards, and an attempt to steal Major General Megee's piano from the other side of the base was thwarted by the officer of the day on patrol. Instead, several officers at K-3 pooled their money to purchase an upgrade on their next leave to Japan. With $300 in hand, Woodbury and John Glenn bought a brand-new spinet piano that was soon delivered to the Atsugi Naval Air Base. Woodbury, however, received orders to return to his squadron immediately.

"I had to leave and he was going to bring the piano back [to K-3]," Woodbury remembered. "But the transport plane that he was supposed to bring the piano back upon somehow got diverted one way or another. So John wound up another two or three or four days before he got back with that damn piano.

"He was mad as hell about it," Woodbury continued, "because he had to get back to Korea because he was missing missions and he wanted to fly again. The version that I got, which I think is pretty accurate, he called and raised so much hell for a [major] in the Marine Corps."

With the improved sound quality Woodbury's O Club act was a hit. Using a songbook that had been passed around squadrons, groups, and divisions, a dozen or so officers sang along with him. Apart from the more obscene songs, mostly about sex, several classics were reworked to include lyrics about jets and North Korean targets.

"The Commie's Lament," sung to "Oh, My Darling Clementine," ended with, "To all Red pilots, here's a warning when out looking for some fun / If you spy us, go on by us or your flying days are done." "On Top of Old Pyongyang," a parody of "On Top of Old Smokey," opened, "On top of old Pyongyang / All covered with flack / I lost my poor wingman / He never came back." And to the tune of Tennessee Ernie Ford's 1951 hit "Mister and Mississippi," MAG-33 officers—many of whom were Reserve recalls—sung the words, "I hope to raise a family when this damned war is through / I hope to have a bouncing boy to tell my stories to / But someday when he grows up, if he joins the Marine Reserve / I'll kick his ass from dawn to dusk for that's what he'll deserve."

Although certainly entertaining, Woodbury and his chorus of half-soused pilots were not as popular as the once-a-month United Service Organizations (USO) shows in the wing mess hall and MAG-33 theater. And as much as banter from Hollywood's Raymond Burr or the sounds of the *Famous Moments in Music* show entertained the Marines, just the sight of a woman riled up the crowd. During April's "You Asked for It" show, singer Ann McCormack and actress Evelyn Russell were by far the main attraction.

"After the performance the troupe came over to the bar for a party," Captain Bill Clem wrote home. "There were five girls in it and wow did the guys knock themselves out trying to get to talk to them. It ended up in a real good brawl."

Other than on leave to Japan, these Marines did not see women very often. Unless, of course, they left the base for liberty, "the authorized absence of an individual from a place of duty not chargeable as leave."

Officers within 311, including John Glenn, occasionally toured Pohang during liberty. Paul Montague frequently led these side missions. The twenty-eight-year-old captain was born and raised in Bandera, Texas, later officially declared the "Cowboy Capital of the World." Boasting a thick

Texas drawl, Tex, as he became known, followed his hometown's traditions. Taught by the Mexican vaqueros who worked on his family's ranch, Montague became an expert roper. By age twelve, he was the featured trick-roper at Texas state fairs and later performed at the New York Rodeo in Madison Square Garden.

Montague, who ran five miles around the base every morning (no matter the weather), was very popular at K-3. He flew for 311 from May through August 1952, received a transfer to forward air controller of the Third Battalion, Seventh Marines, then was transferred back to 311 the following January. By the end of the war, Montague had flown a combined 145 combat missions. Upon his return to K-3, he enjoyed showing off his roping skills to a new batch of Marines. On one winter trip to Pohang, they convinced Montague to try and rope a cow in a nearby pasture. He received permission from someone on the farm, but he didn't have the proper rope, and assured his friends that on their next visit, he would bring the right type. When the time came, Montague roped the cow, causing an elderly Korean man to go berserk.

"The old Pappa-san has come home but he hasn't been cut in on the program and thinks Tex is stealing his cow," John Glenn recalled. "He came tearing out and started jabbering and pleading for them not to take his cow. They had quite a time convincing him they didn't want his cow. So Korean-type rodeos are now definitely out."

Not all stopovers to Pohang were as wholesome and innocent.

Although associating with prostitutes for "immoral purposes" was expressly prohibited, plenty of Marines at K-3 broke the code. Command officers within the First MAW became concerned by their medical staff's monthly reports. A memo on liberty regulations issued by the Headquarters Squadron in May 1953 noted that the "venereal disease rate among Korean prostitutes is extremely high."

To combat the problem General Megee's office employed two methods: education and inspection. Prior to R&R, enlisted Marines were provided prophylactics and they sat through "lectures with visual aids" on venereal disease. The wing's chaplains also gave sermons on "character and self-control in connection with the VD control program." And under the supervision of provost marshal Edro Buchser, a medical team routinely examined the local brothels and prostitutes for signs of infection.

Still, many Marines caught venereal disease, including Ted Williams.

"He confided to a nurse years later, that he had returned from Korea with a social disease," Leigh Montville wrote in his 2004 bestseller, *Ted Williams: The Biography of An American Hero.* "If true—and why would he invent something like that?—syphilis was a final blow to a marriage that was much shakier than it ever had been portrayed in public."

Williams's marriage to Doris had been on the rocks long before he left for Korea. Although he saw others throughout their marriage, as early as 1950 Williams began affairs with two separate women, Norma Williamson and Evelyn Turner, a beautiful blond National Airlines stewardess from Coral Gables. During his retraining at bases in Pennsylvania, North Carolina, Puerto Rico, and California, Williams wrote letters to Turner. At Roosevelt Roads he came close to being absent without official leave (AWOL) from a training exercise to spend time with her in Miami. And from K-3, he wrote Turner more than two dozen letters, several of which she returned with suggestive snapshots of herself that he then shared with his fellow Marines.

While in Southeast Asia, Williams was also afforded a few opportunities to meet women that were unique to the celebrity of his status.

During the spring of 1953, Edro Buchser's official duties as provost marshal required him to visit K-2, an Army base located at Taegu. While there, Buchser planned to visit a nurse, a female friend from high school. He mentioned the trip to Williams, who was thrilled at the prospects of meeting English-speaking, white women. In Buchser's jeep, the two drove forty miles southwest, and by the early evening they had been invited to an impromptu cocktail party held in the mess hall.

"All the nurses were there—about 40 of them it seemed like," Buchser remembered years later. "Of course I wasn't operating, but old Ted was. . . . Old Ted, he had a nurse and she was good looking, too. So the next day we're driving back to K-3 and he's just silent over there in his side of the Jeep. I says, 'What happened last night? Did you get laid?' He said, 'Unhh.' I said, 'Well, you know . . . tell me!' 'She had the fucking rag on.' He was really depressed. The chance of his life and he missed out. I guess he could have had any one of them. He was a good looking guy to women."

Aside from warding off Marines in search of Korean prostitutes and chauffeuring his friend to mingle with Army nurses, Buchser's chief role as provost marshal was keeping K-3 safe. Locals—Buchser called them "spies," Woody Woodbury called them "guerrillas"—frequently entered the base to steal anything they could, particularly at night.

"We always went by the 11th Commandment," said Sergeant Lawrence "Larry" R. Cote of VMC-1, a part of the Second Marine Air Control Group stationed at K-3. "There's the Ten Commandments that everybody preaches. But the Marine Corps has the 11th one: 'Do unto him, before he does it to you.' You stay alive.

"There's always somebody trying to rob the place. Whatever you have, scrap metal, food, anything of any value they will be there. And they're on the runway to sabotage your aircraft so you have to be vigilant and be damn careful where you shoot. Don't ever shoot at aircraft."

Sergeant Cote and other enlisted members of VMC-1 prepared the ammunition and bombs that pilots in 115 and 311 used on missions starting the following morning. Every night 3,800 pounds of GPs were pre-armed, stored for the next day, and guarded by a sergeant with at least six months experience and a .30-caliber M-1 machine gun. Beneath the perimeter was an electrified wire, but the surrounding fence was scalable.

"They would take that 100-pound bomb and they would send it up north," Cote remembered. "The next day, that bomb would be coming back at you."

One night, two thieves climbed over the fence surrounding the ammunition dump. The sergeant on duty gunned down the first intruder but lost track of the second.

"The buddy to this other guy whom he had shot turned around, came back, and cut his throat," Cote said. "It was just pure luck that this fellow here survived. He was able to get three rounds off, they came up and got him and took him down to sick bay and they sewed his throat back up."

Major John Glenn noticed these dangers and hardships when he first arrived at K-3.

"Korea in early 1953 was the old Orient of peasants, low buildings huddled among harsh hills, and a populace that walked or pedaled to get from here to there and supplemented their meager wardrobes with surplus military clothing," he wrote years later. "In Pohang each morning, shuffling men in dark clothes hauled barrels of human excrement for use as fertilizer. About once a week they came to the base to clean out our six-hole outhouse. Officially it was 'night soil' that they hauled away but we called the barrels 'honey buckets,' as if the stench demanded euphemism."

A few weeks into his tour, Glenn realized that he would be missing his daughter's sixth birthday, so he wrote Lyn a lengthy letter. In addition to encouraging her to have an extra piece of cake for him, Glenn provided a brief overview of the evils of Communism and the subsequent need for his absence, as well as a sad glimpse into the world around him.

"Children like you and Dave are very lucky to live in the United States," Glenn wrote. "Children out here aren't quite so lucky."

Glenn was far from the only person to notice the plight of these children. In a letter home to Miami, Woody Woodbury bemoaned the crime—an officer he served with had recently been shot at and attacked while hunting just outside the base—but especially the poverty.

"You can't conceive a land like this," Woodbury wrote. "Ancient women carry loads a GI would shy from. Nearly everyone is thinly clad and barefoot in spite of the bitter cold. Charitable United Nations organizations send clothing and shoes but these are sold on the black market in order to buy food. Children steal everything they can. Youngsters from 4 to 12 crawl through sewer culverts to get onto the base to swipe garbage. What can you do with them? How can you punish children? Besides, they don't consider it stealing. They need the garbage in order to live a little longer. It's a ghastly nightmare . . . and much of that nightmare is back [on] the front, where the dirtiest, hungriest, unhappiest people in the world are scrabbling out a miserable existence."

Decades under Japanese subordination in the early twentieth century followed by the Communist invasion from the North had devastated South Korea. Throughout the fighting of the early 1950s an estimated 10 percent of the casualties were civilians. Millions more were displaced or injured. At one point one hundred thousand orphans lived on the streets and in the mountains of South Korea. Many of them lost arms or legs in the crossfire.

"We keep our animals in better places," a Marine told the press in 1953.

A few orphans became "houseboys," at K-3. Marines gave them leftover rations and pocket change to sweep, straighten up inside their quarters, and haul away trash. Ted Williams had his picture taken with the houseboys, giving them a priceless souvenir. Somewhere near the base Williams found a bicycle and brought it back for his hut's houseboy, a ten-year-old they called Jimmy.

In the hut next door, John Glenn also struck up a friendship with his houseboy, a fifteen-year-old named Kim. That spring, Kim bashfully asked Glenn to help him purchase new school clothes. Korean high school students were required to wear plain, black, high-necked suits with matching black caps, but Kim could not afford new clothes. Glenn promised to help.

On his next R&R to Japan, Glenn stopped at a Daimaru, a department store in Kyoto. Although he struggled to converse with the salesman and did not understand Japanese sizes, Glenn purchased Kim a new outfit for about 7,500 yen.

"Bought it plenty large, so we can get it cut down some if necessary," Glenn wrote Annie. "Very elaborate—gold buttons and all. Gonna be the hottest looking student in school. Gotta have gold buttons, don't you?"

Several Christian orphanages existed in the area. Marines from K-3 visited the children and raised money for expenses. Navy dental officer John Hense assisted the French priest, Father Deslanden, who ran the Catholic orphanage. In March, Hense and Navy medical officer Lieutenant (JG) Patrick F. O'Connell befriended a young orphan whose leg had been amputated two years earlier. They measured the boy, whom they named Mario, and took a plaster impression to mold an artificial limb. With help from a Navy chaplain, Hense and O'Connell raised the necessary $150 for the limb and gave it to Mario in late May.

By then, the First MAW had become involved in the housing and care of Pohang's at-risk and orphaned children. Under the direction of MAG-33's Protestant chaplain, Richard D. Cleaves, the wing sought to build a place that would provide not only a short-term benefit, but one that would thrive long after the war ended.

Through donations, raffles, and Christmas card sales, Cleaves and other missionary leaders raised 1,400,000 won (roughly $234) for a down payment on a piece of land in Pohang. Within a few months housing was built, 870 plots of rice were planted, and an ox was purchased to assist in the farming. Navy medical officers provided care until a full-time local doctor was hired and an educational program was drafted for the newly named U.S. Marine Memorial Orphanage.

On Wednesday and Sunday afternoons a truck left K-3 and shuttled officers and enlisted men to the orphanage, where they taught their "adopted children" baseball and planted more rice. The wing's thirty-one-piece band gave several concerts there each month. The handier enlisted men performed maintenance and installed playground equipment on the facility that spanned 1,230 *pyeongs*, about 43,000 square feet. Sergeant

Larry Cote and several within VMC-1 fashioned a roof for one of the buildings by slicing and flattening their plentiful used Budweiser beer cans.

In less than a year the number of children housed by the orphanage rose from sixteen to seventy. Soon, newborn babies were regularly dropped off at the gate. A considerable increase in supplies and funds was needed, and the Marines at K-3 were eager to help.

"One of our young lieutenants," First Lieutenant Rudy recalled, "he came back and put the word out and we all wrote home and had mama send all the clothes—it didn't matter what size they were—send all the stuff over that they could."

Around this time Ted Williams took a hunting trip with two fellow officers from K-3. Although he and Edro Buchser usually drove a jeep to a nearby spot for a few hours, sometimes an air-sea rescue helicopter snuck Marines up into the mountains to search for duck. Scared off by the loud noises of jet aircraft, the flocks left nearby lakes and rice paddies for higher ground.

Along with Captain Dale Purcell, a pilot in VMJ-1 photographic squadron, Williams hitched a ride into the mountains, where they came across a group of South Korean children.

"The little kids crowded around out of curiosity," Purcell told Ted Williams biographer Bill Nowlin in November 2002. "They looked terribly cold in the winter. We forgot all about the ducks. We were looking at these kids, freezing. No G.I. clothes. Just freezing, and in pretty tough circumstances. We just sat around and visited with them until the helicopter came back.

"En route back, we were talking about those kids, away from any hot food, no G.I.s to get them into an orphanage and not likely that we would be up there very often. Williams was saying we've got to do something. He said, 'I wish we could find a way to get some warm gear and get somebody to get it up there.' I said, well, 'I have a group in my home town. I'll take care of that.' And he said, 'Well, I'll pay for it, but on the condition that no one will ever know about it.' I told him, 'Well, not in your lifetime.'"

Letters home from First Lieutenant Rudy, Captain Purcell, Lieutenant (JG) Hense, and Corporal Paul E. Hestermann of Marine Air Base Squadron-33, soon reached the United States. Throughout the early months of 1953 daily newspapers across the country provided details and encouraged organizations to participate in the clothing drive. Families, churches, women's clubs, retired military groups, college sororities, and the 7-B Club of Meyersdale Joint High School in southeastern Pennsylvania all contributed money, clothing, mittens, school supplies, and food. The Marine Wives Clubs of Minneapolis and St. Paul collected 27,000 pounds' worth of donations.

In March, as shipments from America began arriving, a one-year anniversary celebration of the orphanage's creation was held. Reverend Yun Byung Sick, given the title of "Chairman and Missionary Lion as president of the Orphanage," announced to the crowd, "With one hand the Marine fights. With the other he shows kindness and love to those in need."

A plaque was also erected on the orphanage's grounds.

December 22, 1952

Dedicated to the memory of those officers and men
of the First Marine Air Wing who gave their lives in
defense of the Republic of Korea. May this monument
serve as a page of history and may it be a symbol and an
inspiration to the generations of the future as it records
how free men from beyond the seas came to Korea to
fight for the principles of a free world.

Gratefully and humbly accepted on behalf of
the First Marine Air Wing.

Major General Clayton C. Jerome, USMC
Commanding General

Although it is now called Sun-Rin, and has moved locations several times over the decades, the orphanage still exists today. And under the command of Colonel Dennis Lloyd Hager II, the United States Marines at Camp Mujuk—built on the very same land that once housed VMF-311 at K-3— regularly visit the children there.

CHAPTER EIGHT

Every Man a Tiger

*"Glenn was such a prince of a guy
he could get along with anybody."*

—Rylen Rudy

Almost everyone in MAG-33 liked John Glenn, even the inexperienced Reserve officers forced to follow him on second and third runs through the same target.

His boldness in the air, frequent preaching, and position of authority did cause friction with a few 311 pilots. So too did his penchant for the occasional humble brag.

"Makes me so darn proud when some of our boys really come through," Glenn wrote Annie after a successful interdiction over Pyongyang in May. "I harp and drive and drive on sighting, and techniques, and it seems as though there is no progress, then someone starts hitting like crazy and all the work is worth it. Had several so far who have suddenly gotten the word and have come to me and in effect said 'Hey, this stuff really works that you've been talking about.' Makes me feel like a blood brother."

First Lieutenant John Verdi recalled knowing "only one man who actively disliked John Glenn, and that was an officer who came to me for counsel in a matter which, handled otherwise than I advised him—and he took my advice—would have put him before a general court-martial."

"Glenn was acknowledged as better than the rest of us, and we accepted his leadership because he had the right amount of humility," said Major Jonathan D. Mendes, who succeeded Glenn as operations officer.

Lieutenant Colonel Art Moran had his share of disagreements with him as well. But Glenn ultimately lived up to the recommendation of those two lieutenants who had hoped for his attachment to 311.

"John was," Moran recalled, "everything those young folks thought."

Ted Williams felt the same. Flying on Glenn's wing eight times in a thirty-day stretch during the spring of 1953, Williams saw firsthand a remarkable pilot, or as Williams described him, "a cool cucumber."

"John Glenn? Absolutely fearless," Williams said. "The best I ever saw. It was an honor to fly with him."

Williams also said, "the man is crazy," when asked to describe Glenn's habit of taking risks. But unlike other Reserve recalls at K-3, Williams did not mind serving as his wingman. In fact, he wanted to.

"Any time he'd be in a group of people," Williams's Red Sox teammate Bobby Doerr recalled, "Ted would seek out some person who was extra sharp about something. The story I heard from Ted was that when he went over there [to Korea], and he knew he would be going into combat, he was going to pick someone who was the sharpest and best person to fly with."

Doerr, of course, had it backward. Glenn chose his own wingman, not the other way around. Still, Williams's enthusiasm to learn certainly caught Glenn's attention. As did the sacrifice Williams made. All the men fighting this war, many of whom were fathers to young children, risked their lives every day, especially jet pilots who flew nascent technology thousands of feet above and hundreds of miles into enemy territory. But Glenn, as well as just about every Marine at K-3, recognized that Williams had risked a bit extra, particularly money, awards, baseball records, and fame.

"I never heard Ted complain about that," Glenn said. "Not once. Not a word."

First Lieutenant Richard T. Spencer, a twenty-six-year-old regular Marine in 311, flew with Williams on his wing during several missions, including one over the famous Pork Chop Hill. He did remember Williams bemoaning his reactivation, but called him "an honest man. I really liked him. He made no bones about the fact that he did not care all about being where he was in 1953 and particularly did not care to be doing what he was doing—flying combat. Nevertheless, he did it."

John Verdi also heard Williams complain about his return to the service and losing out on his substantial salary, but he respected his abilities and courage. In his 1969 autobiography, Williams declared, "Everybody tries to make a hero out of me over the Korean thing. I was no hero. There were maybe seventy-five pilots in our two squadrons and 99 per cent of them did a better job than I did." In the years that followed Williams routinely downplayed his abilities as a pilot and his service to the Marine Corps. Verdi thoroughly disagreed, stating, "Ted's [99-]percentile self-rating was backwards. I rate him in the upper-tenth, and I'm a qualified judge who has flown with a lot of people. Whenever I have to go to war again, I'll be pleased to have Ted in the same Ready Room—if he's available!"

Williams knew his place as a late-arriving Reservist with no combat experience. Despite his fame as well as unimpeachable confidence and genius on the baseball field, he did not pretend to be John Glenn. In the early weeks of his tour, Williams showed no interest in reading maps and pinpointing targets: "the fellows ahead of me did that."

"Those guys were all 'Gung-ho,'" he said. "They were younger than I was and I was asked to lead them, but I wanted none of that. They knew more about it than I did. I just wanted to follow; no responsibility."

Major Patrick Harrison and Major John A. Mitchell were Williams's two hut mates throughout the winter and early spring. Both men spoke fondly of him. Upon Williams's return from the USS *Haven*, Mitchell gave him a "Welcome Home" present, a seven-foot-long, four-foot-wide bed that he'd fashioned.

Harrison, a casual baseball fan, had originally prejudged Williams as a prima donna.

"I hoped he fell on his butt every time he chased a fly ball," he said. "I didn't think any athlete was as unsportsmanlike."

But Williams greatly surprised him, first with an overt display of recognition for Harrison's superior rank, then by his performance under the pressure of his crash-landing in February.

"If a few of those infuriated writers who have smeared Ted could only have seen him then as he came back to base!" Harrison wrote a few years later. "If they did, they'd have the same respect and admiration for him that I have. They'd know he was as powerful and as human a man as there is in this world."

But Williams did rub some of his comrades the wrong way, and as far back as his Marine retraining in the spring of 1952. At Willow Grove, the base's public information officer wisely told the press, "Not only has he done well, but he's extremely popular here. Much more popular than on the ball field, I might say."

At the next, far lengthier stop, Cherry Point, his squadron's commander didn't agree. Lieutenant Colonel Hoyle Barr, who had to deal with Williams going AWOL to meet his mistress Evelyn Turner in Miami, called Williams "a spoiled brat-type. He had too much money and had too many people rooting for him. By the time I got ahold of him there was no straightening him out. He was thoroughly spoiled."

During his service with VMF-311, Williams won over some of the men in his squadron, but not all.

"I can wrap up Ted Williams real quick-like: The biggest asshole that ever lived," Rylen Rudy said in 2021. "He got there most unhappy. . . . He was the biggest morale buster I've ever seen. He was not liked by most."

At times during his tour, Williams lived up to his public reputation as an abrasive, self-centered hothead. Major General Megee's aide-de-camp experienced Williams's temper and impatience firsthand during their duck hunting trip. Even among active military personnel in a foreign country, Williams's use of foul language was exceptional. And he was never shy about speaking his mind, including during a dinner prearranged by Edro Buchser with MAG-33 commanding officer Colonel Robertshaw.

"He could cuss like hell. He'd say what was wrong with the war. The brass wouldn't let us fly over the [Yalu] River or near The Holy Land where the peace talks were," Buchser remembered. "Boy, Ted lost his temper. I thought this colonel was going to put the fist on him. . . . I was hitting Ted with my elbows telling him to shut up. I was worried they'd court martial him."

Williams's overwhelming celebrity as a six-figure-annual-salary athlete and spokesman might also have turned off some of his fellow officers. Anyone at K-3 could easily observe the extra attention he received from the wing's senior officers, Marines inquiring about his baseball heroics, or reporters seeking an interview. And as every sportswriter in Boston had learned years earlier, Williams could be moody and supercilious one day, friendly and chatty the next.

Major Patrick Harrison witnessed that Williams placed significant weight on rank, both those higher and lower than his captain's status. Rylen Rudy admitted that as a captain "Williams wouldn't even talk to me, I'm way below him." First Lieutenants Spencer, Verdi, and Larry Hawkins, however, kept Williams in high regard. And as for enlisted men, Williams may have refused to be quartered with Sergeant Nicholas Gandolfo during his stay aboard the U.S.S. *Haven*, but he visited regularly with enlisted Marines during his recovery and at K-3 practiced his photography hobby with Sergeant Curt Giese, a twenty-two-year-old enlisted man.

"There were a couple of pilots in the squadrons who really, they took a dislike to him, but they're the ones who were out of line," Woody Woodbury said in 2021. "I read a couple of things that a couple of guys wrote about Ted, relative to our time in Korea, that were just lies, it was derogatory, and it was said out of either jealousy or written out of malice or whatever. And nobody paid much attention to them."

Personality traits aside, the illnesses that Williams fought while in Korea (and the subsequent impact those health issues had on his participation in missions) caused the most friction with his squadron mates.

Spurred on by his friend Bill Churchman's conversations with the press, reporters speculated that Williams's pneumonia and ear trouble would lead to an early release from the service. An April 19 issue of the *Pacific Stars and Stripes*, a publication circulated widely throughout K-3, featured an Associated Press wire report entitled, "Writer Says Williams May Get Out." The story did not go over well with many Marines. Either they thought the reports were false and became protective of their friend or they did not like the implication that the baseball star would receive preferential consideration. Major Patrick Harrison dismissed that talk, insisting that Williams was a "team player."

In a late April letter home to his family, Captain Bill Clem wrote, "All that stuff about Ted is nuts. He has been back with us since the first of April and has been flying as many missions as anyone. He is a few behind me because of the trip to the hospital but still has about 30. Haven't heard a word from him or anyone else around here about his getting out. Boy do they slaughter the facts when they write about him. No wonder he's always mad at the press. He's here, he's been here and he's staying here till his tour is up."

That proved not to be the case.

Following a nondescript late morning bombing over Sariwon on June 10, Williams suited up again for an afternoon interdiction over identical coordinates, marking the sixth time he had flown multiple missions in the same day. A seven-plane formation began departing K-3 at 1538 hours.

Flight leader Major Jonathan Mendes, who had escorted Williams on his first five training hops a year earlier at Cherry Point, noticed one of the Panthers staying behind. It was Williams.

"He taxied out to join me and he turned back, claiming he had fire warning lights on in his cockpit," Mendes remembered. "He had done this a number of times. This was, I would call, an act of cowardice, that's all, simple as that. After that they sent him home a few days later on a . . . medical discharge."

First Lieutenant Rylen Rudy, whose own impressions of the big-name pilot had been less than favorable, recalled the same.

"He had 'ear trouble,' he didn't have ear trouble, he had a yellow streak up his back," Rudy said. "Sometimes he'd get airborne, but he always found something wrong with the airplane and came back to base instead of going up over North Korea doing missions."

Bill Clem, who considered Williams a friend, said years later, "We were all mad at him. . . . Here we're still over there fighting the damn war, and he's home. That didn't sit too good."

Even Williams's own doctors were skeptical of his physical discomfort. An addendum to the official report written following his medical examination at K-3 on June 25 read, "However, at times this officer has complained of his ears and yet no organic evidence of aerotitis was visible, which led the flight surgeon to believe there was either a psychosomatic element or decreased motivation toward flying." VMF-311 flight surgeon Lieutenant (JG) Catlett signed the addendum.

Both Mendes and Rudy—nearly seventy years after the war—believed that Williams's wheels-up crash-landing in mid-February begat his uneasiness in the cockpit. As Rudy said, "From that point on you couldn't hog-tie him and put him in an airplane." Mendes "never heard anything about [an ear infection.] I know nothing about that. I suspect it was a story made up." And Major Pinky Hollenbeck, whose wing Williams flew on that day, said, "He told me that war suddenly became a wicked reality to him. In the short time I've known him, I never saw him so serious as he was that one time."

But the near-deadly mission over Kyomipo occurred four months before his so-called "act of cowardice." Williams flew three dozen combat missions after being hit on February 16. Nervous, gun-shy, or just plain scared, Williams still flew each of those missions, many of them deep into North Korea and in the face of heavy anti-aircraft fire.*

Williams did abort a mission prior to the episode that Mendes recounts. On May 9, he was assigned to a late afternoon interdiction fifty-five miles northwest of Pyongyang. John Glenn served as the flight leader. Just after takeoff Williams aborted the mission because he could not transfer his fuel. Other than these two incidents, no Command Diaries or mission logs indicate that Williams aborted or returned to base before any mission was completed.

Regardless of any rumors or tales that circulated K-3, in the middle of June Williams was grounded. In multiple letters to Evelyn Turner he expressly stated that his health was the cause. When airborne, he felt fluid and inflammation in his ears, and the base's medical staff suspected an ear infection. Another visit to a Navy hospital ship was needed, news that he asked Turner not to share with his manager, Fred Corcoran, for fear the story would end up in the headlines.

On June 19 Lieutenant G.K. Dwyer, an otolaryngologist or ENT, examined Williams on the USS *Repose* and suggested further treatment aboard the *Consolation*. Dr. Harold Jayne told Williams that the intense discomfort and pressure that he felt in his ears, nose, and throat while flying were the result of hypertrophy of lymphoid tissue around the eustachian orifice. At high altitudes the condition only worsened.

While Williams spent a few days recuperating aboard the Danish hospital ship the *Jutlandia*, the Board of Medical Examiners considered a new

---

* In his book *Ted Williams at War*, author Bill Nowlin details a story told to him by Captain Bill Clem in 2002. According to Clem, late in his service Williams refused to fly a combat mission because he had been assigned an F9F-2 Panther, rather than the improved F9F-4 or F9F-5. "He wasn't afraid or anything, but it was an inferior aircraft," Clem said. "So they had to assign someone else to it. They took the mission. The next day, the C.O. transferred him to the group, out of the squadron. . . . I think the Marine Corps covered it up, because they didn't want that to happen. So then they made up this deal about him being sick." According to official Aircraft Mission Logs, after April 17, 1953, every single mission flown by VMF-311 was carried out in an F9F-5 Panther. Similarly, after May 9, 1953, VMF-115 carried out all missions in either F9F-4 or F9F-5 Panthers. Ted Williams flew ten combat missions for VMF-311 after May 9 and twenty-seven combat missions after April 17.

course of treatment. But the radiation therapy they prescribed was not available aboard hospital ships in the "forward area." Within a few days, Major General Megee approved Williams's orders back to the United States for treatment at the Navy hospital closest to his port of entry.

He returned to K-3 to gather personal items and receive his transfer orders. But before he left, Williams sat for an interview with International News Service correspondent John J. Casserly.

In between rote questions about his health, his return to baseball, and the resurgent first-place Milwaukee Braves, Williams offered his insight on the war.

Throughout the spring of 1953 talk of the conflict winding down had spread like wildfire. In letters home several Marines, including Williams, spoke of an imminent truce between the two sides. A June 12 visit to K-3 by President Syngman Rhee, to present the First MAW a medal for its lengthy support of the Republic of Korea, only furthered speculation that the war was ending. But within a few days, peace negotiations broke down again after Rhee authorized the release of thousands of non-Communist prisoners of war, against U.S. and UN advice. In the days that followed the Communist army advanced on the main line of resistance, prompting increased bombing and close air support missions. The Fifth Air Force reported more Allied sorties (8,476) and more U.S. planes being shot down (19) that week than at any other point in the war.

During all this John Casserly interviewed Ted Williams. Fitting of a man who had never wanted to be there in the first place and was scheduled to return home with no end to the fighting in sight, Williams didn't hold back.

"We've had the atom bomb for the whole three years of the war," he told Casserly while reclining in his quarters at K-3. "Guys are getting killed every day in the line. Do you think we are trying? . . . We've sat on the 38th Parallel for a year and a half and more. Still we sit there. And still more guys die. Do you think we are trying? We're not trying one-tenth of what we could."

Next, he turned his indignation from military brass and the politicians in Washington, D.C., to the American people. In Williams's mind, he had been forced to serve, just like the "guy with six kids" in the quarters next door, "who can't get out because there is no one to take his place."

"Many Americans have forgotten this war," he added. "The United

States of America ought to be ashamed of itself the way this thing is going on out here. You can ask any guy in the squadron."

Casserly did just that. He sought input from other members of MAG-33, but not regarding the nuances of the war or their own sacrifices, but rather about Williams and his relationships around the base. VMF-115 First Lieutenant Lloyd Merriman told Casserly that Williams was "one of the finest men I know."

Another Marine, who chose to remain anonymous, offered his opinion.

"Ted Williams—he doesn't make friends easily, but when he does it is all the way."

———

With a series of Navy transports whisking him away from South Korea to California, Ted Williams finally received his wish to leave K-3 permanently. For him, the fighting was over. That same month John Glenn also left K-3, and his wish too was granted in the process. But for Glenn, the fighting—true aerial combat—had just begun.

Glenn took great pride in every one of the sixty-three combat missions he flew for VMF-311, just as he had in completing fifty-seven combat missions during World War II.

"But I also hoped for air-to-air combat," he admitted. "That was the ultimate in fighter flying, testing yourself against another pilot in the air."

Glenn saw his chance in late May.

The United States Marine Corps did not have squadrons dedicated specifically for air-to-air combat. Since the days of World War I, the purpose of Marine aviation was to assist ground forces in landings and provide air support to troops on the ground. Aerial combat missions were carried out by the Navy or the Army Air Forces, which later became the United States Air Force. Still, the Marine Corps recognized the importance of air superiority, and during the Korean War an exchange program allowed one or two Marine pilots from individual squadrons to undertake a ninety-day temporary additional duty (TAD) to fly air-to-air combat missions with the Air Force.

25th Fighter-Interceptor Squadron (FIS) was one of these squadrons that rotated Marine Corps pilots in and out. A part of the larger 51st Fighter Wing, the squadron was stationed at K-13 on the western side of the Korean Peninsula. 25th FIS had a very specific job. Throughout the war, Soviet-made MiGs targeted Allied fighters across North Korea. The elusive and amply-produced MiGs came from Manchuria, the northeast-ern-most region of Communist China, and destroyed hundreds of Allied planes. The forty-some pilots within 25th patrolled south of the Yalu River, the area known as "MiG Alley," to *intercept* these planes.

Captain Harvey L. Jensen of Sioux City, Iowa, flew ninety-two missions for VMF-115 beginning in October 1952. By the spring he had applied and been accepted for transfer to the Air Force exchange program. Attached to 25th FIS, Jensen instantly loved the work.

"This is fun compared to the fighter-bombers, but this place gives you the ulcers," he said after nabbing his first MiG on May 18. "Those damn MiGs run away from you and everyone here wants a MiG so bad he can taste it."

In addition to the challenge posed by air-to-air combat (referred to as "dogfights"), the main reason Marines sought the transfer was a chance to pilot the F-86 Sabre. Created by North American Aviation in the late 1940s, the Sabre shattered the world speed record within a year of its com-pletion. Eleven months after Chuck Yeager and the Bell X-1 broke the sound barrier above the Mojave desert, Air Force Major Richard L. John-son piloted the plane to a world record 671 miles per hour, over Cleveland, Ohio, of all places. Four years later, Air Force captain Slade Nash shattered Johnson's mark, pushing an improved F-86D Sabre to 698 miles per hour.

When loaded up with two thousand pounds of bombs, napalm tanks, and rockets, the Sabre could not reach the same blistering speeds, but it vastly outperformed the Panthers operated by pilots in MAG-33 and lev-eled the playing field when engaging MiGs. If the Panther was a city bus—durable, dependable, utilitarian—the Sabre was a Ferrari.

"I loved the bird," Jensen recalled decades later. "They liked me, they said, 'He's a hunter.' A lot of people are not hunters. You get into the com-bat situation a lot of people would just fly airplanes that don't want to get too damn close to anything. They just take off and land again. Boy, we saw that all the time, but I went after my targets and they paid off."

John Glenn was a hunter. When Jensen's TAD ended in June, Glenn took his place with 25th FIS: "I've been waiting for ten years for a chance to do this," he wrote his wife. And in his mind, Annie should have been just as excited.

"Hope I have the orders to the AF exchange when I get back," he wrote to her while on R&R in late May. "Get a little bit of that safe type flying in for a change. I know you don't believe me on that, but it is actually much safer than what we are now doing. Can't outguess AA. . . . Every guy I've talked to out here has said the same thing."

Glenn believed in himself. He was confident, not cocky, in his skills and decision-making. And he was not shy about his abilities.

Dropping bombs, mostly in a coordinated, large formation of planes, left much to chance. VMF-311 missions required flying low to the ground in a tight formation with the wingman following right behind his leader. Anti-aircraft fire from the ground often missed one Panther only to hit another inadvertently.

"The North Korean and Chinese gunners, cannon-people, nobody had ever taught them that to shoot at this airplane you shoot out over ahead of him so he beats the bullet out there eventually," Rylen Rudy said. "The gooks would shoot right straight at you, which is where you want them to shoot because by the time the bullet gets there you're a hundred yards down the road."

After the mission that ended with his crash-landing at K-13, Ted Williams told Pinky Hollenbeck—on whose wing he flew—"You son of a gun, they were shooting at you and they got me!"

But 25th FIS missions rarely included more than eight planes. And in dogfights, often high in the air, separated from the rest of the formation, Glenn did not consider random fire a concern.

"Just keep a good lookout, that's the whole thing," Glenn assured Annie. "As long as you are alert every second, they can never touch you. Only if one sneaks up on you, can they get you, and if you're blind enough or stupid enough to not keep looking, then you should 'get got.' . . . That's where the years of training pay off. Really knowing how to get the most out of an airplane is it."

From the outset of his arrival at K-13, Glenn fit right in.

Chastised for reckless maneuvers while flying missions for 311, Glenn and his eagerness to take risks were actually encouraged by his superiors in 25th FIS. With no inexperienced Reserve recall on his wing, and no fear of secondary explosions or small arms fire attacks from the ground, Glenn was free to pursue enemy combatants high in the air.

Working together, be it with a wingman or as part of a formation, was critical to the success of any squadron, including 25th FIS. Glenn and his wingman—or Glenn and the pilot for whom he served as wingman—eluded or attacked MiGs in unison. On one mission in particular, when his wingman suffered engine trouble during a dogfight, Glenn flew circles around him to provide a shield from enemy fire. Upon completion of his tour with the Air Force, at the request of MAG-33's commanding officer, Glenn wrote a seventeen-page memo outlining his observations and recommendations for improving Marine aviation.

"Teamwork among the F-86 pilots is carried to a high degree," he stated. "No one stays 'on the river' alone. A wingman must stick. Teamwork is constantly stressed."

However, Glenn quickly realized that missions for 25th FIS were far more independent and autonomous than dive-bombing atolls in the Marshall Islands or dropping GPs into a cloud of white phosphorous smoke north of Pyongyang. The purpose of these interceptor flights was to seek, pursue, and destroy a deadly, unpredictable, moving target. Just below the paragraph in his report that espoused the virtues of teamwork, Glenn stated, "Aggressiveness is greatly encouraged. . . . 'Every man a tiger' was the word and the theme drummed into new pilots. Corny, but it pays off in an aggressive flying attitude. For the majority of the interceptor pilots, to say that they have an aggressive attitude toward getting MiGs is a gross understatement."

As much as Glenn considered himself a team player, a dutiful Marine—and he was—in this arena, each pilot was largely on his own, a lesson he learned two weeks into his tour.

On June 16, Glenn joined Mission Maple 01, flying on the wing of Lieutenant Colonel John C. Giraudo. The squadron's commanding officer, Giraudo had already flown ninety-eight missions, destroying at least two MiGs and possibly damaging or destroying three more.

Patrolling low to the ground, just above the Yalu River, Giraudo and Glenn spotted anti-aircraft artillery.

"We better get out of here," Glenn told the lieutenant colonel over radio. "They're going to shoot us up."

"No sweat, John," Giraudo answered. "We're flying too fast."

"Famous last words," he later said.

Anti-aircraft fire hit Giraudo's Sabre, which spun out of control. He ejected at five thousand feet and landed safely in a wooded hillside. Glenn repeatedly circled the area to keep a lock on his position as he radioed for help. But rescue planes never arrived. Running out of fuel, Glenn climbed to forty thousand feet and dead-sticked the plane back to K-13, then jumped back into another fully-fueled Sabre to return and continue the search for Giraudo.

Glenn had tremendous respect for Giraudo, who endured eighteen months as a prisoner of war (POW) of the Nazis during World War II. And he enjoyed flying his wing, telling Annie after one of their earlier missions, "This Giraudo is a real airplane driver and he spares nothing on these hops. He was surprised that I stuck with him today in some of his maneuvers." But Glenn was also infuriated by his fruitless efforts as a wingman to stick with Giraudo on the June 16 mission.

"Never had anyone going down affect me like that one did for some reason," Glenn wrote. "Never felt so helpless in my life. Sit and fly with a guy literally fighting for his life and not be able to help, then the rest of that day, the flameout, second trip, etc."

Although Glenn observed him safely hidden from the enemy, Giraudo was taken prisoner by the North Koreans. When the war ended and the prisoner exchange Operation Big Switch returned Giraudo to the Allies, Glenn sniveled his way into attending the ceremony at Freedom Village in Panmunjom in early September 1953.

"You son of a bitch," Giraudo said upon first seeing Glenn. "I had it in for you."

"Why? What's wrong?" a startled Glenn responded. "What happened?"

"You caused me all kinds of problems," Giraudo said laughing, not actually angry with his wingman.

"I was trying to get you out of there, for gosh sakes."

"I know you were, but let me tell you what happened."

Giraudo then informed Glenn that he had landed safely, but not far from a collection of North Korean troops. Attempting to hide his parachute and survival gear from the enemy, Giraudo accidently inflated his life raft. On his trail, a Communist soldier shot Giraudo through the shoulder and began dragging him to a POW camp.

"It hurt enough as it was," Giraudo told Glenn. "But then you came back and started circling. Every time you came over, they'd throw me in a ditch and sit on me. It hurt like hell. I was thinking, 'John Glenn, would you please just go home.'"

While Glenn, the Air Force, and Giraudo's wife, daughter, and sick mother awaited any news on the fallen pilot's whereabouts, missions for 25th FIS continued.

The squadron that Glenn had joined measured success differently than Marine pilots at K-3. Each MiG that they destroyed represented a tangible achievement, different from blowing up a bridge or providing air support for ground troops. Whenever a MiG was downed, two flags flew high above the base, one with a skull and crossbones, the other with a giant red star.

"Kills" were credited to individuals, recorded in official Air Force logs, and commemorated with a three-inch-tall red star painted on the hull of the pilot's plane. (Unlike protocol within VMF-311, pilots in 25th FIS flew the same aircraft on every mission, usually with their names or nicknames elaborately painted on the side.) And when the squadron reached one hundred total kills in mid-June, right after Glenn's arrival, a celebration took place at the Officers' Club.

Five kills were rewarded with the unofficially official title of "Ace." When he first arrived at K-13 to join the squadron, "Glenn was not shy. He boasted to everyone that he was going to be the second Marine ace of the Korean War." (A few weeks earlier, VMF-115 pilot Major John F. Bolt had joined 39th FIS, and shot down six MiGs by early July.)

But in his first month Glenn did not have many chances to bag a MiG. As was the case when he joined 311, Glenn had to study handbooks and take fam hops in the Sabre. All the while, the same news of an impending truce that hit K-3 that June also hit K-13.

"The peace news today has had me scared to death," Glenn wrote Annie. "Afraid they'll end this thing before I even get to fly wing up there. Wingmen don't shoot up here unless it's a very unusual circumstance. The wingmen are just there to clear the leader's tail when the shooting starts. Their only job is to stick, and I mean stick, with their element (section) leaders . . . so I'll probably get no shooting for some time, but at least I'll get a look at the vaunted MiG."

Even once he began flying missions, first as a wingman, and eventually as a section leader, Glenn remained hungry to notch a MiG on his record. Air Force officers could see how unfulfilled and impatient their new comrade was. They took to calling him the "MiG Mad Marine," which they painted on his Sabre in beautiful red-and-yellow lettering, along with the names Lyn, Annie, and David.

"It was very disappointing to be all keyed up for a big mission, fly the mission, and make no contact," he said.

Despite a decade of training, studying, and instructing military aviation, both in peacetime and wartime, stalking enemy aircraft was a largely new experience for Glenn.

"There was a lot of real wild flying," he told an interviewer decades later. "And that's where it was so much faster, because if you have an airplane coming toward you at 550 or 600 miles an hour and you're doing the same thing toward him, you're closing at 1,000 miles an hour, and your decision-making and your maneuvering have to be really accelerated on a speeded-up basis. But you're not using the kinds of weapon systems we have now. We didn't have radar to pick people up. It was all visual. And you had six .50-caliber machine guns mounted on your airplane, and you had to maneuver in behind the other airplane and get in to within about 800 to 1,000 feet with him maneuvering, too, and draw a bead on him."

Although unquestionably the most advanced plane he had yet flown, with unparalleled agility and world-class speed when flying in a straight path, the Sabre had its limitations. MiGs were smaller and lighter, which meant they could climb higher than the Sabre.

"So there were times when you found yourself flying around under MiGs and you just couldn't quite get up there," Glenn recalled. "It was like, you ached to get up a little bit higher and couldn't do it."

On July 12 Glenn led an attack on two low-flying MiGs. At extremely close range he opened fire, securing direct hits to the enemy's fuselage and wing. Barely fifty feet in the air, Glenn observed the plane explode on the ground below him.

"Dearest Annie, Dave, and Lyn," he wrote that evening. "Tonight I am singing a slightly different tune than my last few letters. Today I finally got a MiG, cold as can be. Of course I'm not excited at this point. Not much!"

Upon his return to K-13, as he taxied along the runway, enlisted men, officers, and even the base's Catholic chaplain came out to cheer on the MiG Mad Marine's first kill.

A week later, over the Suiho reservoir, Glenn's formation encountered sixteen enemy planes. Reinforcements arrived to assist, and the Sabres and MiGs split into smaller groups of dogfights. Amid tremendous chaos, Glenn trailed and destroyed one MiG, assisted his wingman in another kill, then when he ran out of ammunition, returned to base to claim his second star.

His next kill came much quicker. On July 22, in traditionally aggressive fashion, Glenn initiated an attack on a team of four MiGs. Unloading hundreds of .50-caliber cartridges, Glenn and two other members of the formation each took out a MiG of their own. Three kills in ten days.

Glenn's local newspaper, the *Zanesville Times*, chronicled the exploits of the Central Ohio star by publishing excerpts from his letters to Annie. The front page of the Sunday, July 26 edition featured multiple images of Glenn—in his Marine Service Alpha uniform; beside the Corsair he flew in World War II; a family portrait with Annie, David, and Lyn; even one of his baby photos—accompanied by an article entitled "New Concord Jet Pilot Tells of First Kill."

Above those words, in far larger print, another headline read "Signing of Truce Set for Today; 3-Year-Old Korean War to End."

During a ten-minute ceremony within the walls of a modest wood-paneled building quickly assembled in the village of Panmunjom, a cease-fire agreement was reached. Representing the United Nations, United States Army lieutenant general William K. Harrison, Jr., signed for the Allies, and Nam Il, representing North Korea and China, signed for the Communists. South Korean president Syngman Rhee refused to sign. Just as the Korean War was never technically a war authorized by Congress, the fighting ended technically without a peace treaty. And because poor weather had kept his squadron grounded over the previous few days, it also ended with the MiG Mad Marine a couple of kills short.

"I really didn't want the war to end," Glenn told a fellow pilot sixty years later, "because I had three and I needed two more."

So John Glenn's dogfights above the Yalu River with North Korean and Chinese pilots flying Soviet-made MiGs were over. But his mano a mano battles with the Communists had just begun. And soon enough, his aching "to get up a little bit higher" would be relieved.

CHAPTER NINE

Big Shot

On July 9, 1953, a Marine R5D transport plane touched down at Naval Air Station Moffett Field outside San Jose, California. Aboard was Captain Ted Williams, still bothered by pain and fluid in his ears, especially after a twelve-hour transpacific flight.

Upon his arrival Williams told a collection of sportswriters outside the airfield exactly what they wanted to hear.

"I'll always be able to hit a baseball," he assured them.

During an impromptu press conference Williams backtracked from the scorched-earth interview he gave John Casserly before leaving Korea—"I was in a bad mood that day," he explained—then detailed the reason for his return to the United States. Doctors at Oak Knoll Naval Hospital in Oakland hoped that the experimental treatment of inserting a radium-tipped rod into his nose, known as nasopharyngeal irradiation, would cure his symptoms.

After signing autographs, praising his fellow Marines at K-3, and joking that his impaired hearing would help block out insults and boos from the fans, Williams reiterated that his service commitment would not end until October. With the Red Sox ten-and-a-half games out of first place, postseason baseball did not seem very likely for Boston.

But Red Sox general manager Joe Cronin let it slip to reporters that Williams had called him from Oakland to learn about any new pitchers on American League rosters.

"That sure sounds like he's coming back to us, doesn't it?" Cronin said.

The following morning, Williams received transfer orders to the Naval Medical Center in Bethesda, Maryland. Before resuming treatments, he was granted a few days' leave, which he spent watching Major League Baseball's annual All-Star Game in Cincinnati, Ohio.

At Crosley Field, home to the Cincinnati Redlegs—baseball's oldest professional club was rebranded that April to avoid any association with Communism—Williams received a hero's welcome. To open the twentieth edition of the Midsummer Classic, Williams threw out the ceremonial first pitch to Brooklyn Dodgers catcher Roy Campanella, then sat in the visitors' dugout as an honorary member of the American League team. In between socializing with New York Yankees such as Yogi Berra, Hank Bauer, and manager Casey Stengel, Williams continued to tease reporters and fans, saying "It's possible I might get out in a few weeks."

Williams had already submitted his formal request for an early release and hoped that those with whom he'd served would also get out soon. Even after the war ended, officers of VMF-311 continued to fly air patrol missions over North Korea. John Glenn, still with the Air Force, was reprimanded weeks after the cease fire for flying over North Korean territorial waters, which he denied.

"The big deal now is to get my buddies back from Korea as soon as possible," Williams told a reporter at the end of July. "I left a lot of wonderful guys over there and I'd like to see them all get safely home."

One day after Communist and United Nations forces reached their tenuous peace agreement in Panmunjom, Ted Williams arrived fifteen minutes late to a brief ceremony at the Navy Gun Factory in Washington, D.C. Surrounded by reporters, photographers, and television cameras, Marine barracks commanding officer Colonel Kenneth B. Chappell thanked Williams for his service and handed over his official discharge from the United States Marine Corps.

"Ted, I understand that your future address is Fenway Park, is that correct?" Chappell said.

"Well, as of now that's where I'm scheduled to go, Colonel," Williams replied. "I plan on being up there tomorrow, and needless to say I'm anxious to see if I can still hit."

He could.

Pinch-hitting late in the finale of a three-game series against the St. Louis Browns, Williams popped up against veteran screwballer Marlin Stuart. Three days later, Williams strode to home plate at Fenway Park to pinch-hit for shortstop Johnny Lipon.

Trailing 5–2 in the bottom of the seventh inning, Williams faced Cleveland's two-time twenty-game-winner Mike Garcia. Two low sliders put Williams ahead in the count. The hard-throwing right-hander was renowned for relying on his fastball when caught in a jam, and Garcia did not believe that the thirty-five-year-old fighter pilot could catch up to his heater. With Williams ahead 3–1, the "Big Bear" threw a third consecutive fastball, which Williams belted over the right field bullpens. Although the crowd of nearly twenty-seven thousand roared as he rounded the bases, Williams appeared grim.

"It seemed as though a tragedy had struck him," Indians third baseman Al Rosen noticed. "His face looked awful pale—and when I tried to stare him in the eye, he looked down with his mouth clamped tight. I'll bet maybe he was trying to hold back some tears. Because nowhere, no time, have I ever seen a man look like he did when he hit a home run."

An hour later, following the Red Sox 9–3 loss, Williams shaved, showered, and ducked out of the Red Sox locker room to avoid the press.

After fifteen months away from baseball, Ted Williams—theatrical, enigmatic, brilliant—had now truly returned.

Appearing on the front page of the *Zanesville Times* made John Glenn something of a local celebrity in the summer of 1953. Still stationed at K-13 and flying missions for 25th FIS after the war ended, he received his first fan letter, from a woman living a few miles outside New Concord. Bedridden for years after contracting rheumatic fever, Bettie Smith of Cambridge, Ohio, wrote Glenn asking him to autograph three parlor cards featuring his photograph. He obliged the surprising request.

Glenn finally left Korea in January 1954, but unlike Ted Williams, he was a military lifer. After a brief reunion with his family, he reported to the naval air station at Patuxent River, Maryland.

Founded in 1945, the United States Naval Test Pilot Training Division at Patuxent River produced its first batch of graduates in December 1948. Considered at the time "more like Albert Einstein and less like Jack Armstrong," the inaugural class of sixteen did far more than just fly as fast or as far as possible. Intense study of aerodynamics, physics, and calculus forced pilots to calculate center of gravity or longitudinal, latitudinal, and directional stability on their aircraft when, for example, an instructor cut off three of the plane's four motors.

"People think a test pilot is a strong-armed Joe who dives a ship until its wings come off," the school's assistant director, Navy lieutenant commander Emil P. Schuld, said after proctoring the first class's exam. "These pilots already know how to fly when they came here. . . . Now they know why. Knowing why, they can help the Navy make new ships better."

During the final months of World War II John Glenn had tested aircraft at Patuxent River, and although he loved the work, he did not apply to the test pilot program for several years. As an ambitious young officer, he believed that leaving Marine duties for a naval training assignment would hurt his career advancement plans. By the end of the fighting in Korea, he felt his record was strong enough to pursue the Navy program. Besides, he had already requested and accepted a transfer to temporary duty with the United States Air Force.

Glenn, who did not finish his undergraduate degree, lacked the academic pedigree of many of his classmates, mostly products of the United States Naval Academy or pilots with graduate degrees. Teaching himself several of the necessary basics to understand advanced calculus, Glenn completed the six-month program and graduated in July 1954.

"It was a very rigorous course," Glenn said. "It was like we used to joke about, going to the academic side of test pilot training was like getting a drink out of a fire hydrant. You get a little in you and a lot over you."

In addition to many late nights of study, the trainees at Patuxent River frequently flew new and experimental aircraft. Throughout his training and afterward as a full-time test pilot, Glenn became skilled at handling the FJ-3 Fury, a jet comparable to the Sabre but outfitted with a Wright J65 engine. Pushing the engine to its maximum ability was certainly part of the duty of a test pilot, but anticipating and exploring an aircraft's limitations in combat were their top priorities.

On one of Glenn's earliest assignments in the Fury, both the seal on the canopy and the oxygen regulator failed. At more than forty thousand feet in the air, over the Atlantic Ocean, in a depressurized cockpit, he began to suffocate. With his last ounces of energy, he located the emergency oxygen tank in his parachute pack, filled his lungs, and pulled out of the steep nosedive.

Just a few weeks after he graduated from Patuxent River, Glenn was sent to the National Aircraft Show to give a public demonstration of the Fury. Formerly known as the National Air Races, the annual event drew hundreds of thousands of spectators over Labor Day weekend, and had recently moved to Dayton, home of the Wright Brothers. For years, one of the show's signature competitions had awarded the Allison Trophy to the pilot who flew a predetermined straightaway course (several hundred miles in length) in the fastest time.

To usher in the jet age, the show's organizers changed the 1954 edition of the event. The award would go to the pilot who climbed to an altitude of ten thousand feet in the shortest time. Needing two minutes and seven seconds to reach that height in his F-89D Scorpion, Air Force Second Lieutenant William J. Knight claimed the Allison Trophy as well as national headlines. Glenn wasn't as impressed.

"I can do better than that myself," he told several of the Marines at Dayton's James M. Cox Municipal Airport.

The next day, Glenn lit up his Fury, readied the dashboard stopwatch, and raced down the runway. According to his eye, he reached ten thousand feet in one minute, fifty-nine seconds, besting Knight's time by eight seconds. Although unofficial, the mark that Glenn had set satisfied his hunger for competition. More importantly, he proved to himself an ability to conceive, plan, and execute—or simply snivel—a historic aviation achievement.

After more than two years at Patuxent River, Glenn was transferred to the Navy's Bureau of Aeronautics (BuAer) in Washington, D.C. Rather than testing planes every day, he worked as a desk officer, touring aviation factories, looking for ways to cut costs, and sitting through interminable meetings.

"It was all paperwork," he said. "So I didn't enjoy it nearly as much as I had my previous assignment."

During one of his visits to the Chance Vought factory in Dallas, Texas, Glenn dreamed up a project to get himself back in the game.

Capable of flying over a thousand miles per hour, Vought's F8U Crusader was considered the Navy's fastest fighter, but it was not yet combat ready. The Crusader's engine, a Pratt & Whitney J57, had strict limitations on its afterburner; otherwise, its manufacturer believed, the engine would overheat and catch on fire.

Rather than conducting several separate tests on the engine's prolonged use of afterburner, Glenn proposed a cross-country test of the engine that would have the added bonus of challenging the transcontinental speed record.

"They were going to do some high-speed tests on the airplane, sustained high-power tests on the engine anyway, actually in flight, not just on a test stand, and so I proposed this idea," Glenn said years later. "Although the real reason, what I wanted to do was go at this thing and get the speed record in addition to the engine test."

For decades, flying nonstop from one coast to the other signified an aviation milestone. Army pilots Lieutenant John A. Macready and Lieutenant Oakley G. Kelly completed the first such flight in May 1923. In a Dutch-made Fokker T-2 the trip took nearly twenty-seven hours. Fourteen years later, aviation icon Howard Hughes cut the time to under eight hours while at the controls of his Hughes H-1 Racer.

By 1955 United States Air Force Lieutenant Colonel Robert R. Scott had shaved the official mark down to three hours and forty-six minutes. Piloting a Republic F84F Thunder jet, Lieutenant Colonel Scott covered the distance from Los Angeles International Airport to Floyd Bennett Field in Brooklyn at an average of 649 miles per hour, but the new record was far from supersonic. (Given the changes in atmosphere, the speed of sound at an altitude of thirty-five thousand feet is about 670 miles per hour.)

Glenn believed that he could best that record. Knowing the Crusader's capabilities, he intended to become the first pilot to average supersonic speed throughout a nonstop transcontinental flight. That feat would also reaffirm United States dominance over the skies at a time when the Soviet Union had reportedly begun supplying its newest supersonic fighter, the mass-produced MiG-19, to East Germany, Egypt, and Syria.

With the assistance of Vought engineers, Glenn mapped out the entire journey, then sought the permission of his bosses at the Bureau of Aeronautics. Rear Admiral Thurston B. Clark, the commander at Patuxent River, and Admiral Robert E. Dixon, appointed chief of the department by President Dwight D. Eisenhower that May, approved the plan, which a team of Navy and civilian engineers had thoroughly vetted. Glenn named his efforts "Project Bullet."

From the outset, fuel emerged as the most critical aspect of the mission. The Crusader was capable of flying up to 1,425 miles, but prolonged use of the afterburner significantly reduced its range. A flight from Los Alamitos Naval Air Station in Orange County, California, to Floyd Bennett Field stretched 2,446 miles. To remedy the discrepancy, three midair rendezvous with Navy twin-propeller tanker planes would refuel the Crusader once it descended to twenty-five thousand feet and slowed to three hundred miles per hour. A probe extending from the port side of the fuselage would receive fuel from a long drogue released by the tanker's aft. In less than seven minutes the tanker could resupply the plane with fifteen hundred gallons of JP-5 fuel. Midair refuelings were planned over naval air stations in Albuquerque, New Mexico; Olathe, Kansas; and Indianapolis, Indiana.

"That was a high pressure operation," Glenn recalled. "You're flying like a son of a gun, then you've got to drop down to find the tanker. You've got to locate the tanker pretty fast because you're running low on fuel."

On the morning of July 16, 1957, Glenn walked through the muggy summer air of Southern California and jumped into his shiny, silver aircraft. Utilizing an F8U-1P, the unarmed photographic reconnaissance model of the Crusader, Glenn took off at 6:04 a.m. and within minutes reached supersonic speeds ten miles above the ground.

"It was a beautiful trip on a beautiful, clear day, and a lot of fun," he recalled fifty years later. "I'd like to do that again."

Although he lost sight of the tanker over Indianapolis—"I couldn't find him and I was very, very low on fuel, it was nail-biting time"—Glenn refueled at each of the designated checkpoints. And as he crossed above states, cities, and neighborhoods at over one thousand miles per hour, his wake shattered windows across the Midwest.

In Terre Haute, Indiana, Glenn's Crusader swooped so forcefully over the home of Mr. and Mrs. Louis Howerton that the ceiling of their home on North Sixth Street crashed into the floor. New Concord, Ohio, residents swore they heard a sonic boom as he soared overhead. "I guess Johnny must have dropped a bomb," local spectator W. S. Dixon phoned to Glenn's father later that day. And in Pittsburgh, Pennsylvania, police and newspaper switchboards lit up with so many calls from homes in the South Hills reporting a "mysterious blast" that the National Guard was contacted.

As he made his approach into Brooklyn, with his fuel tank down to just forty gallons, Glenn knew he had bested Scott's two-year-old mark. And by his meticulous calculations—which he logged in the cockpit every three-and-a-half minutes—his supersonic goal was in sight. At 12:27 p.m. the Crusader touched down at Floyd Bennett Field. Apart from slowing down to refuel, Glenn had employed the afterburner for virtually the entire flight, but the engine never overheated or caught on fire. Flying the plane so fast, at such a high altitude helped to keep him safe.

By covering the 2,446 miles in 3 hours, 23 minutes, and 8.4 seconds, Glenn's average speed was over 722 miles per hour. At his average altitude of nearly 35,000, that easily surpassed the speed of sound. But it wasn't quite fast enough to Glenn, who announced that he would gladly do the flight "all over again tomorrow."

"Give me a break in the weather, we can make the same flight in under three hours," he said.

Major Glenn was already sniveling his next assignment.

———————

With a pinch-hit home run in his second at-bat since leaving for the Korean War, Ted Williams seamlessly settled back into his place among baseball royalty. He just as easily settled back into his tumultuous life away from the batter's box.

Despite weak legs and insisting "I could do with a vacation," Williams returned to the Red Sox regular lineup in mid-August 1953, starting in left field for twenty-six of Boston's final thirty-four games. Hitting .407 during that truncated season, Williams clubbed thirteen home runs in his ninety-one official at-bats, by far the highest homer-to-at-bat ratio of his entire career, higher than even Babe Ruth's finest season. One member of the Baseball Writers Association of America even listed Williams tenth on his ballot for the American League Most Valuable Player award.

Finally granted that vacation, an extended off-season trip to Florida, Williams caught four sailfish during the 9th Annual International Light Tackle Sailfish Tournament in West Palm Beach. Williams's three-man team won the tournament, while he claimed the event's award for Top Fisherman.

Headlines for his fishing prowess came at an optimal time. That same week, professional golfer Sam Snead bought a large percentage of Williams's newly formed fishing equipment company and was appointed a vice president. With two household names at the helm, each their respective sports' highest-paid figure, Ted Williams, Inc., aimed to take the sporting goods market by storm. Their first product was a light rod ideal for bonefish which Williams began hawking in the Keys.

Williams was in need of more income: A month later, Doris filed for divorce in Dade County, claiming that for six years he "indulged in a course of conduct in which he [had] mistreated and abused" her. She petitioned the court for ownership of their Miami home, the blue Cadillac he received at Ted Williams Day in 1952, attorneys and court fees, child support, and full custody of their six-year-old daughter, Bobby-Jo. On his fifteen-minute Sunday evening radio show on ABC, famed gossip columnist Walter Winchell immediately speculated that Williams might soon marry Evelyn Turner. Through the Associated Press, Turner insisted they were "strictly friends."

With his marriage ending and much of the goodwill he had earned for serving in Korea gone following allegations that he had "hit, beaten, and struck" Doris, Williams turned his focus on baseball. But ten minutes into his first workout at Red Sox spring training in Sarasota, Williams dove for a line drive hit by teammate Hoot Evers and crashed into the ground, fracturing his collarbone. A surgeon inserted a steel pin into his shoulder and Williams missed the first month of the regular season. Three weeks into his comeback, a June bout of pneumonia sidelined him for the Red Sox' next twenty-one games.

He would be thirty-six years-old that August. Between his recall to the Marines, a broken elbow in the 1950 All-Star Game, and now another injury- and sickness-riddled season, Williams had missed large chunks of four of the previous five years. That April, he penned a column (as told to Joe Reichler and Joe Trimble) in the *Saturday Evening Post* entitled "This Is My Last Year." At the conclusion of the 1954 season, with Boston sixteen games under .500, Williams reaffirmed his intention to retire.

"There's no question about it," he said an hour after homering in an 11–2 victory over Washington. "This is my last day in baseball."

Williams went to Florida. Doris occupied their lavish home in South Miami, but he had also purchased a spot in the Matecumbe neighborhood of Islamorada on the Keys. Throughout that winter, which included a fishing trip to Peru, Williams assured sportswriters that he was through with baseball. And when Boston's spring training opened, he remained at Islamorada, happy to fish, run his business, and watch his manager Fred Corcoran try and sell Hollywood producers on a biopic starring Williams in the lead role.

"If I had enough dough, I would never play baseball again," he had said the previous year. "I'm not kidding. First of all, I'd never miss baseball. You let in for a lot of criticism and take a lot of gaff."

But that winter word leaked to the *Akron Beacon Journal* that Ted

Williams, Inc., was in considerable financial trouble. Spending $87,000 on advertising in its first year had caused interest in their products to boom during 1954. The small business, with its president and vice president busy on the diamond and the links, respectively, failed to meet the demand. Behind in production, the company canceled many orders.

On May 14—five days after a circuit judge granted Doris her divorce—Williams signed an $80,000 contract to rejoin the Red Sox.

"My arm is sore, my back aches, my hands hurt from hitting, and I'm still 10 pounds heavier than I want to be," he said after a workout at Fenway Park. "But my legs don't hurt. They're too dead. Otherwise, I'm fine. Swinging a bat, I feel real good. Strong."

Each of the next three seasons adhered to the same script: coaxed out of certain retirement to play for a ball club that never really contended for the pennant, Williams flourished while simultaneously courting both batting titles and controversy.

Perhaps the most infamous moment of his entire career occurred during a Tuesday afternoon game with the Yankees on August 7, 1956. In the eleventh inning of a scoreless pitchers' duel between Boston's Willard Nixon and the Yankees' Don Larsen, two months before he would throw a perfect game in the World Series, Mickey Mantle popped up to shallow left field. Williams misplayed and ultimately dropped the ball. The near-capacity crowd at Fenway unloaded a chorus of boos. The very next batter, Yogi Berra, smashed a hard liner toward the wall that would have easily scored Mantle from second. Williams leapt to make a sensational catch and end the inning.

The grab may have saved the game, which Boston won in the bottom of the eleventh on Williams's bases loaded walk, but it was his actions in between innings that made news. As he jogged off the field, toward the Red Sox dugout, he spat in the direction of the right and left field stands. In separate games the previous month, Williams also appeared to spit at the press box, including once as he crossed home plate following his four hundredth career home run. Fans, reporters, and team owner Tom Yawkey were outraged. Team president Joe Cronin levied Williams a $5,000 fine, matching the largest player fine in baseball history. Although he expressed contrition to both Cronin and reporters that day, he also said, "I'd spit again at the same people who booed me today," then blamed the press for his actions.

"[Williams] should quit baseball before baseball quits him," *Boston Globe* columnist Harold Kaese wrote the following day. "His body is wearing out and so, apparently is his nervous system. He never could take it very well. Now he is near the point where he can't take it at all."

In light of another row with the press, Williams declared that the season would be his last. But when spring training came around the next year, he rejoined the team in Sarasota, just in time for another bad publicity tour.

That March, the New York State Selective Service Draft board ordered Brooklyn Dodgers pitcher Johnny Podres to report for induction into the United States Army. Podres, a twenty-four-year-old from Upstate New York, had become a hero to championship-starved Brooklyn fans the previous fall by tossing a complete game shutout in Game Seven of the World Series. In the Dodgers' first-ever Series victory, Podres won both his starts over the mighty Yankees.

"Podres is paying the penalty for being a star," Williams told reporters after a spring training exhibition game. "If Podres had lost those World Series games he would probably still be with the Dodgers.

"Gutless draft boards, gutless politicians, and gutless baseball writers, that's what we've got," he added. "He wins a couple of games, gets famous and some two-bit draft board puts the arm on him. They're going to take 20 percent of the kid's money-earning time, and for what? Are we at war? No. Do they need him? No. It's just a big act by the government and some politicians."

The story eventually quieted down. Until the next spring. Following an exhibition game in Louisiana, the Red Sox flight to Sarasota was delayed for several hours. Crozet Duplantier, sports editor of the local *New Orleans States*, approached Williams for an interview. A Marine combat correspondent during World War II and still in the Reserves, Duplantier asked Williams if he had resented being recalled to service in Korea. Duplantier claimed he approached Williams to "get Ted to say something nice which will help encourage the Marine Corps Reserve."

Instead, Williams unloaded on the Marines, the United States military, and the federal government. While making a spitting gesture several times throughout the interview, he outlined the unfairness of his recall to the service and his scorn for those who had failed to secure his deferment five years earlier.

"I used to admire Senator Taft, I thought he was a wonderful man," he said. "We've got a lot of gutless politicians in this country. I didn't want to meet the President [Eisenhower], nor did I want to meet Harry Truman. I don't like politicians."

The interview hit the wires the next morning, setting off a frenzy of national headlines. Duplantier fiercely defended his reporting. Williams issued a written rebuttal through the Red Sox public relations department.

"I have too many friends and I have spent too much time in the Marine Corps not to know that that organization is tops," it read in part.

Although Williams insisted that Duplantier had been "drinking excessively" before the interview, the written statement ended with an apology, which he essentially retracted upon opening his mouth.

"What I said about the Marines and Taft goes . . . but charges against Truman and the government, that's a damn lie. If I did say it, I don't remember it. But if I'd say it, I'd remember. I remember everything else," he told the Associated Press. "I got a raw deal from the Marines and I've said before I've got no use for them."

Again, Williams withstood, deflected, or just ignored the considerable criticism from his remarks and channeled his anger toward American League pitchers. Twice in the first half of the 1957 season Williams hit three home runs in a single game on the road. And on the last day of June his colossal three-run home run at Fenway Park lifted the Red Sox to their eleventh win in thirteen games, pulling them within seven games of the first-place Yankees.

Rejuvenated by a few days off during the all-star break, Williams's torrid pace resumed. During a five-game road trip through Detroit and Cleveland, he pounded out seven extra-base hits, including five home runs. Following a doubleheader against the Indians, in which Williams homered in both games, the Red Sox headed to Kansas City for a three-game set with the Athletics.

Trailing 2–1 during a ninety-degree summer night, Williams came to the plate with one out in the top of the ninth. He hit the first pitch thrown by veteran right-hander Virgil Trucks over the right field fence to spark a Red Sox comeback victory. For the fifth straight game he socked a home run, the sixth in his last eleven at-bats. He was just one shy of tying the American League record for consecutive games with a home run. With a league-leading twenty-six home runs, Williams now trailed Mickey

Mantle, the reigning American League Triple Crown champion, by just one point in the race for the batting title.

"Theodore Samuel Williams won't be washed up as a great hitter," *Boston Daily Record* reporter Joe Cashman wrote from Kansas City, "just so long as he can drag himself to a plate and swing a bat."

That July 16 morning had been a typical day on the road for Williams. The team's eight-hundred-mile train ride from Cleveland had taken more than twenty-one hours. While his teammates slept before resuming their eleven-game road trip, Williams woke up early to enjoy his standard breakfast: orange juice, two lamb chops, and double orders of bacon and liver. But unlike his younger days, instead of touring a new city or stopping by the movie theater to see a Western, Williams remained in his hotel room. Room service and valets brought him everything he needed.

Although sportswriter Edwin Pope later explained that the thirty-eight-year-old Williams "had begun husbanding his strength by resting for much of the playing day," he was just as content to hide out from reporters and autograph-seekers until much closer to game time.

At some point that day, however, he did see a familiar face.

News of Major John Glenn's transcontinental supersonic flight saturated television and radio airwaves as well as the afternoon editions of hundreds of American newspapers. The *Kansas City Star* mentioned the milestone on the front page, while pieces in the *St. Louis Post-Dispatch* and Missouri's *Springfield Leader* were accompanied by large photographs of the Marine in his sleek tan flight suit.

By early evening Williams was ready to leave his solitary confinement for the ballpark. But before heading to Kansas City Municipal Stadium, he had to make a stop. At a local Western Union station he sent a telegram to the rear entrance of the Main Navy and Munitions Building adjacent to the National Mall in Washington, D.C. The message, addressed to Major John Glenn, Jr., read, "CONGRATULATIONS ON RECORD I AM BIG SHOT NOW TELLING EVERYONE I FLEW WITH YOU IN KOREA TED WILLIAMS."

When he returned from Brooklyn to his post at BuAer in Washington, D.C., Glenn picked up the telegram. He held on to it for more than fifty years.

CHAPTER TEN

Life Begins at 40

"There's a man who could make this team. He is just what we need—somebody in position to catch a fly ball."

—New York Mets manager
CASEY STENGEL
on John Glenn, February 20, 1962

From the moment he popped open the Plexiglas canopy of his F8U-1P, John Glenn puzzled the New York City press gathered along the runway at Floyd Bennett Field.

"At 36, Major Glenn is reaching the practical age limit for piloting complicated pieces of machinery through the air at speeds that can only be compared with those of sound and of the earth's turning on its axis," the *New York Times* wrote. "But he looked a lot more like a youth than a supersonic man when he climbed out of his jet Crusader."

Sporting "thinning red hair, freckles, and a boyish grin," Glenn eschewed a ladder set up for him, sprang out of the cockpit, and bounced off the fuselage onto the ground to embrace his family. He handed his children mementos (David's pocket knife, Lyn's Siamese cat charm) which they had asked him to make "supersonic."

Throughout the informal press conference, reporters found easy copy in Glenn, who deflected praise by saying "any bouquets around here should be tossed to [Admiral Clark]."

While referring to the Crusader as his "Old Girl" and "a scalded duck," he shrugged off his remarkable achievement as another day at the office.

"Flying at 1,000 miles an hour you don't feel speed as much as you do driving 70 miles an hour on the highway," he said. "Speed is just something you read on the dials."

No longer simply a Central Ohio celebrity, Glenn became an overnight national figure. In addition to newspaper, radio, and television coverage of the flight, an Ed Herlihy–narrated *Universal-International Newsreel* featured Glenn. Tens of thousands of moviegoers across the country saw him wave goodbye from Los Alamitos, soar high above the clouds, then touch down in Brooklyn.

The publicity tour carried on throughout the rest of the summer. While still in New York, he appeared on *I've Got a Secret* and *The Ed Sullivan Show*. Even Annie and the kids were guests on Arlene Francis's nationally syndicated daytime talk show *Home* as Glenn executed Project Bullet. After returning to Washington, D.C., where he collected the telegram from Ted Williams as well as his fifth Distinguished Flying Cross, from Secretary of the Navy Thomas S. Gates, Jr., Glenn visited his hometown in September.

To kick off "John Glenn Day" at Muskingum College, the local Board of Trade honored the favorite son with a parade, banquet, and the unveiling of the "Major Glenn Trophy," to be awarded each year to the New Concord High School student with the top grades in mathematics. Held inside the college's Brown Chapel, the ceremony concluded with everyone walking down to the basement to attend the New Concord Potato and Vegetable Show. Glenn awarded prizes in the contest for best scale model airplane, but not the five different potato events: best Irish Cobbler, Red Triumph, Chippewa, Katahdin, and largest of any variety.

The following week, Glenn was back on the East Coast at a slightly different beauty contest, the Miss America Pageant in Atlantic City. A guest speaker to the annual convention of the National Exchange Club, Glenn joined the rest of the conventioneers in witnessing Miss Colorado, Marilyn Van Derbur, take the crown. But the main reason for his trip to the Tri-State Area was to attend nationally televised programs as a contestant, not a spectator.

The day after his historic flight, a television producer spotted Glenn, in his Marine officer's uniform, walking through a Manhattan Macy's department store and asked him to appear on the CBS game show *Name That Tune*. Intrigued by the possibility of good PR, Navy administrators encouraged Glenn to participate. Paired with a ten-year-old from

Mississippi named Eddie Hodges, Glenn was poised and engaging during a five-week run on the popular Tuesday evening program. Correctly identifying songs such as "South America, Take It Away," "Where the Blue of the Night Meets the Gold of the Day," and "Roaming in the Gloaming," Glenn and Hodges claimed the show's grand prize of $25,000, which they agreed to split evenly.

Glenn applied his share of the winnings to a college fund for David and Annie, but the exposure he received from the national broadcast proved far more lucrative than the money.

News of the Soviet Union's successful launch of *Sputnik* in October 1957 signaled that the United States had fallen behind in the burgeoning space race. While he and Eddie Hodges were competing for the penultimate $20,000 prize on *Name That Tune*, the show's host, George DeWitt, asked Glenn about the first-ever artificial satellite, launched by the Soviets into Earth's orbit four days earlier.

"To say the least, George, they're out of this world," Glenn said, inciting studio audience laughter. "It's the first time anybody has ever been able to get anything that far out in space and keep it there for any length of time, and this is probably the first step toward space travel or moon travel, something we'll probably run into maybe in Eddie's lifetime, here, at least."

Even before the Soviets' success of *Sputnik*, the National Advisory Committee for Aeronautics (NACA) had already begun recruiting candidates to fly their "rocket planes." That April, NACA selected Navy aviator Scott Crossfield to pilot the North American X-15, a hypersonic rocket-powered plane believed to be capable of reaching 3,600 miles per hour and an altitude of one hundred miles. By the following spring, Air Force Captain Iven C. Kincheloe and NACA pilot/physicist Joseph A. Walker had joined the team.

But before the end of the year, NACA was disbanded, and effectively replaced by the newly formed National Aeronautics and Space Administration (NASA). NASA then began to search for an entirely new batch of recruits, who would not simply fly airplanes propelled by rockets, but operate "spaceships," a term now regularly used by eminent aerospace engineer Werner Von Braun.

On NASA's radar thanks to Project Bullet and its de facto press tour during CBS's Tuesday night fall schedule, Glenn was one of 110 men asked to audition for the assignment dubbed "Project Mercury." Having sold Annie on yet another dangerous career choice, Glenn happily accepted. In late February 1959, as NASA whittled down the list, candidates were stealthily sent to the Lovelace Clinic in Albuquerque, New Mexico.

"They gave us fictitious names out there and registered into a motel with fictitious names," Glenn remembered. "We had these fictitious names during the time we were being poked and prodded and all the medical tests that they gave us there."

For a week in Albuquerque, followed by several more days at Wright-Patterson Air Force Base in Dayton, Ohio, each recruit was subjected to a draining battery of physical, mental, and emotional examinations intended to test every human limitation that doctors and engineers could conceive. These included extended periods spent in an isolation chamber, a vibration chamber, a heat chamber, spinning in a centrifuge at roughly thirteen hundred miles per hour, repeated barium enemas, ingesting large doses of castor oil, and for some reason, a sperm analysis. Glenn impressed the observers by writing poetry—in the dark—during his extended stay in the isolation chamber.

Each candidate also received orders during their testing: "do not discuss Project Mercury unless authorized to do so."

In early April, however, Glenn spilled the beans to his former VMF-311 wingman.

———

Twenty years old throughout most of the 1939 Major League Baseball season, Ted Williams hit .327, smashed 86 extra-base hits, and drove-in a still-standing rookie-record 145 runs. The .406 batting average he posted two years later has barely been approached, let alone matched, across the eight ensuing decades. And in 1949, while setting career highs with 43 home runs and 159 runs batted in, he came within one one-hundredth of a percentage point of winning the batting title to claim an unprecedented third Triple Crown.

But the 1957 season was Ted Williams's crowning achievement.

In the month following his ninth-inning home run in Kansas City—the one he hit a few hours after sending John Glenn a congratulatory telegram—Williams collected forty-five hits in ninety-two at-bats to raise his average thirty-three points. Hitting a league-best .390 on August 14,

Williams crushed an opposite field home run to lift Boston to a 6–4 victory over the Yankees. The three-run blast off World Series MVP Don Larsen gave him thirty-one home runs on the season, just one behind league-leader Mickey Mantle. After the home run, a large group sitting directly behind the Yankees dugout at Fenway Park raised a twenty-foot-long banner reading, "TED WILLIAMS!!! GREATEST AMERICAN *SINCE* GEORGE WASHINGTON."

Williams's pace fell off toward the end of the month, then a chest cold sidelined him for more than two weeks, but he returned in mid-September to pinch-hit at Fenway Park. Beginning with a four-hundred-foot smash into the right field bleachers, which gave the Red Sox a victory over Kansas City, Williams homered in each of his next four official at-bats. (He set a new major-league record that year with thirty-three intentional walks.)

"Funny thing about that," he said later. "I really wasn't feeling good when I returned to the lineup. But the writers started saying I was through for the season and that burned me up. So I made up my mind that I was going to play even if it cost me the batting title."

During a season-closing home stand with the Yankees, Williams collected three more hits, including two doubles. It was not enough to reach the fabled .400 mark again, but by hitting .388 at the age of thirty-nine, he became the oldest batting champion in baseball history, and remains the oldest man ever to lead all of Major League Baseball in batting average.

To honor the star player on the final day of the season, Massachusetts governor Foster Furcolo publicly declared September 29, 1957, Ted Williams Day at Fenway Park. But Williams wanted no ceremony or celebration that afternoon. In fact, after a pinch-runner replaced him in the third inning, he left Fenway Park to begin a two-week fishing trip in Canada. Catching landlocked salmon in Labrador interested him even more than the $15,000 that NBC offered to provide guest commentary during the World Series. He did make an appearance at the fifth annual "Tops in Sports" awards banquet in Maryland the following January. On the dais at Lord Baltimore Hotel, Williams sat beside his friend Stan Musial, the thirty-seven-year-old St. Louis Cardinals slugger who had won the National League batting championship the previous season.

"Ted and I have it all figured out," Musial told the crowd. "We've got the young fellows all down on us anyway. So we're gonna go out this year and lead the [league] again!"

Williams did just that. Although he badly damaged his ankle while eyeing salmon from the rocks of Labrador, Williams gave retirement no consideration that off-season. The $130,000 contract he signed made his decision easier. And despite a miserable opening two months to the season, the newly forty-year-old hit over .400 during the final six weeks to claim a second consecutive American League batting title in 1958.

But in classic Ted Williams fashion, the triumphant season was marred by outbursts. Toward the end of July, he spat at fans in Kansas City. And in late September, at home against the Senators, Williams struck out looking to end the third inning. Irritated at leaving two runners on in a one-run game, Williams chucked his bat toward the dugout, only to see it bounce up into the stands and strike sixty-nine-year-old Gladys Heffernan in the head. As Heffernan—Joe Cronin's housekeeper—was taken to the first aid station and later Sancta Maria Hospital, the Fenway crowd booed Williams.

In between innings, he hid in the dugout where home plate umpire Bill Summers spotted him in tears.

"I felt ready to just die," Williams said.

Jovial and forgiving from her hospital bed, Heffernan had suffered no serious damage, unlike Williams's reputation. National columnists took familiar shots at him from afar. By now, he was used to it. The previous winter, the Baseball Writers Association of America had caused great controversy by awarding Mickey Mantle, not Williams, the 1957 American League MVP. Multiple writers listed Williams as low as ninth or tenth on the balloting.

"It doesn't make any difference to me," he said after a member of the press told him the results of the voting. "I'm through with you guys."

As usual, once the 1958 baseball season came to a close, Williams took off for the serenity of South Florida. But while casually demonstrating his swing for a friend beneath a coconut tree in his Islamorada backyard, Williams pinched a nerve in his neck. Although he fought through the injury for a few weeks during spring training in Scottsdale, Arizona, by late March he could barely turn his head without writhing in pain.

Sent back to Boston, Williams checked into New England Baptist Hospital, where a neurosurgeon prescribed three weeks of intensive cervical traction. Depressed by both the pain in his neck and the angst of yet another season-interrupting injury, Williams perked up when someone brought him fan mail. One letter was from recently promoted Lieutenant Colonel John H. Glenn, Jr.

"He was writing to tell me he was going through the centrifuge, the weightlessness chamber, and I'd really get a kick out of it," Williams recalled in his 1969 autobiography. "Then I threw the letter away. Just after that they announced the astronauts and John Glenn was the one from the Marines. I wish I had that letter."

On April 9, 1959, the day after photographers crowded Williams to snap shots of him leaving the hospital in a foam neck brace, NASA introduced Glenn and six others as America's first astronauts.

At a nationally televised press conference, the media-savvy Marine took command of the stage, answering reporters' questions with jokes, enthusiasm, and a charming naivete of the uncertainties of space exploration. As much as it clashed with his meek instincts, Glenn realized that the space program needed a confident, likeable poster boy.

"I was careful about my image while an astronaut because there were people who were against the manned space program," Glenn later admitted. "And I didn't want to do anything to tarnish my image and hurt the program."

Despite the excitement, the manned space program had become rife with setbacks.

Six weeks after showcasing the first astronauts for the world, NASA launched a Jupiter rocket three hundred miles into the atmosphere. But no human was aboard. A rhesus monkey named Able and a squirrel monkey named Baker were strapped inside the nose of the rocket. The "monkey business" and "top banana" headlines wrote themselves. Other early rockets such as McDonnell's "Little Joe" series either failed in tests or were severely limited in capability. The more sophisticated rockets also went through a series of failures in the program's first eighteen months.

By 1960 NASA's missteps, funded by the American taxpayer, had become a political hot potato in a presidential election year. Science advisors to the national Democratic Party called Project Mercury "costly . . . highly publicized . . . risky." After hearings in the United States House of Representatives, *Newsweek* reported that the Mercury Program's budget had nearly doubled from $200 million to $350 million. In the spring, NASA Administrator T. Keith Glennan told a Senate Space Committee that the United States would need to spend as much as $15 billion over the decade to compete with the Soviets.

Meanwhile, the men competing for the first assignment aboard the seemingly overpriced, ineffective projectiles underwent extensive training. At NASA headquarters in Hampton, Virginia, as well as the Navy's Aviation Medical Acceleration Laboratory in Johnsville, Pennsylvania, Glenn and the others trained for zero gravity and G-forces while becoming experts in astronomy, astrophysics, ballistics, fuels, geography, guidance systems, and meteorology.

"If we didn't know what to expect, we might be like the Ubangis in Africa, suspicious of everything and afraid of every leaf that stirs," Glenn said in late 1959. "When you're educated, you're no longer afraid. In this field, there are only a handful who understand, and they are not fearful."

The astronauts were dubbed "The Mercury Seven," but at various points in NASA's earliest years they were hardly a cohesive team. Glenn, and to a lesser extent Navy aviator Scott Carpenter, emerged as the self-righteous, unabashedly moral faction of the group. Physical, emotional, and mental acuity were critical to the choosing of America's first star voyagers, but so too was selecting men of character . . . faithful, Christian, family men of character.

Beginning in May 1959 much of the training phase for Project Mercury migrated to a Florida Air Force facility known as the Cape Canaveral Missile Test Annex. At Cocoa Beach and other spots along the strip the celebrity astronauts found plenty of leisure time in their off hours. At dirt cheap prices local dealerships offered them Chevrolet and Ford sports cars, which some raced well above the speed limit. Well-wishers offered them free drinks. And according to author Tom Wolfe's celebrated book *The Right Stuff*, women in the region offered sex, then bragged about how many astronauts they had slept with.

With Carpenter, viewed as his "sidekick," Glenn urged the rest of the Mercury Seven to stay out of trouble. He playfully put up a sign on one of their office walls that read, "I cut out smoking. I cut out drinking. I cut out women. Now I cut out paper dolls," a contemporary joke about being locked up in an insane asylum.

The situation eventually came to a head, pitting Glenn against fellow astronaut Alan Shepard. A highly decorated Navy aviator who had served in the Pacific during World War II, Shepard was passionate about the

Mercury program, but perceived by the press as "regal, cold, on edge." Behind closed doors, he also reportedly had an "understanding" with his wife regarding his extracurricular activities.

During the astronauts' tour of an aeronautics facility in Southern California, Shepard took a detour to Tijuana, Mexico. While he was there, a reporter and photographer caught him with a woman that was not his wife. Told about the situation by a NASA spokesman, Glenn personally phoned the newspaper.

"I talked to both the reporter and to the photographer and later the publisher or the night editor," he said. "I talked about the Russians, 'godless Communists,' how 'you gotta let us get back in the race.' I pulled out all the stops. . . . The story did not appear in the papers. But it well could have if I hadn't talked to them."

Shepard, whom John Glenn viewed as "an enigma," may well have reminded him of another moody, headstrong pilot capable of damaging his reputation with impulsive behavior: Ted Williams.

After the incident in Tijuana, Glenn confronted the group about the issue.

"As time went by," Tom Wolfe wrote in *The Right Stuff*, "the Glenn position became: Look, whether we like it or not, we're public figures. Whether we deserve it or not, people look up to us . . . We've got to be above even the appearance of doing wrong."

At thirty-eight, Glenn was at minimum two years older than the other Mercury astronauts. And of the seven, he was the only Marine: three were Navy, three Air Force. Before developing a kinship with Carpenter, he started the program as an outsider.

The image that Glenn seemed to be crafting also complicated his relationship with the others. Glenn did not crave the spotlight, but he didn't shun it either. He seemed to actually enjoy talking with the press. An early profile on the astronauts named him "most articulate of the group." Often his remarks centered on his faith and religion, which did not necessarily endear him to the others. Neither did the exaggerated public perception that he never smoked, drank, or swore. He was also the only member of the group not to take advantage of the local dealers' generous sports car prices. He remained perfectly content to drive a far less sporty NSU Prinz. Wolfe went so far as to call Glenn "the flying monk, or whatever the Presbyterian version of a monk was. A saint maybe; or an ascetic; or maybe just the village scone crusher."

Glenn's training regimen only added to a holier-than-thou aura. In the early days of the Mercury program, the astronauts were stationed at Langley Air Force Base in Hampton, Virginia. They had been advised to stay in shape, but it was not enforced, and most of them hated exercise. Glenn had chosen not to uproot Annie, David, and Lyn from their home on North Harrison Street in Arlington, Virginia, and instead lived alone inside the base's Bachelor Officer Quarters. In a display considered showy by his fellow astronauts, Glenn jogged miles around the base every morning.

With NASA's move to Florida, he, and sometimes son David, jogged the beaches in another transparent exhibition of his dedication to the program. *Life* magazine reported that Glenn's commitment to diet and exercise took him "from a somewhat paunchy 195-pounder to a trim, muscular 165 pounds."

Division between Glenn, and to a much lesser extent, Carpenter, and the rest of the group peaked as the program advanced closer to manned space launches. Each wanted to be the first to go to space. In the press, Glenn became the odds-on favorite to win the job. But a secret "peer vote" taken among the astronauts ended his chances.

Without selecting themselves, each was asked to rank their preference for the first ride. Not long after the votes were tallied Administrator Glennan informed the group that Shepard would make the first trip. Glenn believed that it was merely a popularity contest, which he lost largely by admonishing the others "to keep their pants zipped and their wicks dry." He expressed his anger in a letter to the head of NASA's Space Task Group—after all, the letters he wrote asking to serve in Korea had worked—but nothing came of it. Upon his return to Arlington, Glenn moped around the house for weeks. Tom Miller, his friend, fellow Marine pilot, and now his next-door neighbor, confronted Glenn, saying "You're making everybody miserable because your damn pride is so high."

"We're just afraid," Glenn had said at the start of the Mercury training, "that all America is interested in is firsts. That's the way Americans work and that's the way they play. They want to be 'first' in sales, 'first' in the major leagues, 'first' in every endeavor."

———

Hampered all year by the pinched nerve in his neck, Ted Williams slogged through a miserable baseball season in 1959. Five weeks into his return to the starting lineup he was hitting .173 with just two home runs and had already been benched by Red Sox manager Pinky Higgins.

"I know a lot of people are saying the old guy is washed up, but it just isn't true," he insisted in late June.

By season's end, Williams gave little indication otherwise. In 103 games, he had hit just ten home runs and batted .254, nearly a full one hundred points below his career average. Still, he signed a contract the following January to return for one more year.

Opening Day for the Red Sox was at Griffith Stadium in Washington, D.C. President Dwight D. Eisenhower, in his final year as commander in chief, threw out the game's ceremonial first pitch. In the top of the second inning, Williams walked to the plate for his first at-bat of the season. Seated next to his boss, Vice President Richard M. Nixon told Eisenhower, "Ted Williams is coming up this inning and it will probably be his last season. I'd like to see him get off to a good start. Let's root for him to get a home run." On cue, Williams smashed a Camilo Pascual pitch so high and so far over the 31-foot-tall, 420-foot deep center field wall that it was called "one of the longest home runs ever witnessed in Washington."

Nixon—one week after an unopposed victory in the Illinois Republican presidential primary—was so impressed that he wrote Williams a letter that evening.

"While both the President and I were rooting for the Washington Senators today, I can assure you that no one could have gotten a bigger charge out of your tape measure homer than we did," the letter read. "After all, we 'old men' (in our forties that is) have to stand together."

At forty-seven, the vice president was hardly an old man, especially among his colleagues: the United States Senate over which he presided included seven members at least seventy-five years old. At forty-one, however, Ted Williams was the oldest player in Major League Baseball. And in the chilly East Coast April weather he struggled to play consecutive games without a day off. On the afternoon following his Opening Day home run in Washington, Williams smashed another. The blast down the right field line, fittingly at Yankee Stadium, was the 494th of his career, and with it he surpassed Lou Gehrig for fourth on the all-time list. But while round-ing second base, he pulled the calf muscle in his left leg, relegating him to pinch-hitting duties for the next several weeks.

Back in D.C. for a series in late April, Williams remained on the bench for the duration of a Saturday afternoon victory over the Senators. The Red Sox' third win in four days made for a cheerful scene beneath Griffith Stadium, perfect for Williams to introduce an old friend to his teammates.

John Glenn, up from Hampton, Virginia, that weekend to visit his wife and children in Arlington, was noticeably thinner than Williams remembered.

"He looked like he had malnutrition, but he must have been running those five miles every day," he said. "He didn't do all that running in Korea."

Williams proudly paraded his slender friend around the clubhouse, telling teammates and sportswriters, "I don't know what they're going to have this man do, but if it can be done he'll do it."

"John came in the clubhouse after the game," recalled Red Sox utility infielder Don Gile. "The Washington clubhouse was set up in cubicles. I was in the same one that Ted was in. Ted told us that [he and] Glenn had flown together, and Glenn was telling us about his current space training. We were all looking at each other like, 'What is he talking about?'"

Glenn even came with an enticing invitation for his friend.

"He was going through the space program, the weightless chambers, the centrifuges, and all the rest, and I was still in baseball," Williams said nearly forty years later. "He said 'I wanna take you down there and maybe show you what we're doing.' Well I never did get a chance to go down there."

The nagging injury that prevented John Glenn from actually seeing his friend swing the bat during that visit to Griffith Stadium took weeks to improve. Williams remained unable to do anything more than pinch-hit. And once his calf did heal—in the middle of a ten-game Boston los-ing streak—he caught a virus and laryngitis, which kept him bedridden in hotels during a lengthy road trip. Pressed for comment, team trainer Jack Fadden added insult to injury, saying "at his age you more or less have to figure that he will be subject to frequent injury or illness if he tries to play regularly."

Finally, by early June he had returned to the starting lineup, just in time to catch fire by hitting twelve home runs over the next month. And on a cool night at Cleveland's Municipal Stadium, Williams smacked a high, outside slider from rookie right-hander Wynn Hawkins over the left-center field wall. With the home run Williams joined Babe Ruth, Jimmie Foxx, and Mel Ott as the only members of the exclusive "500 Home Run Club."

Talking to the press the next afternoon, Williams announced that season would be his last.

"My mind is made up in regards to next year," he said. "And you know what it is. The only reason I'm playing this year is because I wanted to vindicate myself and I also wanted those 500 home runs."

A handful of times since his recall to the Marine Corps in 1952 Williams had declared *that* season to mark the end of his playing career. Despite five months at war in Korea, severe viruses and injuries, and several ugly feuds with both fans and the press, he had always changed his mind. But this time, he meant it. Late in the season, the Red Sox even confirmed Williams's retirement plans with a public statement from team owner Tom Yawkey.

Content to close out his career at Fenway Park with a mid-week series against Baltimore, rather than during a season-ending weekend series in New York, Williams played his last game on a rainy late September day. After a walk his first time up, he just missed home runs in the third and fifth innings.

"I hit two balls that I think some days would have gone out for sure, but this day they didn't, caught 'em up against the fence," he recalled. "But the last time up, I got the count 2–0 on [Jack] Fisher. And I missed a ball, I don't know yet how I missed that ball, and I know he thought he threw it by me. . . . I could just sense he said, 'Gee, give me that ball, throw another one by him.' And I could just see all of that developing in his own mind.

"And sure enough he come back with the same pitch and I hit it good and it went for a home run, which is kind of a storybook finish."

While Williams rounded the bases for the final time, appreciative, wistful Boston fans chanted his name. After touching home plate, he trotted back to the dugout. Teammates urged him to acknowledge the crowd.

"I had a really warm feeling," he said later, "but it just wouldn't have been me."

Williams stayed true to his word about retirement that winter, although he did return to the Red Sox as a spring training instructor. That March in Arizona, he mentored his assumed replacement in left field, a twenty-one-year-old rookie from Long Island, New York, named Carl Yastrzemski. But on Opening Day 1961 Williams was in Fort Myers, Florida, not Fenway Park, for Boston's afternoon tilt with the Kansas City A's. In December he had signed a five-year deal worth six figures annually to endorse and field test sporting equipment for Sears, Roebuck and Co. He also promoted Sears, Roebuck–sponsored events such as a spring Ted Williams Florida Fishing Tournament, which awarded $29,000 in cash and merchandise. At each of the event's eighteen promotional stops across the state, reporters and fans of all ages still crowded around the retired star.

"I felt all through spring training, that I had made the right decision. I had reached the end of the line and knew it," he said while the Red Sox lost their first game to Kansas City. "Still, not being there on opening day hit me more than I thought it would."

Williams's business deal fit conveniently with his personal life. Sears, Roebuck's national headquarters were in Chicago, also home to Williams's new love interest, Lee Howard. Tall, blond, and a fashion model, Howard had changed her last name from Houda while pursuing a movie career years earlier. She lived in the Riverside suburbs with her parents and two teenage children. Williams had met the thirty-four-year-old divorcee in Florida during the winter of 1959. He even phoned Howard from the Red Sox clubhouse right after his career-punctuating home run. A year later, they were married by a justice of the peace at the district courthouse in East Cambridge, Massachusetts.

Essentially paid to pursue his hobbies on Sears, Roebuck's dime, Williams began a life of leisure upon return from his honeymoon in the fall of 1961. Over the next several months, he hunted for deer in Maine, played thirty-six holes at Winged Foot Golf Club in Westchester County, New York, caught a 557-pound bluefin tuna during a tournament in Galilee, Rhode Island, and filmed the twenty-minute instructional "Batting with Ted Williams," available at all Sears, Roebuck stores. And for a fourth consecutive summer he made occasional cameos at the annual Ted Williams Camp held on 180 rural acres in Lakeville, Massachusetts. In front of locals and campers aged eight to nineteen, Williams regularly put on a show by crushing deflated softballs over the fence.

A year into his tenure with the thriving retail chain, Williams was appointed to Sears, Roebuck's newly formed advisory committee. A collection of prominent "sportsmen," the committee included Illinois football hero Buddy Young, Masters and PGA champion Doug Ford, NBA all-star Jack Twyman, and legendary mountaineer Sir Edmund Hillary. Twice a year the twelve committee members met in Chicago to make recommendations to Sears, Roebuck board members and manufacturers. As the resident expert for three sports (baseball, hunting, and fishing) Williams was named chairman.

"He tested them too," Twyman recalled. "He'd make the buyers cry. They'd have some new product and he'd say, 'This is just a piece of crap.'"

On Tuesday, February 20, 1962, Williams was in Chicago for three days of meetings with Sears, Roebuck executives. But he spent that morning at the home of his in-laws, Mr. and Mrs. Robert M. Houda. Along with millions of Americans watching on television, Williams sat in awe of Lieutenant Colonel John Glenn.

Passed over for the first—and ultimately the second—NASA flight, Glenn had pulled himself together following a "time of self-doubt and anxiety."

There was a silver lining to watching two other Mercury astronauts launch before him. Both Alan Shepard (May 1961) and Gus Grissom (July 1961) made their voyages sitting in a capsule atop Redstone rockets. Capable of seventy thousand pounds of thrust, the Redstone rocket did not have the power necessary to break into the Earth's orbit. As a result, each man's *suborbital* flight was fairly short, less than sixteen minutes.

By the summer of 1961, the Soviet space program had already completed two manned orbital flights. In April the USSR's Yuri Gagarin not only became the first human being in space, he became the first to reach orbit, circling the globe in 108 minutes. Four months later, fellow cosmonaut Gherman Titov completed a full seventeen revolutions of the Earth's orbit during the course of more than twenty-five hours.

The United States was losing the space race, and NASA, the American people, and especially the new President knew it.

"We have a good many very talented scientists, but we did not make a major effort in this area for many years, and we are now behind," President John F. Kennedy said in August 1961. "We are making a major effort which will cost billions of dollars. But we cannot possibly permit any country whose intentions toward us may be hostile to dominate Space."

Within three months, Glenn learned that he would attempt America's first orbital flight, aboard the Atlas rocket. Like the Redstone, the Atlas rocket had gone through a series of high-profile failures, although with 367,000 pounds of thrust it was capable of reaching orbit.

In May 1959, with each of the just-introduced Mercury Seven astronauts observing, an Atlas had taken off from Cape Canaveral, reached ten miles in the air, then exploded. "That's our ride?" one of them remarked. It was the fourth consecutive failed launch. More than a year later the Atlas remained a NASA boondoggle. On the morning of July 29, 1960, Glenn and the other six astronauts again sat inside the blockhouse to witness the eighty-five-foot-tall Atlas blast off. It headed toward the heavy clouds, disappeared, then crashed into the Atlantic Ocean after sixty-five seconds.

"The Atlas was a peculiar bird. It was made out of stainless steel one-sixteenth of an inch thick. It was nothing but a steel balloon. You had to keep pressure inside of it, keep it inflated or it would fall down," Glenn remembered. "What they did to fix that was put on what they called a belly band. It was a stiffener made out of more stainless steel that went about four feet down the side of the booster, just under the spacecraft . . . We had three successful launches after they fixed it like that. So I had good confidence it was going to work okay."

Although his mind was eased by the successful unmanned launches, multiple delays due to weather and other equipment failures exasperated Glenn. Three times in early 1962 he was strapped into his self-titled *Friendship 7* space capsule and awaited the launch countdown only to see the mission canceled. For the impatient astronaut the moment was like taking to the skies in his F-86 Sabre and not even seeing an enemy MiG over the Yalu River.

"As soon as I was up there, it was a disappointment. When you go through all that and get ready and get yourself psyched up to go and all ready, then they cancel the flight and you have to get unstrapped and get out and come down and start all over again—a big disappointment," he recalled.

"It was a lot of stress. I think probably more stress for the family; I wouldn't say it was more than it was for me, that wouldn't be true I guess. But the family, when something would happen that meant a flight was canceled, then that cast some doubt in the family's mind I'm sure, Annie's mind and the kids, about the safety of this whole thing. That we couldn't just go up and get in it and take off like you did in an airplane."

On the morning of February 20, 1962, Glenn climbed into his space capsule for a twelfth attempted launch. This time, there were no setbacks, no delays, no cancelations. At 8:48 a.m. the Atlas rocket broke free from the ground pad and raced up into the atmosphere, leaving a trail of smoke and fire.

Throughout the next several hours Glenn achieved a series of those "firsts" over which he believed Americans obsessed. Already the first American to enter the orbit, Glenn became the first American to snack in space: the orange juice, coffee substitute, two scrambled eggs, toast with jelly, and filet mignon that he had for breakfast were not enough to sustain him for more than an hour of flight time. Through a small hole in his helmet, he sipped a beef-vegetable paste and applesauce from aluminum squeeze tubes.

By 10:20 a.m. he completed the first full orbit—around the world in eighty-eight minutes and twenty-nine seconds—followed by a second roundtrip ninety-four minutes later. During his third revolution, he learned that NASA was monitoring a warning light that indicated a problem with the *Friendship 7* heat shield. Without a secure heat shield, the vessel would incinerate upon re-entry. Panicked engineers had hidden their concern from Glenn as long as possible (although testing later revealed that it was the indicator light that had malfunctioned, not the heat shield), so much of his attention during the third and final orbit centered around addressing the problem. He was advised to leave the retropack in place to serve as a buffer between the capsule and the tremendous heat and pressure caused by re-entering the Earth's atmosphere.

Upon re-entry, the retropack burned up in a spectacular blaze. But those listening to Glenn over NASA's direct audio feed heard no fear or concern, only excitement and wonder.

"My condition is good, but that was a real fireball, boy!" he announced.

During his four-hour, fifty-six-minute voyage Glenn had enthusiastically narrated the spectacular scenes that he viewed: A mirror affixed to his flight suit reflected images that appeared through the capsule's two-foot-wide trapezoidal window. From hundreds of miles above, he saw the Mississippi Delta, dust storms blowing near the African Coast, and shining lights from the homes and streets of the Western Australian city of Perth. And the famous shower of yellow-green particles—only later did he describe them as "space fireflies"—that he saw while in orbit, which were not sparks or ignited fuel or some sort of hallucination, as some NASA scientists feared. Neither were they living creatures as some hoped. Rather they were miniscule ice particles that melted in the changing temperatures within orbit.

"Man, this is beautiful," he told the Canton Island tracking station in the South Pacific, seventy-four minutes into the flight.

Early in the Mercury program, before any successful manned space launch, the astronauts had predicted what they might see while streaking through orbit at thousands of miles per hour.

"If we're looking straight down," Glenn opined, "we'll be able to see light reflected from earth. We may even be able to see a blacktop road across a desert in the broad panorama of the spinning globe. Looking up, I think we'll be able to see the stars."

"I'm betting a steak we won't be able to see any stars," Gus Grissom replied.

"Maybe I'll throw in a fifth of whiskey on that," Glenn answered.

"I think you're in trouble on that steak bet, John," astronaut Wally Schirra said.

In the end, Glenn would have won the wager with Grissom. Throughout the journey he told several of the NASA tracking stations listening to his transmissions that he saw stars and even some constellations, including Orion.

"I was rather surprised that you could not see more stars," he said the following week. "I think it is more like being out on the desert on a very clear, dark summer night, when you can look up and the stars just seem to jump right out at you."

He was not surprised, however, that another heavenly light failed to reveal itself.

A year after orbiting the globe seventeen times, Soviet cosmonaut Gherman Titov visited the 1962 World's Fair in Seattle, Washington. Reporters wanted to know if the "godless Communist" had experienced any religious feelings during the twenty-five-hour voyage. "I looked around," Titov replied. "I saw no god or angels." A few days later, Glenn attended the National Conference on the Peaceful Use of Space, also in Seattle, where reporters asked him the same question.

"The God I pray to is not small enough that I expected to see him in outer space," he said.

Glenn always considered himself a religious person. For years his father was an elder at Presbyterian church in New Concord and both his parents were active members of the congregation. His mother, Clara, studied the Bible regularly and also became an elder not long after her son joined the Marines. During his teenage years, Glenn led Sunday School programs and discissions at the church.

"It was a community that was centered a lot around the churches and religious life, and it was a good thing to grow up in that kind of environment," he said. "I think it gives you a sense of ethics and values that most people don't get unless they are involved with some sort of religious activity like that."

As an adult Glenn carried on his Christian faith. He married Annie at the United Presbyterian church in New Concord, and the two committed to raising their children with a strong sense of religion. And during the months of mission delays leading up to the *Friendship 7* launch, Glenn's minister in Virginia, Reverend Frank Erwin, became a reliable source to the press.

Throughout his years in the Mercury program Glenn spoke freely about faith, God, and the Bible. To help show that this irritated the other Mercury astronauts, Tom Wolfe frequently referred to Glenn as the "Presbyterian Pilot" in *The Right Stuff*.

But Glenn's Presbyterian upbringing and practices never defined the man whose entire life hinged on career choices best described as "sniveling."

"The church I grew up in, in New Concord, I remember the preacher preaching some sermons on predestination," he said. "I always had trouble with that. I never liked the idea that somehow I was just placed here on Earth and everything I was going to do was all programmed out, no matter what I thought about it."

A week after he returned from space, Glenn, along with Alan Shepard and Gus Grissom, testified before a United States Senate subcommittee.

In addition to Nevada's Howard W. Cannon gleefully stating that a prominent military leader had been pleased to see that "the idol and the hero of the American teenager and youth today had changed from the rock and roller to [Lieutenant] Colonel John Glenn," several senators praised Glenn for his religious convictions.

At the start of the hearing, the committee chairman, Senator Robert S. Kerr of Oklahoma, congratulated Glenn for "his spirit of reverence and his faith in God. By his example and by his performance, [Lieutenant] Colonel Glenn has made a tremendous contribution to the spiritual uplift which has stirred the hearts of so many people in this Nation and around the world."

Later, Senator Alexander Wiley of Wisconsin, a former Lutheran ministry student, asked Glenn multiple questions about his faith and its relation to the voyage of *Friendship 7*.

"I can't say that while in orbit you sit there and pray, or anything like that," Glenn testified. "It is a very busy time. There have been people in the past who have tried to put words in my mouth that at a certain time I suddenly lapsed into a prayerful state, or something like that, and this just isn't the case."

Glenn may not have prayed while riding through Earth's orbit strapped inside a capsule that he thought had a faulty heat shield, but millions of Americans did.

State legislatures in Michigan, Pennsylvania, and Arizona paused for a moment of prayer during Glenn's ride. Twelve hundred spectators watched a live television broadcast of the mission from inside Muskingum College's gymnasium, where John Glenn, Sr., made an appearance to announce, "our prayers were answered."

In 1964, World Book Encyclopedia published a collection of hundreds of letters written to Glenn by people across the globe. The letters weren't all rosy and full of praise. A family in Concord, North Carolina, actively scolded Glenn for not publicly "thanking God or giving God credit for anything you had accomplished. We're sure that there are thousands of families all over the United States that felt this same disappointment as we did." Another (anonymous) letter went even further, telling Glenn, "Glad you got back safe but do you know your trip was a sin. God made people for the earth—not the sky or moon. . . . They are making an idol of you. This is pagan."

But the vast majority of the people who wrote to Glenn expressed deep appreciation for his achievement and wanted to share with him their prayers.

"I think you are the most wonderful man in the world," a ten-year-old girl from Omaha, Nebraska wrote. "I said prayers for you all day long."

Pope John XXIII, who received Robert F. Kennedy the next morning in Vatican City, told the United States attorney general that he too had prayed for Glenn.

Even those with far less religious devotion pleaded that day for the forty-year-old's safe return to the Earth.

During the 1920s and 1930s, while John Sr. and Clara Glenn raised their only son to be a thoughtful, humble, steadfast Presbyterian, practically no one had raised Ted Williams at all. Growing up, he saw very little of his alcoholic, wandering father, Samuel. His mother, May, was more devoted to her job as a foot soldier seeking donations for the Salvation Army than to her two children. Ben Bradlee, Jr., author of the highly acclaimed 2013 biography of Williams, *The Kid*, believed that Williams carried a "festering resentment against his mother for her service to the Lord through the Salvation Army, which Ted believed came at his expense."

On an official application for his acceptance to Pensacola Naval Air Station, Williams listed "Protestant" under "My religion is _____," but aside from a few late-in-life encounters with devout, almost proselytizing Christians, he did not participate in any organized religion. He did not begrudge anyone who did, and held great respect for specific religious leaders, such as the Reverend Billy Graham and Cardinal Richard Cushing, the longtime archdiocese of Boston. And he acknowledged the presence of some sort of higher power, during his crash-landing at K-13, for example. But throughout his adult life Williams developed a combative relationship with religion, often blaming God for perceived slights or the inequities of the world.

"Once, I remember him cursing God and Jesus so badly that I wished for Dad's sake that God really didn't exist because, if He did, He would surely punish Dad for what he was saying," Williams's youngest daughter, Claudia, wrote. "Simply put, Dad was angry with God . . . My father was a very logical man, determined to think for himself and accept the consequences of each and every one of his actions."

But for John Glenn, the Presbyterian Pilot, Ted Williams—the Agnostic Athlete—made an exception.

"I don't pray," Williams said the morning after Glenn's successful *Friendship 7* mission, "but I said a little prayer for him."

As far back as the triumph of Project Bullet, Williams had bragged to teammates, friends, and reporters about simply knowing Glenn. In March 1961, during his first spring training as a Red Sox instructor, Williams shared all that he knew about his friend's much-publicized participation in the space race.

"Williams hoped that Glenn would get the first orbital assignment because he knew that Glenn was so sure of everything that he did that it would be a successful experiment," Boston scout Charlie Wagner recalled.

Johnny Pesky also saw Williams that spring training, during exhibition games in Ocala, Florida. Pesky, the first-year manager of the Red Sox Triple-A affiliate in Seattle, remembered Williams singing the praises of his astronaut friend.

"Williams called Glenn the most sincere guy he ever had met. Ted said that everyone felt pretty safe flying a mission with Glenn, because he was so sure of himself and the things he could do."

Glenn's connection to the Splendid Splinter was hardly common knowledge. So in the spring of 1962, when the *Boston Globe* hired Williams as a guest writer, his friendship with America's newest hero became the starting point for his first column.

In a June piece entitled "When to Quit" Williams focused on Glenn's calm and self-control in the face of danger during the Korean War. He mentioned that upon their first encounter Williams experienced an "intuitive feeling" that Glenn was "destined for something great." And he pointed out that while they were both shot down over North Korea, they were not shot down on the same mission: "You can carry 'togetherness' a little too far," he quipped.

But as much as Williams respected his friend for heroism in war and grace under pressure while coasting through the Earth's orbit, there was something else that he admired about Glenn: his age.

Retired, well past his physical prime, and no longer able to thrill or silence massive crowds with one swing of his bat, Williams had learned what it meant to be just another spectator watching history on television.

"We've always heard the adage that life begins at 40," the forty-three-year-old Williams wrote. "What a wonderful thing it would be if people of 40 could still have the same physical reflexes and coordination that they have when they're 20. Unfortunately, it doesn't happen, at least not yet; which is why there is a personal identification for all of us when we hear about some great exploit being made by a man 40 or older. John's flight was a special victory to us 'old-timers.'"

In some ways, Glenn's life *was* beginning at forty. His country, and much of the world, had begun to celebrate him as a conquering hero. Williams's best years were behind him. So while Little Leaguers, middle-aged diehard Red Sox fans, Air Force colonels, and even the sitting vice president of the United States still looked up to Ted Williams, Ted Williams looked up to John Glenn.

CHAPTER ELEVEN

The Slow Boring of Hard Boards

"We had some great political discussions,
things I won't say with those recorders running.
He was not one to hold back. And neither was I."

—JOHN GLENN on Ted Williams

Eight years old when the stock market crashed, John Glenn grew up during the Great Depression. He saw his father's plumbing jobs dry up along with most small businesses in Central Ohio as unemployment rates sky-rocketed throughout the United States. But beginning in 1935, President Franklin Delano Roosevelt's New Deal put millions of Americans back to work with projects such as the Works Progress Administration (WPA). Given his plumbing background, John Sr. became a foreman on a sewer system upgrade in New Concord. The steady work helped the Glenns avoid foreclosure of their home, a frequent topic of discussion for the family and one that "struck mild terror into an 11-year-old heart."

Despite Roosevelt's profound impact on his youth, as well as his parents' long-standing commitment to Democrats, John Glenn, Jr., remained unattached to a single political party. By the early 1960s, he described himself as both "somewhat of an independent" and "a conservative Democrat or a liberal Republican." He had supported both parties in previous presidential elections, explaining "I'm not registered as either one. I vote for the best man." In 1960, he voted for Republican Richard Nixon.

But once NASA announced that Glenn would become the first American to orbit the Earth, he became a regular guest of the man who had defeated

Nixon less than two years earlier. President John F. Kennedy, a bold and ardent supporter of the space program, took an instant liking to Glenn.

On February 5, 1962, a few weeks before the successful *Friendship 7* mission, Glenn visited the White House. The two men sat inside the Oval Office—Kennedy in one of his iconic rocking chairs—while reporters irritated Glenn with inquiries of "how Annie is getting her hair fixed," rather than scientific questions about the Atlas rocket or re-entry procedures.

Later that month, after the crew of the USS *Noa* hauled Glenn out of the Atlantic Ocean, Kennedy personally congratulated him over a direct radio hookup. Seizing on the newly minted American hero's image, Kennedy appeared with Glenn at several public celebrations, including a Welcome Home reception inside the West Wing, an "inspection" of Glenn's slightly charred space capsule, and a White House space summit with Soviet Cosmonaut Gherman Titov. Each event was well covered by photographers and camera crews.

Over the next several months Glenn practically became an honorary member of the Kennedy family.

Curious to meet the famed astronaut during a visit to Florida with her father, President Kennedy's four-year-old daughter, Caroline, asked Glenn, "Where's the monkey?"

"He's eating bananas," Glenn replied, fighting back laughter. "All this and I didn't get a banana pellet on the whole ride."

In June, Attorney General Robert F. Kennedy invited Glenn to an extravagant party at the family home known as Hickory Hill, in honor of actor Peter Lawford and his wife, Patricia Kennedy, the President's sister. Sitting at a table on a narrow plank stretching across the swimming pool, Glenn chatted with the party's hostess, Ethel Kennedy, whose chair slipped, sending her into the water. Guests and society columnists noted that Glenn "remained dry, just as he did when his capsule plummeted into the ocean after his triple orbit around the earth."

He did not remain dry the following month during a trip to Hyannis Port, Massachusetts. In July, President Kennedy invited the Glenns to the family compound for a weekend of seafood, sailing, and swimming. After water-skiing in tandem with First Lady Jacqueline Kennedy—they both fell into Lewis Bay—Glenn sailed privately with the President aboard his yacht, the *Patrick J*, as it toured Nantucket Sound.

Like the Kennedys, the public could not get enough of Glenn. Television affiliates across the nation broadcast live coverage of his return to his hometown of New Concord. An hour-long documentary of Glenn's space flight became a global hit. Produced that spring by NASA, the 16 mm color film entitled *Friendship 7* was translated into ten languages and widely distributed throughout Europe, Africa, and Eastern Asia. Reviewers in Sweden called the film "a fantastic drama . . . a thriller." And in early March, four million New Yorkers cheered for Glenn along an eighteen-mile ticker-tape parade through Lower Manhattan.

"He's the head of state today," Mayor Robert F. Wagner, Jr., declared.

That same week, Glenn appeared, alone, on the cover of *Life* magazine for the second time in a month. For 20 cents, *Life* promised to reveal "The Glenn Story Nobody Saw: At Home with Annie and the Kids While John Orbited the Earth." But before turning to several detailed articles about the journey and a series of large photographs—fretful Annie watching television coverage of the mission, shots of the *Friendship 7* capsule floating in the Atlantic Ocean, and JFK beaming as Glenn raised two thumbs up to onlookers at Cape Canaveral—readers of the weekly issue saw the image of another Korean War veteran who flew with the Marine Corps's VMF-311.

A two-page spread within that March 2, 1962, issue of *Life* featured Ted Williams striding at the plate, hands back and cocked, awaiting the pitch. Opposite the timeless, oversized color photograph a headline read "Why Sears signed Ted Williams—as a playing manager."

Explaining that the company hired Williams "to add a cold, professional viewpoint on the quality of every piece of Sears sports equipment *before* it gets into the Sears catalog or any one of the 740 Sears department stores," the advertisement boasted about the retired slugger's input on numerous products.

"Most sleeping bags seem to be made for midgets," one of Williams's suggestions read. "Let's make them longer and a whole lot wider—so that people can really stretch out. Who wants a sleeping bag that fits like a straitjacket?"

Ted Williams's partnership with the world's largest merchandising enterprise remained beneficial for both sides. During the 1963 fiscal year, Sears' annual net sales increased by more than 11 percent—to well over $5 billion—while Williams continued to receive his six-figure annual salary in exchange for his unvarnished, honest opinions. And given relatively light responsibilities with Sears, Williams scheduled fishing tours, hunting trips, and spring training with the Red Sox whenever he pleased.

He also ate and drank whatever he pleased. The breakfasts of liver and bacon, coupled with a penchant for beer, martinis, and tropical rum drinks, had begun to catch up with him. Several reporters who ran into the retired Williams noted that, at roughly fifty pounds above his rookie year playing weight, "the former 'Splendid Splinter' is still splendid but he's no splinter anymore."

Williams certainly enjoyed his freewheeling lifestyle, but his wife did not. Two-and-a-half years into her marriage, Lee Howard filed for separation. The following year she sued Williams for divorce, claiming mental cruelty.

"I couldn't do anything right," she told a *Miami News* reporter during the hearings. "If we went fishing—and I took up fishing to please him— he would scream at me, call me a dumb bitch and kick the tackle box."

Williams countersued on the grounds that Howard had been "moody and indifferent" toward her husband, disappearing for long periods of time. Repeated efforts to reconcile never materialized, and eventually a Dade County court granted Williams his second divorce in twelve years.

He did not remain a bachelor for long. In May 1968 he married Dolores Wettach, a twenty-nine-year-old *Vogue* model. Four years earlier, aboard a flight home from a fishing exhibition, Williams had lobbed her a hastily scribbled note that read, "Who are you?" A former Miss Vermont, the five-foot, nine-inch brunette had recently screen-tested for the role of Pussy Galore in the 1964 James Bond film *Goldfinger*. A *Newsweek* blurb about the marriage noted that Wettach bore a striking "resemblance to Jackie Kennedy." Already several months pregnant, Wettach agreed to a prenuptial agreement then quietly eloped with Williams in Jamaica, later telling reporters that they had been married the previous fall.

Dolores gave birth to Williams's first son, John-Henry, that August. As he had with the birth of his first child, daughter Bobby-Jo, Williams missed his son's arrival. He was away on a fishing trip. Three years later, Dolores gave birth to a daughter, Claudia. But the marriage was always tumultuous. Not only did Dolores stand up to his bullying, which only further infuriated him, but Williams regularly flirted with other women, allegedly even propositioning some. And he still received love letters from "old flames." He and Dolores divorced in less than five years.

Williams had never been quite domesticated enough for married life and fatherhood. Accustomed to living out of his suitcase in hotels one road trip at a time or tracking tarpon and kingfish across North America, he was too itchy and impatient to truly settle down.

"Fact is, Ted doesn't chase (while we were together anyway)," a friend said during Williams's marriage to Dolores, "but he *is* chased. After all, for three decades as a superstar—a regular American pop/folk hero—he nailed down everything that *moved*, and it must be hard to altogether halt that kind of momentum."

A few years after his first divorce from Doris Soule in 1954, a reporter asked Williams, "When are you going to get married again?"

"Not me!" he snapped. "I'm NEVER going to get married again!"

"What if you meet a beautiful gal who likes to fish?" someone interjected.

"Nope. Not even if she can fish."

The only absolute resolution that Williams issued with more certainty than never marrying again was never managing a big-league team.

Late in his career with the Red Sox, reporters and fans often asked him about eventually calling the shots from the dugout. Known as one of the game's most cerebral players, Williams had amassed decades of strategy, knowledge, and experience that would benefit any ball club. Hall of Fame players from the previous generation, such as Ty Cobb, Rogers Hornsby, Mel Ott, Tris Speaker, Eddie Collins, and Walter Johnson, managed major-league teams late in or not long after their playing careers.

"Never," he said in the summer of 1958. "I'm not interested. Managing is a thankless task. And if the press second-guessed me this much as a player think what they'd do to me as a manager!"

Even early into his retirement from baseball, he held firm when *Boston Globe* reporter Will McDonough gauged Williams's interest in managing, particularly managing the Red Sox.

"No, definitely not," he said. "I don't think I'm geared for it. And I'd never try it."

Ted Williams did not keep that vow either.

———

On February 27, 1962, exactly one week after *Friendship 7* splashed down in the Atlantic, a small group of Las Vegas, Nevada, citizens gathered at a suburban residence on Gilder Street. Although the homeowner, Mrs. Marguerite Kennedy, acknowledged that her husband's roots traced back to that famed political dynasty on the East Coast, she and all her guests that evening were staunch Republicans.

The purpose of the meeting was to establish a new, informal organization with one specific goal: make John Glenn the next Republican nominee for President of the United States.

"He's head and shoulders above us all," the club's spokesman declared. "We don't know if he is a Democrat or Republican. We'll take him just like we did Herbert Hoover and Eisenhower."

A local Republican county chairman refused to support the group's cause but did acknowledge, "I think [Glenn's] better qualified than the incumbent."

John Glenn would hardly have agreed. After his visits to Hickory Hill and Hyannis Port, Glenn had aligned himself with the Democratic Party, exactly what Bobby Kennedy had hoped for with those summer invitations. With an eye on his brother's 1964 re-election campaign, Kennedy asked Glenn to inject new life into the party by running for the United States Senate. Glenn, who had served as the 1937–38 junior class president at New Concord High School, was flattered by the administration's suggestion. But after thinking over the offer, he turned down Bobby Kennedy and chose to remain with NASA.

"I still wanted to make my own contributions to the [space] program," Glenn said. "We hadn't had that many people go into space, and each one of us that went up had a duty, I felt, to really work with and get the other upcoming people prepared for what they were going to do, so we got the best return out of every space flight."

At the time, Glenn had no idea that President Kennedy had secretly grounded him from any further space flights. Some sources say that Kennedy did not want to risk the safety of America's most cherished astronaut in another space mission. Other accounts indicate that Kennedy's goal for a NASA journey to the moon was the reason. He only wanted flights by astronauts who would presumably be young enough for those far-off lunar missions, and Glenn would be close to fifty by the end of the decade.

But following President Kennedy's assassination in November 1963, Glenn reconsidered politics and announced a primary challenge of the seventy-four-year-old Democratic incumbent Ohio senator Stephen M. Young.

"I guess along with every other American, I just sort of sat back and thought about our responsibilities to the country and how we could contribute the most." Glenn said years later. "And it was a time when a lot of people were doing the same thing. I decided that I would run."

Some political strategists received the decision with excitement. "The average American would hesitate to vote against Glenn," one said. "It would be like voting against the flag." But Bobby Kennedy told Glenn it was too late to build a viable campaign for an election taking place in less than a year. And several members of the political establishment, even within the party he had just officially joined, also opposed the idea of Glenn springboarding from NASA to politics.

"He has chosen to enter politics at the very top of a space platform built by the taxpayers of the United States," Ohio Democratic Representative Charles A. Vanik told the *New York Times*. "The high office of the United States senator from the state of Ohio should not be made a hero's pawn—no matter the breadth of our gratitude."

In January 1964 Glenn formally requested his release from both NASA and the United States Marine Corps and began forming a staff. But as he awaited the official military discharge necessary to run for public office, he slipped and fell in his bathroom, smacking his head against the bathtub. With the candidate hospitalized by a concussion, several campaign-launching events were canceled. Between the late start, the embarrassing headlines, and persistent dizziness and headaches from damage done to his inner ear, Glenn ended the campaign six weeks before the primary contest.

He had spent most of his savings on the race and forfeited both his full-time salaries with NASA and the military. Although he earned a healthy pension following his promotion to colonel and subsequent release from the Marines—like his friend Ted Williams, an ear ailment had sped up his discharge—Glenn needed a job. For a handsome salary and interest in the company he joined Royal Crown Cola in the fall of 1964. He insisted on working as an executive rather than endorsing, pitching, or hawking products.

"I'm not going to allow my name and picture to be used on billboards," he explained. "My specific duties haven't been determined yet, but I'll be taking part in board of director meetings, helping discuss policy matters."

Despite being a civilian and private citizen for the first time in nearly a quarter century, Glenn stayed in contact with people from NASA and the Marine Corps. He also developed his new friendship with Bobby Kennedy, now the junior United States senator from New York. Alongside Bobby, Ethel, and the Kennedy children, Annie and John went kayaking on Idaho's Snake and Salmon Rivers in the summer, then skiing in Waterville Valley, New Hampshire, and Sun Valley, Idaho, before Christmas. And once Kennedy announced his late bid for the Democratic presidential nomination in early 1968, Glenn spoke at campaign stops in Ohio, Indiana, Nebraska, Alabama, South Dakota, and Oregon. In March, Glenn introduced Kennedy at Vanderbilt University's prestigious Impact Symposium, prompting Kennedy to facetiously remark to the massive crowd, "I thought you gave a little too warm a reception to John Glenn, I thought you perhaps forgot who the candidate was . . . Makes me think of my warm friends in the Senate."

That June, Glenn accompanied Kennedy to a contentious meeting with the Black Panther Party in Oakland, California, then joined the candidate and his family at Disneyland, where they all went on the Pirates of the Caribbean ride, which had just opened the year before. Two days later, inside a suite at the Ambassador Hotel in Los Angeles, the Glenns and the Kennedys watched the results of the California Democratic primary on television. With his victory assured, Kennedy went down to the ballroom to give a speech. Glenn and Annie remained in the suite.

Just after midnight, Kennedy was shot in the hotel's kitchen. Ethel Kennedy, pregnant with the couple's eleventh child, asked John and Annie Glenn to accompany the five younger Kennedy children back to Virginia. At Hickory Hill, Glenn played touch football with twelve-year-old David and ten-year-old Michael, then swam in the pool with the others. In "one of the hardest things I've ever had to do," John Glenn told each of the children the next day that their father had died.

"John Glenn had great courage, both physical and moral," Robert Jr., the second eldest son of Bobby Kennedy, said fifty years later. "But what many people don't know is what a compassionate and tender man he was. My father had many friends. This was more than that. He considered John Glenn to be his brother."

Five months removed from a second tragic Kennedy assassination, Richard Nixon won the 1968 presidential election by defeating Democratic Vice President Hubert H. Humphrey. One of Humphrey's top aides during the campaign was his close friend and fellow Minnesotan Robert E. Short. A businessman who owned the Minneapolis Lakers then sold the team five years after moving the franchise to Los Angeles, Short served as the national treasurer of the Democratic Party during Humphrey's campaign. To console himself following his friend's defeat, Short purchased the Washington Senators baseball team one month after the election. His first objective as owner of the last-place club was to make a big splash in the hiring of a manager. He set his sights on the sport's two greatest retired stars, Ted Williams and Joe DiMaggio.

Both men adamantly turned Short down, but he played to Williams's weakness, his "responsibility toward the game, toward the country, toward Nixon." Williams agreed to meet in person at the Marriott Hotel in Atlanta, Georgia. Short's persistence intrigued him, as did the offer of a stake in the club to supplement his yearly salary. Encouraged to take the job by his former manager, American League president Joe Cronin, Williams agreed to an unprecedented arrangement. Given the additional title of vice president, he signed a five-year, $100,000-per-season contract, that included the option of purchasing up to 10 percent of the franchise. He also could not be fired.

"You have always flatly rejected the idea of being a manager," a reporter reminded Williams. "Can you look back now and say when your thinking began to change?"

"Two days ago," Williams answered. "I met Short and we talked turkey and he really impressed me. I had discouraged him the first few times we talked. The first time, I was pretty emphatic but he came back at me. He's a hard guy to say no to."

"What did you expect," the reporter added. "As national treasurer of the Democratic Party he had to raise Humphrey's campaign funds, and they don't give that job to guys who are easy to say no to."

"Is that what his job was?" a shocked Williams replied. "He told me he was a big Humphrey man, but I didn't know he was that big. Well, I'm not going to let that change my mind now."

Throughout his entire life, Williams had been a dyed-in-the-wool Republican. His original birth name was actually "Teddy," not "Theodore," in honor of Republican hero Teddy Roosevelt. Williams's father either hinted or outright claimed to have served in Roosevelt's fabled Rough Riders unit during the Spanish-American War. Only years later did Williams cross "Teddy" off his birth certificate and write in "Theodore," which he preferred.

Ted Williams's allegiance to the Republican Party did not stop with his namesake. In 1970 Williams called Republican president Herbert Hoover one of the two men he most admired.

"As a young boy, my family, we're struggling along when he was President," said Williams, who graduated from San Diego's Herbert Hoover High School. "I remember how thoroughly he was defeated by [Franklin] Roosevelt and over the next 20 years how he was blamed for the Great Depression. How people blamed him for so many things that he certainly wasn't the fault of. How little credit he was given for things that actually were brought into law that he had thought of prior to his being ousted as president, or being voted out of presidency.

"In my heart, I'd have had ill feeling, being blamed for a lot of things you weren't responsible for. But that man, for the rest of his life, tried to do everything he could to make this a better government. He did everything he could to help the underprivileged of the world. He did everything he can to help the powers in office in any way that he could."

For years, he had hoped to meet Hoover and pay his respects to the man who helped create the Young Republicans. Through a mutual friend, Williams asked then Vice President Nixon to arrange a visit with Hoover in New York City. Hoover's declining health and eventual death kept Williams from sitting down with the 31st President, but his relationship with Nixon, soon the 37th President, blossomed.

The letter that Nixon wrote Williams in April 1960 was not the first time he had reached out to the Splendid Splinter. Arguably the most sports-obsessed American president, Nixon had sent a personalized message to Williams following his winning the 1957 Associated Press Outstanding Male Athlete of the Year award. Nixon also sent a congratulatory telegram to the Red Sox clubhouse beneath Cleveland's Municipal Stadium following Williams's five hundredth career home run. And in May 1960, Nixon aide Colgate "Coke" Prentice wrote a memo to the campaign's top advisors explaining that "a college associate of mine is a good friend of Ted Williams. He informs me that Williams is a <u>very</u>

strong Nixon fan and thinks we could secure his endorsement for use at the right time in any way we wish."

Prentice's intel proved accurate. On October 18—three-and-a-half weeks before Election Day—Williams flew to South Florida, where both Nixon and Kennedy addressed the American Legion Convention. At the Miami International Airport he and Nixon spoke and posed for the cameras. Williams even wore a Nixon campaign button. Kennedy, whose plane landed at roughly the same time, had hoped for the same photo op, especially given Williams's Boston celebrity. But Ted Williams did not care for the Kennedy clan.

He looked down on the family patriarch, Joseph P. Kennedy, Sr., believing him to be a "glorified bootlegger who had acquired much of his wealth through ill-gotten gains." He reportedly held a grudge against the former ambassador to the United Kingdom for burning him on bad stock advice. As for the next Kennedy generation, John had failed on his promise to obtain Williams a deferment from military service after his recall to the Marines. Not long after Kennedy's victory in 1960, Williams flat-out refused an invitation to meet the newly elected President by saying, "Tell him I'm a Nixon fan."

In fact, he became more than just a fan.

Apart from Southern California upbringings and contempt for most reporters, Williams and Nixon shared the same political ideology. An avid hunter who promoted Sears rifles, automatic-action and single-barrel shotguns, and scopes, Williams fervently backed the National Rifle Association. And although he strongly supported the Civil Rights movement of the 1950s and 1960s, Williams despised the other social revolutions of the times and unequivocally defended law enforcement. At one point, his station wagon brandished a bumper sticker that read, "If You Don't Like Policemen, The Next Time You Need Help Call A Hippie."

Throughout Nixon's 1968 presidential campaign his staff collected endorsements from star professional athletes like currency with the creation of the "Athletes for Nixon" committee. Spearheaded by Nixon ally and businessman Robert "Cy" Laughter, the committee circulated recruitment pamphlets across the sports industry which stated that Nixon's "championship qualities, plus his unmatched experience in national and international affairs, make him the logical choice for the Presidency in 1968."

In a short time the movement boasted such names as Olympic hero Jesse Owens, two-time Super Bowl MVP Bart Starr, NBA legend Wilt Chamberlain, and professional golf icon Arnold Palmer. But Ted Williams, who had participated in the similar "Celebrities for Nixon" campaign in 1960, was the charter member. Well before Nixon formally declared his candidacy for President in February 1968, Williams wrote to his advisors asking to help in any way possible. For the Athletes for Nixon recruitment pamphlet, Williams lent the endorsement, "Why start a rookie when we've got an established pro like Dick Nixon on our team?"

Nixon never forgot Williams's support. On the one-year anniversary of his narrow victory in the 1968 election's popular vote, he sent Williams a box of golf balls with the Presidential Seal on it as a token of his appreciation.

"The help you gave us meant a great deal to our success at the polls," the accompanying note read, "and I will always be grateful for your participation in the campaign."

———

Although the two men who brought him into politics were both brutally assassinated, John Glenn remained committed to serving the public. And in 1970, eighty-year-old incumbent senator Stephen Young chose not to run for re-election, which left the party's nomination wide open. Glenn campaigned vigorously for it, but one day after the student shooting at Kent State University in Ohio, Glenn suffered "one of the biggest disappointments of my life," losing the state's Democratic primary to political insider and businessman Howard Metzenbaum.

"And then I had to make a real decision," Glenn recalled. "Was I going to stick with politics or was I going to do other things? There were a number of things. I could go back to school and I could do teaching and lots of things I thought about doing. But I decided that if I really wanted to devote a chunk of my life to being in politics, well, we were far from being rich. I had made enough money in those intervening years that we were a little more financially independent than we had been before. And so I decided that I'd stick with it."

Turning his attention to the other Senate seat in Ohio, Glenn set about sniveling his way to the nomination. Over the next four years he tried to attend every Democratic function and local rubber chicken dinner in all eighty-eight counties across the state. Again facing Howard Metzenbaum, who lost the general election in 1970, Glenn secured his first-ever political victory with an uncharacteristic public display of anger and passion during a debate at the Cleveland City Club.

Metzenbaum—a self-made millionaire who often derisively referred to his opponent as "the Colonel"—attacked Glenn throughout the campaign with insults that his service in NASA and the Marines meant that he had "never held a job." Given the recent withdrawal of American forces from Vietnam, Metzenbaum was playing to the military's tremendous unpopularity. But in a retort that became known as "The Gold Star Mother Speech," Glenn's impassioned defense of himself, the military, and military families galvanized the audience of 650 spectators, many of whom gave him a twenty-two-second uninterrupted ovation.

"Howard, I can't believe you said I have never held a job," Glenn said. "I ask you to go with me, as I went the other day, to a Veterans Hospital and look those men, with their mangled bodies, in the eye and tell them they didn't hold a job. You go with me to any Gold Star mother and you look her in the eye and tell her that her son did not hold a job."

Four days later, Glenn won his party's nomination with 54.2 percent of the vote, then trounced Republican Ralph J. Perk by more than a million votes in the general election. Joining a Congress that had been in Democratic control for nearly two decades, Glenn soon became an authority in the Senate on issues such as veterans' rights, national security, and foreign relations. During the summer of 1976 he was on the short list to be Georgia governor Jimmy Carter's running mate in that year's presidential election.

Glenn was most adept at working with his Republican counterparts. His crowning legislative achievement, authoring the Nuclear Non-Proliferation Act of 1978, passed 88–3 in the Senate.

But in 1980 actor-turned-California-governor Ronald Reagan cruised to an Electoral College victory over President Jimmy Carter as Republicans won control of the Senate and made key gains in the House. The prohibitive favorite to combat the GOP resurgence, Ted Kennedy, chose not to seek his party's nomination in 1984, opening the door for Glenn.

On April 21, 1983, the national media descended on the small town of

New Concord. Inside the gymnasium of John Glenn High School—which had opened just months after the successful *Friendship 7* mission—he formally announced his campaign to 2,000 spectators, including 160 high school seniors eager to cast their first vote for the hometown hero.

Given Glenn's place as a revered, global figure, his campaign hit the ground running. An early Gallup Poll showed him six points ahead of Reagan. Soon *Newsweek, Time, Rolling Stone,* and the *New York Times* viewed him as enough of a serious contender to cover the campaign with lengthy profiles. That fall, a part-biography, part-campaign-memoir written by *New York Daily News* columnist Frank Van Riper was released. A series of excerpts from the book, which was entitled *Glenn: The Astronaut Who Would Be President,* appeared in several newspapers across the country. And in October the legend of John Glenn—portrayed by actor Ed Harris—came to the silver screen with the release of *The Right Stuff.* Based on the book, the film gave Glenn's presidential campaign mounds of free publicity.

"Something is out of whack here," a *Newsweek* special report stated in October. "It was bad enough, for those who like their politics serious and pure, when Hollywood produced an honest-to-gosh president in the person of Ronald Reagan—a confusion of real substance with mere celebrity, a blurring of the lines. But now the Great American Dream Machine has upped the ante—and within a few weeks, just as the presidential season begins in earnest, the lords of Tinseltown will uncork a popcorn epic, 'The Right Stuff,' which threatens to elevate presidential pretender John Glenn from the honorable status of national hero to the dangerous level of myth."

Glenn was skeptical that the film could have a sizeable impact on the outcome of a presidential election.

"I think most people at that time thought that it was going to help," Glenn said a quarter century later. "I did not. I was in the minority at that time and I had not seen the movie. We had no connection with the movie whatsoever. A lot of people think that we had some interest in it, the astronauts had some interest in that movie, and we didn't. . . . It was not the documentary of the early space days that they advertised it to be in fact. And I think the way it came out, the way the characters were portrayed in the movie, for me it was not a big plus, let's just put it that way."

Glenn not only disliked the attention the movie brought to the campaign, he disliked the entire process of campaigning. As far back as his first run for Senate in 1964 he had hated courting donors and raising money, "more than just about anything else in the world." On one occasion, advisors insisted he call a particular wealthy Democratic donor for a contribution. The next time they all gathered in a room, Glenn mimed the call in front of his staff, holding down the buttons on the phone with his hand so there was no dial tone. "The room we were in was lousy with mirrors," one aide remembered. "Everyone could see what he was doing."*

Still, Glenn raised $6 million dollars in 1983.

Despite the strong war chest, promising early poll numbers, and name recognition from *The Right Stuff* and its eight Oscar nominations, the campaign was beset by missteps.

"We made so many mistakes," he said years later. "We weren't properly organized for a national campaign."

For all he had achieved as a two-term senator, Glenn was not a natural politician. Similar to his quarrel with Alan Shepard and other Mercury astronauts, his idealism and dedication could be mistaken for self-righteousness. While negotiating the specifics of the second Strategic Arms Limitations Talks (SALT II) in 1979, Glenn displayed an obsession with minutiae that prompted a Carter administration official to note, "He isn't just a man who looks at the trees. He looks at the bark on the trees."

"Everybody was getting exasperated with him," a fellow Democratic senator told the *Wall Street Journal*. "You've seen people dig in their heels. Logic would not change him."

---

* In 1989, Glenn became caught up in a savings and loan scandal, the only real blemish on his political career. Along with four other United States senators (the so-called "Keating Five") Glenn was accused of providing political favors to embattled financier Charles Keating in exchange for campaign contributions. Glenn reportedly did receive $200,000 in undisclosed corporate donations to his political action committee, but he emphatically denied any wrongdoing. At the end of a fourteen-month Senate ethics investigation, he was found to have "exercised poor judgement" but broke no laws or regulations. One of his presidential campaign advisors, Scott Miller, said in 2021 that Glenn's disdain for fundraising may well have led to his involvement in the scandal. "I think when the Keating thing came along, they said, 'Here's a chance to go in, spend fifteen minutes with this guy, and you could end up with, whatever it was, $100,000, $200,000 for your campaign.' I'm sure he just said, 'Yea, I can't wait to get out of this next cocktail party or fundraiser and just get it all at once.' I'm sure that's how it happened."

Even members of his staff noticed that Glenn sometimes failed to see the larger political picture.

"His thinking is not focused," a former aide said. "It's exploratory. He's wandering around in the forest."

Stubborn and often distrusting of professional political advisors, he preferred to lean on his family and close friends for advice. During the primary, his daughter Lyn served an unspecified but prominent role within the campaign, meeting with voters, addressing reporters, and speaking to crowds and party representatives. But three different campaign managers in the first six months signaled disorder and instability to the press.

And thanks to some, particularly his Democratic opponents, *The Right Stuff* did hurt Glenn's credibility.

Following an early primary debate, New York governor Mario Cuomo endorsed a different candidate, explaining that Glenn had "started to remind people that we selected a president (Reagan) on the basis of celluloid images. That's not what we want to do again."

Glenn took offense at the implication that he was a "celluloid" hero like Reagan.

"I wasn't doing *Hellcats of the Navy* on a movie lot when I went through 149 missions," he said. "When I sat atop that booster, it wasn't *Star Trek* or *Star Wars*."

By the start of 1984 the Democratic race featured several rivals to Glenn, most notably Colorado senator Gary Hart, Reverend Jesse Jackson, and the front-runner, former vice president Walter Mondale. But from the outset of his campaign Glenn focused his attention on the sitting President.

"During his 1980 campaign, President Reagan often spoke of a shining city on a hill," Glenn said the day he declared his intention to run. "It is no shining city that denies education, destroys jobs and diminishes opportunities. . . . Unfortunately, its deeds have fallen short of its words. They aren't promoting excellence, they're discouraging it. They aren't fostering compassion, they're reducing it."

On paper, Glenn was a worthy, even formidable challenger for Reagan.

"If I were you, I'd be terrified of Glenn," political analyst Mark Shields told Reagan's chief of staff Jim Baker prior to a 1983 segment on CBS's *Face the Nation*.

"Why?" Baker asked.

"He doesn't have to make up military experiences," Shields answered.

"He's with his original wife—he's very much in love with her—he's got a high school in his hometown named after him. This is the genuine article."

"And Jim Baker flinched," Shields remembered decades later. "The idea of John Glenn against Ronald Reagan, that terrified him as a matchup."

But Glenn's persistent attacks on Reagan throughout the early months of the campaign did not move the needle with Democratic voters. As primary season neared its opening contest, he was mired in second place, twenty-nine points behind Mondale. Still, he remained determined.

As much as he disliked campaigning and raising money, he felt compelled, almost obligated to carry on. At one early campaign stop, a reporter asked him "Why does John Glenn—former astronaut, folk hero, U.S. senator—want to be president?" Before responding with a series of jabs at the Reagan Administration's tax cuts and rollbacks to education and research spending, Glenn stated, "It's not so much 'want to' as it is for the good of the country that we better change some of the policies that we have."

"I think he felt somewhere in the recess of his mind that he had earned the rank of president," remembered Scott Miller, the campaign's media advisor. "With Glenn you're just never not aware that this guy was the true American hero, and the irony of '84 was running against Reagan, and Reagan was sort of an ersatz American hero . . . Passion was not something that came easily to Glenn. And he would not raise his voice, he wouldn't get angry, and he wouldn't swear. . . . [Reagan as President] just so bugged him. And yet at the time America was willing to accept a celluloid hero over the real deal."

In Iowa, Democrats accepted Mondale, Hart, former South Dakota Senator George McGovern, and California Senator Alan Cranston well ahead of Glenn, who earned just 3.5 percent of the delegates. A week later, Glenn did slightly better in New Hampshire, taking third place with 13 percent of the vote, but any momentum gained died with last-place finishes in Vermont and Wyoming.

Glenn struggled in the early primary contests for several reasons. He backed progressive platforms on abortion, gun control, school prayer, gay rights, and tuition tax credits but dragged his feet on solutions to combat acid rain, a key environmental issue in New Hampshire, and believed military production of deadly nerve gas was a necessary deterrent against the Soviet Union. And unlike each of his primary opponents, he strongly opposed cutting defense spending.

But more costly than his policy choices, Glenn failed to connect with primary voters. One reporter assigned to the campaign noted that Glenn's "speaking style was charitably described as wooden."

By the time of his father's presidential run, David Glenn, now thirty-eight years old, had become an anesthesiologist. Stump speeches often included this fact about his son, followed by Glenn's remark that "he puts people to sleep. Like father, like son."

In unscripted remarks, Glenn's shortcomings were magnified. Even before running for president, Candidate or Senator Glenn's messages often got lost in a bevy of numbers, scientific jargon, and step-by-step plans. David Broder of the *Washington Post* dubbed Glenn "Mr. Checklist."

"He's a technocrat," a fellow senator said. "He really doesn't like politics."

Throughout the campaign, one of Glenn's favorite topics of discussion was scientific innovation. In his very first speech as a declared presidential candidate, he issued a warning that "new technologies promise great opportunities and pose great dangers."

"We must have leadership that understands the potential of modern science both for good and for ill," he said. "We must be the masters of the new technology, not its servants or victims."

Although the calendar matched George Orwell's famed dystopian novel about the connection between totalitarianism and technology, audiences did not warm to Glenn's nine-point plan for curbing the spread of nuclear weapons and the need for more radar picket ships in the Arctic to answer the Soviet Union shooting down Korean Air Lines Flight 007.

"He did not think thematically, he was an engineer," remembered Greg Schneiders, the campaign's press secretary. "Classic case of 'ask him what time it is, he'll build you a watch.'"

During a question-and-answer session at Western Iowa Community College in Sioux City, Glenn shared with a group of spectators his wish for the future of energy: "Better electrical energy storage." He then reeled off intricate details about an aluminum air battery in development at a laboratory in California and a Chinese invention similar to a septic tank that produced cooking gas from food scraps. A producer for network coverage of the forum noted that the crowd had practically fallen asleep.

"Now, it turns out he was very prescient," Schneiders remembered. "He was thinking like Elon Musk, a long time ago, that if we had better batteries we could capture energy and have renewables. But nobody in the audience had any idea what he was talking about, they were thinking 'Double A's?' Classic Glenn. Not that he was wrong but that he came at every problem from an engineer's point of view and that didn't translate very well into a compelling visionary message in a presidential campaign."

Looking ahead to Super Tuesday, Glenn's campaign needed a spark. In addition to a swing south, one of the nine states holding its primary on March 13 was Massachusetts, with its 100 delegates, two fewer than the first four contests combined. With a victory, Glenn could gain considerable ground, but over the previous two months, his polling numbers in Massachusetts had fallen from 19 percent to 12 percent for a distant third behind Mondale and Hart.

Someone within the campaign floated the idea of a celebrity endorsement. And who better to approach than Glenn's old war buddy, the greatest sports figure in the history of Massachusetts?

Ted Williams and John Glenn did not see much of each other in the thirty years after the Korean War.

They kept in touch through telegrams and letters. Williams—or perhaps an assistant—sent Glenn beautiful Christmas cards, although they weren't personalized or signed. And in addition to their rendezvous in the clubhouse at Griffith Stadium in April 1960, the two men met in person on a few occasions.

At a sporting goods show in Chicago during the mid-1960s Glenn spied his former wingman teaching children the proper way to cast a Sears fishing rod. In the early 1970s Annie and John attended a Washington Senators game then dined with the team's manager and his wife at Williams's favorite French restaurant.

But they both had wives, children, and demanding, high-stress, high-paying professions. They also lived hundreds of miles apart and traveled extensively, not just across the country, but across the world.

Besides Sears promotional trips and later lengthy West Coast road swings with the Senators, Williams went on safari to hunt lions along the

Zambezi River in Zambia and on fishing trips, such as the one in Auckland, New Zealand, where he caught a 587-pound thresher shark.

As head of Royal Crown Cola's international division, Glenn traveled the globe for several years. Once he became a senator, he spent weekdays inside the Capitol Building or joining congressional delegations to China or the Middle East, then personally flying his $230,000, six-seat, twin-engine Beechcraft Baron 58P home to Ohio each weekend.

Still, Glenn's campaign staff reached out to Williams in the late winter of 1984 to ask for a public endorsement, either via statement or by recording a radio or television advertisement ahead of the Massachusetts Democratic primary and Super Tuesday.

By that time, Williams was no longer in baseball.

His 1969 debut as a manager of the Washington Senators had been promising. For the first time in seventeen seasons, the cellar-dwelling franchise boasted a winning record at the all-star break, good timing given that the Midsummer Classic was held in Washington, at the recently renamed Robert F. Kennedy Memorial Stadium. Although the team finished in fourth place, twenty-three games behind the Baltimore Orioles, Williams won the Associated Press Manager of the Year award in his first season.

The season was remarkably profitable for both the Senators and Williams. More than 918,000 patrons came to RFK Stadium in 1969, by far the largest attendance figure in the nation's capital in twenty-three years. By all accounts, Williams earned his six-figure salary. And in addition to his Sears endorsements, he also earned a considerable payday from another side job: writing.

Ghostwritten by John Underwood—a young *Sports Illustrated* reporter whose company he enjoyed—Williams's autobiography *My Turn at Bat: The Story of My Life* hit bookstores in June 1969. Called a "portrait of an original who is unrepentant about being better than anybody else" by *New York Times* reviewer John Leonard, the book appeared in sports pages and stores across the nation. On a September night in Boston, Williams autographed more than a thousand copies at the Jordan Marsh department store. One newspaper called the ninety-minute event "the biggest signing session in Boston book store history." The next summer at RFK Stadium children under the age of fourteen received a free copy of the book prior to the Senators' July 17 game against the California Angels.

My Turn at Bat spent six weeks in the top ten on the *New York Times* bestseller list and reached a fourth printing by the end of summer. Reportedly two movie studios and a national television network wanted to turn the book into a feature film. Again, Williams's manager Fred Corcoran insisted Williams play the leading role. Simon & Schuster, the publisher of *My Turn at Bat*, wanted more Ted Williams content, and by early 1971 a sequel of sorts had been released.

Based on a *Sports Illustrated* collaboration between Williams and Underwood, *The Science of Hitting* offered no insight into Williams's personal life and quarrels with the press. But the ninety-five-page manual unintentionally revealed the obsession with details and nuance that had made Williams the greatest hitter of all time.

Williams may have been blessed with quick hands, a sinewy frame, and uncanny eyesight, but hard work facilitated his .344 career batting average, still the highest of anyone born in the twentieth century. To him, training and preparation meant much more than just taking batting practice. Williams invented the concept of bat speed, revolutionized the hitter's mental approach to the plate, and refined the mechanics of the swing into an art form. He studied and cataloged opposing pitchers' strengths and weaknesses, opposing catchers' pitch-calling tendencies, and the quirks and subtleties of each American League ballpark.

"He knows the slant of the batter's box. . . . He knows the throwing power of every outfielder," his former manager, Joe Cronin, once said. "His sweat shirts have to fit just right. He breaks in shoes a year in advance . . . a poor fit might distract him. He'll rip out a worn shoe-lacing. Right down to the smallest detail, everything has to be just right. . . . Sure, he's impulsive, explosive. Complacent people never are great athletes, or great pianists, or great actors, are they?"

The Science of Hitting did not appeal to mass audiences. Casual baseball fans probably did not enjoy or appreciate the lengthy section on the importance of hip and wrist action or the value of guesswork at the plate.

"It's as professorial as a volume on the amoeba," famed *Los Angeles Times* sports columnist Jim Murray noted in his review of the book. "Williams is a Ph.D. in hitting and his book is as pedantic as Einstein's. He makes hitting seem like the Quantum theory and it's described by morphological boxes, diagrams illustrating the cosine of the angle of impact, arrows showing the progress of the hips, and shadow outlines for the movement of the body or the flight of the ball."

The book did, however, become a cornerstone of baseball teachings. The next generation of ballplayers who picked up a copy heeded the words that Williams wrote in the book's dedication: "To the young baseball players of America, who dream, as I did, of becoming great hitters. May this help them on their way." It certainly helped a frustrated high school senior named Wade Boggs, whose father checked *The Science of Hitting* out of a Tampa-area library and told his son to "read the book cover to cover." Immediately, Boggs learned that "there are certain good pitches to hit [and] I started looking for those." Seven years later Boggs won his first of five American League batting titles, each as a member of the Boston Red Sox.

Even Cy Young award–winning pitcher Greg Maddux benefitted from Williams's book. By reading *The Science of Hitting,* Maddux (or more accurately the fictionalized version of Maddux that appeared in a popular 1999 Nike television commercial) fulfilled his quest for home run power and discovered that, indeed, "chicks dig the longball."

While Williams's career as an author took off, his ball club fell back to the bottom of the standings. In 1970, the Senators lost their final fourteen games to finish dead last in the American League East. The next season Washington finished thirty-three games under .500 and attendance at RFK Stadium fell by nearly one-third from Williams's first year at the helm. Prior to the 1972 season, owner Bob Short moved the franchise to Arlington, Texas, and renamed the team. Even in a strike-shortened season the Texas Rangers lost one hundred games. Following a third consecutive losing season, in which the club never reached higher than fifth place in their division, Williams resigned, citing "personal reasons."

But throughout Williams's failed three-year term in Washington, D.C., one of his biggest fans remained the President of the United States. When he received the Manager of the Year award, Richard Nixon sent him another congratulatory telegram and occasionally visited Williams inside the clubhouse at RFK Stadium. In April 1971, Williams—wearing his now trademark bolo tie—led a small group of baseball executives into the Oval Office to present Nixon with a season pass to American League games. Later that week Nixon called Williams from Camp David to congratulate him on the Senators' early season victory over the Yankees.

And when political turmoil surrounded Nixon, Williams jumped to his defense through the press.

Asked about Nixon's unpopular decision in May 1972 to conduct "Operation Pocket Money," an aerial mining of ports in North Vietnam, Williams told the *Washington Post*, "Nixon had to do it, regardless of the consequences. We have 60,000 guys over there we have to protect."

During Nixon's re-election bid in 1972, Williams not only called him "the greatest president of my lifetime," he publicly disparaged the candidates vying for the Democratic nomination, saying "those four guys make me puke." The two men also spoke on the phone a few weeks before Nixon's landslide victory over Democrat George McGovern.

Even at the peak of the Watergate scandal, Williams told a reporter, "Good God, I think the man is great. Who could have done a better job in ending that Vietnam mess? I believe he did it as fast and as honorably as it could have been done. I support him completely."

Nixon resigned the presidency the next summer, but Williams never wavered on his praise for Republican office holders and candidates.

On May 1, 1982, Williams participated in an Old Timers' Day game at Fenway Park. Although the sixty-three-year-old with gray hair around the temples and a slight paunch hanging over his belt went hitless in three at-bats, more than thirty-two thousand fans cherished seeing Teddy Ballgame swing the bat. That day Williams met Samuel A. Tamposi, a minority owner of the Boston Red Sox and prominent East Coast real estate developer. Over the next few months Tamposi convinced Williams to become the pitchman for a new community he was building in central Florida called Citrus Hills.

In addition to the $300,000 annual paycheck that he offered, Tamposi won over Williams with his politics. For years, Tamposi had raised large donations for several successful Republicans, including Richard Nixon. And throughout the early 1980s, he served as New Hampshire's finance chairman for candidate-then-president Ronald Reagan. Tamposi's daughter Elizabeth, a state representative, also served as the state's Republican finance chair, then resigned that role to take over as chairman of the statewide voter registration drive for President Reagan's re-election in 1984.

So when Ted Williams—a lifelong Republican, a devoted Richard Nixon supporter, and now business partners with a top Reagan fundraiser—was asked to endorse the man looking to defeat Reagan in 1984, he was torn.

Williams mulled over the request from the Glenn campaign while enjoying his semiretired bachelor's life in Florida. A week after the New Hampshire primary, Williams and a team of retired ballplayers took third place at an Old Timers' golf tournament held at Longboat Key Club, south of Tampa. He remained in Tampa that winter to join the Red Sox as a spring training instructor. At Chain O'Lakes Park in Winter Haven he worked in the cages with reigning American League batting champion Wade Boggs, watched rookie Roger Clemens blow away hitters with his fastball, hit flies to outfielder Tony Armas, and joked with his old-protégé-turned-hitting-instructor the recently retired Carl Yastrzemski.

While Williams held court at Winter Haven, "constantly swinging his bat with a vengeance that suggests he still could hit .300," one observer noted, John Glenn toured that same region. Like Massachusetts, Florida would also hold its primary during the upcoming Super Tuesday. That week, Glenn made campaign stops in Pensacola, Orlando, Tampa, and Lakeland, which was about fifteen miles west of Red Sox spring training.

A small group of national and Boston baseball reporters, no doubt aware of the Korean War connection, asked Williams about his friend's floundering presidential campaign.

Although he professed infinite respect for Glenn, calling him "one of the most natural leaders I've ever met . . . the most important mission I flew, I flew with him," he also explained, "I can't vote for him because he's a Democrat."

"God it killed me that I couldn't support him for president," he told sports broadcaster Bob Costas four years later. "But I didn't."

"Who did you support?" Costas inquired.

"Ummmm," Williams said, racking his brain. "Whoever the Republican candidate was."

Well aware of Williams's political leanings, neither Glenn nor his aides had really expected much to come from their request for an endorsement. Still, Glenn was hurt.

"He was momentarily crushed," recalled Steve Avakian, the campaign's communications director. "He was angry."

After several decades, Glenn learned something about his friend that day. When it came to politics, no one, not even hardheaded John Glenn, was as stubborn as Ted Williams.

November 30, 1943:
One week before graduation from the United States Naval Air Station in Bunker Hill, Indiana, Aviation Cadet Ted Williams (seated) learns to pilot the Boeing-Stearman N2S Trainer with guidance from Chief Flight Instructor Lieutenant Duane M. "Red" English of Binghamton, New York.
The Cleveland Public Library

Circa 1944: Stationed in the Marshall Islands during World War II, First Lieutenant John Glenn, the assistant operations officer for VMO-155, sits atop the wing of an F4U Corsair.
The John H. Glenn Archives at The Ohio State University

April 30, 1952: At Fenway Park prior to his final game before returning to active duty in the United States Marine Corps, Ted Williams receives a brand new $5,000 Cadillac as a going away present.
Associated Press

Winter 1952: On the runway of Port Columbus Airport, Major John Glenn says goodbye to his wife, Annie, and two children, David and Lyn, on his way to service in the Korean War.
The John H. Glenn Archives at The Ohio State University

Circa 1953: Lieutenant Colonel Robert F. "Bob" Conley boards his Douglas F3D Skyknight prior to leading a VMF(N)-513 mission over North Korea.
Courtesy of J. Christopher Conley

1953: Major Glenn, Captain Williams, and each of the Marines stationed at K-3 slept inside these canvas tents, which provided little warmth during the cold Korean winter. The tin roofs atop each tent became frequent targets for pranks known as krondyking.
Courtesy of Robin Campbell

1953: The sign posted outside K-3 Airfield near Pohang, South Korea.
Courtesy of Robin Campbell

Circa 1953: Developed by the Grumman Engineering Aircraft Corporation in the late 1940s, the F9F Panther was the only airplane flown by pilots within VMF-311 during the Korean War.
Courtesy of Northrop Grumman Corporation

HOLE IN ONE CLUB

THIS TO CERTIFY THAT Maj. J.H. Glenn, Jr.
WHILE PLAYING ON A STRANGE COURSE,
THE NORTH KOREAN COUNTRY CLUB,
SCORED A "HOLE-IN-ONE" ON 22 March, 1953
BY PICKING UP A 'SUKOSHI HOLE' FROM ..?
FROM ENEMY GROUND FIRE!
SIGNED
COL. USMC

CHARTER MEMBER

March 22, 1953: VMF-311 pilots whose planes were struck by enemy fire were awarded a Hole in One Club card, such as this one presented to Major Glenn. Captain Williams received the squadron's first Hole in One Club membership card five weeks earlier, on February 16, 1953.
The John H. Glenn Archives at The Ohio State University

February 16, 1953: His plane struck by either small arms or anti-aircraft fire, Captain Williams crash-landed his flaming, failing Panther at K-13, the Air Force base located near Suwon.
Courtesy of Bill Nowlin and Roger McCully

March 22, 1953: During Mission Number Intake 05 Major Glenn's plane was hit by enemy anti-aircraft fire, blowing a massive hole out of his Panther's tail. Sergeant Curt Giese, a Marine photographer based at K-3, took this photograph of Glenn in front of his damaged plane.
The John H. Glenn Archives at The Ohio State University

Spring 1953: Major Glenn (seated left) occasionally stopped by the Officers' Club at K-3, where the lively atmosphere consisted of music, card games, and alcohol. *Courtesy of Patrick Canan*

Spring 1953: Captain Williams shares his baseball knowledge with a local nicknamed Jimmy, who served as a houseboy at K-3. In exchange for pocket change the houseboys at K-3 cleaned up inside the Marine's quarters. *The Marvin Koner Archive*

Spring 1953: Captain Williams (left) and Major Glenn (right) discuss matters on the K-3 runway alongside an unidentified Marine. *Courtesy of Skip Rothrock*

Spring 1953: Major Glenn (left) listens to Captain Williams (right) narrate maneuvers during a free moment within the Officers' Mess Hall. *The Marvin Koner Archive*

Spring 1953: Captain Williams on Rest and Recreation (R&R) at Maruyama Park in Kyoto, Japan.
Courtesy of Elizabeth Cushing

June 29, 1953: Inside his quarters at K-3, Captain Williams packs his belongings in preparation for his return to the United States.
Associated Press

Circa 1946: During a road game Boston Red Sox star Ted Williams hacks at a pitch.
National Baseball Hall of Fame

February 20, 1962: Mercury astronaut John Glenn climbs into his *Friendship 7* spacecraft.
Courtesy of the United States Marine Corps

April 9, 1971: Washington Senators manager Ted Williams chats with President Richard M. Nixon during a ceremony inside the Oval Office. Williams and several baseball executives presented the President with a season pass to American League games.
Courtesy of the Richard Nixon Presidential Library and Museum

June 2, 1968: A frequent surrogate on the 1968 presidential campaign trail, John Glenn appears with Senator Robert F. Kennedy and his family in Garden Grove, California, three days before the state's Democratic Primary. *The Orange County Register*

August 17, 1953: Outside Boston Children's Hospital, Ted Williams signs autographs for a group of young Jimmy Fund cancer patients prior to the Ted Williams Welcome Home banquet at the Statler Hotel. *Courtesy of the Boston Public Library, Leslie Jones Collection*

Circa 1984: Senator John Glenn campaigns for the Democratic party's presidential nomination. *The John H. Glenn Archives at The Ohio State University*

November 10, 1988: Ted Williams and Senator John Glenn share a laugh at Boston's Wang Center during "An Evening with Ted Williams, No. 9 and Friends: A Fireside Chat." *Jim Bourg for The New York Times*

Circa 1995: John Glenn and Ted Williams inside Williams' Citrus Hills, Florida home.
The John H. Glenn Archives at The Ohio State University

Circa 1995: (L to R) Annie Glenn, Ted Williams, John Glenn, and Lyn Glenn gather together at Williams' Citrus Hills, Florida home. *The John H. Glenn Archives at The Ohio State University*

*To John Glenn
An American Hero and my friend
your old wingman
Ted Williams
1997*

Circa 1997: Autographed photograph of Ted Williams sitting inside the cockpit of his Panther, sent to Senator John Glenn. The inscription reads "To John Glenn, An American Hero and my friend. Your old wingman, Ted Williams, 1997." *The John H. Glenn Archives at The Ohio State University*

December 11, 1998: At the DoubleTree Hotel in Cocoa Beach, Florida, Ted Williams greets John Glenn after a parade celebrating the return of NASA's STS-95 *Discovery* shuttle mission. *Peta G. Adovasio via The John H. Glenn Archives at The Ohio State University*

November 18, 1991:
President George H.W. Bush
and First Lady Barbara Bush
present Ted Williams with
the Presidential Medal
of Freedom.
*Courtesy of the George H.W.
Bush Presidential Library*

May 29, 2012:
President Barack Obama
presents John Glenn with the
Presidential Medal of Freedom.
Courtesy of NASA / Bill Ingalls

July 22, 2002: John Glenn appears at the Fenway Park memorial for Ted Williams.
Jim Mahoney / Boston Herald

April 6, 2017: Through the rain, Marine Body Bearers (back) and the Caisson platoon of The Old Guard of the Army's Third Regiment (front), escort the body of Colonel John Glenn to his final resting place at Arlington National Cemetery in Virginia.
Courtesy of NASA

CHAPTER TWELVE

My Greatest Regret

"There is always something we can do
for some youngster somewhere"

—TED WILLIAMS,
August 17, 1953

Late in the afternoon on a warm summer day in 1953 Ted Williams
trotted out to left field at Fenway Park. It had been fifteen months and
thirty-nine combat missions over Communist North Korea since he last
stood guard beneath "The Wall," the thirty-seven-foot-high structure later
known as the Green Monster.

Upon receiving his discharge from the United States Marine Corps,
Williams had rejoined the Boston Red Sox in early August of that year.
Weak from both a painful ear ailment and experimental treatments at
four separate naval medical facilities from Korea to Bethesda, Maryland,
Williams felt too out of shape to chase fly balls or bat multiple times in
a single day. Two weeks into his return to the club all he could do was
pinch-hit.

But after sitting out the first game of a Sunday doubleheader against
Washington, Williams started the second game in left field. Following a
hard line-out in the first and a ground rule double in the third, he walloped
a Frank Shea slider inside and well beyond the right field pole, bringing the
Red Sox within one run of the Senators.

Still not back to full strength, Williams pulled himself from the game
after the blast and sat out the rest of Boston's 7–4 loss.

"I feel awful good up there at the plate," he told reporters in the clubhouse before stepping on the scale to notice that he still weighed over

two hundred pounds. "But my legs are telling me I'm not ready to play a full game yet."

The fourth-place Red Sox had that Monday off, but nevertheless Williams arrived at Fenway Park the next afternoon to jog, stretch, and take batting practice alongside rehabbing shortstop Milt Bolling. When the workout ended, he showered and dressed in his familiar outfit, a stylish dark suit with an unbuttoned, wide-lapel dress shirt. Just in case, he stuffed a necktie inside his pocket. He then exited the clubhouse, walked to the nearby parking lot, and jumped into the backseat of a brand-new Cadillac that was flanked by police motorcycles. He wasn't thrilled about all the attention and praise he was about to receive that day, but the "Ted Williams Welcome Home" banquet would be for a good cause.

Thirty-seven cars—most of them packed with past and present Red Sox teammates—followed Williams's convertible down Jersey Street. As it proceeded along Boylston Street, then south on Brookline Avenue, and through the Intown Shopping District, he waved to the thousands of fans.

"They weren't out to see me," he said. "They were just going home to dinner."

When it reached 35 Binney Street, the motorcade stopped and a swarm of children surrounded Williams. Dressed in hospital gowns and pajamas, they were all cancer patients at nearby Boston Children's Hospital, a place Williams visited frequently.

"Ted is not a new friend," explained one of Boston Children's doctors. "He has visited our hospital and cheered our patients on many an occasion."

Long before he halted a sightseeing tour through Kyoto to toss shadow batting practice for a pack of Japanese boys, Ted Williams loved bringing a smile to the face of a child, particularly a sick child.

During his rookie season in 1939, Williams received a letter from George Nicoll, a resident of the West Roxbury neighborhood in Boston. Nicoll's eleven-year-old son, Don, was very ill with a ruptured appendix and peritonitis. Just twenty years old himself, Williams arrived at Faulkner Hospital with a ball signed by several Red Sox stars. Don eventually made a full recovery, but Williams continued to visit the Nicoll home for dinner, bringing bats and other memorabilia to the family. Soon Williams was regularly treating Don to breakfast then admission to Fenway Park for a Red Sox game.

Eight years later, while in Chattanooga, Tennessee, for an exhibition game against the Cincinnati Reds, Williams was stopped on the street by another local man asking for a favor. Ben Seessel told Williams that he had hoped to take his son Tommy to the game but the nine-year-old was bedridden with influenza. Williams not only agreed to stop by the Seessel home and meet Tommy, he promised to hit him a home run. In the second inning of that afternoon's game, he smashed a ball an estimated 450 feet.

"I'd heard this Williams was not the friendliest fellow in the world," Ben Seessel told reporters. "But you'll never prove that to me. He was wonderful. I've never heard anyone talk so kindly to a child as he spoke to Tommy."

The very next month, once the regular season had brought the team back to Boston, Williams heard an even sadder story about a boy in nearby Malden, Massachusetts. Eleven-year-old Glenny Brann had been so badly "burned at the stake during a game of Cowboys and Indians" that both of his legs were amputated. Along with teammate Joe Dobson, Williams visited Glenny in the hospital, presented him with an autographed ball and a game-used bat, then promised him a home run. A few hours later, as Glenny and the other children at Malden Hospital listened to the radio broadcast on a sunporch, Williams clubbed two home runs in a Red Sox 19–6 victory.

Once polio began to spread across the nation in the late 1940s, Williams started to draw requests from parents and friends of children suffering with the deadly epidemic for which there was not yet a vaccine. Young polio victims such as Jack Mason of Accomac, Virginia, and Bob Peterson of Omaha, Nebraska, received signed, personally dedicated baseballs from Williams.

The Jimmy Fund, a cancer research foundation affiliated with Boston Children's, multiplied the number of needy children that Ted Williams could treat. Originally aligned with the Boston Braves, the Jimmy Fund became the Red Sox' official team charity in 1953. By then Williams had already become a mainstay on the cancer ward.

On the condition that no reporters follow him and no photographers take his picture, Williams regularly ducked in and out of Boston Children's to visit patients.

"He's very, very good medicine for the children who are sick," said Dr. Sidney Farber, the pioneering cancer specialist who in tandem with the

New England Variety Club founded the Jimmy Fund. "I say Ted Williams is a very big human being. Ted comes in here quietly, by the back door, so to speak. He's careful there is no publicity. He's a genuine man. He's himself. His visits here are dignified and genuine and they have no ulterior motives."

There was, however, an ulterior motive for the August 1953 Ted Williams Welcome Home parade and celebration: fundraising.

After an hour of signing autographs and greeting the patients at Boston Children's, Williams got back into his Cadillac and led the procession north onto Blackfan Street, through Brookline Village and Kenmore Square, then stopped on Park Square. At the luxurious Statler Hotel, a $100-per-plate banquet was being held in Williams's honor. All the event's proceeds would go to the Jimmy Fund. Emceed by television star Ed Sullivan, the evening raised more than $125,000, including a $50,000 donation from the Joseph P. Kennedy, Jr., Foundation. Twenty-one-year-old Harvard sophomore Ted Kennedy hand-delivered the check.

Uncomfortable with all the tributes, awards, and gifts, Williams most dreaded the speech he'd been asked to make, especially since Ed Sullivan personally put Williams's necktie on for him.

"In closing I only wish I was worthy and deserving of all the things that have been said and happen to me," he told the audience of more than a thousand. "Please let me, on behalf of the kids, thank everyone who is helping in this magnificent effort. You should be proud and happy to know that your contribution will some day help some kid to a better life."

As much as hitting a baseball with proper hip and wrist action, fishing for the *Salmo salar*, or supporting conservative Republican candidates, the Jimmy Fund and bringing joy to young cancer patients became one of Williams's greatest passions for the remainder of his life.

On Saturdays at Boston Children's, he stopped in patients' rooms, then drove the toy train that transported them to treatment. His example inspired other Red Sox to give their time and energy to the Jimmy Fund or visit—without photographers and reporters—Boston Children's. But in New England, no sports star or celebrity could compare with Williams, who also made house calls to cancer-stricken children.

"It was like heaven when he came walking into a house," friend Al Cassidy said. "He walks into a house of average means, and, gosh, that kid would just, you know—he couldn't believe it. All the kid could do was lay in bed and listen to his radio, and here comes Ted Williams into his room to see him."

Over the decades Williams raised millions of dollars for Jimmy Fund research. In addition to fundraising events and contributing plenty of his own money to the foundation, he donated souvenirs to be auctioned off, such as his five hundredth home run ball. His name alone also encouraged philanthropy. Upon his selection to the National Baseball Hall of Fame in 1966, 120 anonymous Williams fans donated a combined quarter-million dollars to the Jimmy Fund on his behalf.

He also tried to attend Jimmy Fund exhibition games, usually at Fenway Park, where the ticket and concession sales went to the cause. Fans in attendance hoped to see the retired hero swing the bat. Sometimes he did. In 1967 a twenty-seven-year-old women's softball pitcher named Joan Joyce struck him out on four pitches during a game in Waterbury, Connecticut. Five years later, while managing the Texas Rangers, he appeased the Fenway Park crowd of nearly thirty-four thousand by participating in a Home Run Derby prior to an exhibition between his club and the Red Sox. The game netted more than $100,000 for the charity.

"I'd do anything asked to help the Jimmy Fund," he said that night.

And he meant it, so long as he wasn't asked to wear a tie or be the center of attention at another testimonial or banquet like the one at the Statler Hotel.

But in the summer of 1988 Jimmy Fund organizers approached their de facto finance chairman once again.

"Every year we wanted to honor Ted, but he'd never agree to it," Red Sox broadcaster and Jimmy Fund trustee Ken Coleman said. "Five years ago, I asked Ted if we could honor him, as usual, but this time he said, 'Check back in five years.' Maybe he was just putting me off, but I stored it in my computer and last summer I reminded him the five years were up and true to his word, he agreed."

Nearing seventy years of age, Williams had started to mellow in the eyes of those who knew him. Although still animated, loud, even pugnacious, he wasn't quite as irritable or quick to anger. And he had largely forgiven the sportswriters and fans who had hassled him from the press boxes and grandstands so many years ago. Within a few years, he would even tip his cap to the crowd at Fenway Park during Ted Williams Day in May 1991.

So while he still insisted that "I've gotten 10,000 times more credit for this than I deserve," Williams agreed to be honored by the Jimmy Fund in the fall of 1988 with a public celebration.

Budweiser was lined up as a corporate sponsor. David Hartman, cohost of ABC's *Good Morning America*, was tapped as master of ceremonies. Newspaper advertisements were printed and promotional radio spots aired. Tickets costing as much as $200 were printed up. And the plush Wang Center in Boston was booked.

Finally, invitations were sent out to local luminaries, Jimmy Fund personnel, and the friends Williams wanted to attend. One was mailed to the following address:

HONORABLE JOHN H. GLENN, JR.
United States Senate
503 Hart Building
Washington, DC 20510

———

Super Tuesday 1984 was not kind to John Glenn. Despite telling reporters that "I plan to win" in Alabama and Georgia, Glenn finished no higher than third in eight of the day's nine contests. In Alabama, a state to which he had devoted considerable resources, Glenn tied for second with Gary Hart. In Massachusetts, he did not receive a single delegate. All in all Glenn collected just 15 of the 505 delegates up for grabs.

Dismissed by the pundits and national press as finished, Glenn remained defiant, insisting that his candidacy "is very much alive." But reality set in the next day. With the campaign more than $2.5 million in debt, Glenn sixteen pounds heavier than he wanted to be, and virtually nothing to show for it, he withdrew from a primary race that he called "a poor way to select a president."

In addition to decrying the influence of money in politics, the problems with televised campaigns, and the ineffective format of live debates he explained that there was plenty of blame to spread around.

"I know that we're not properly informing the people of the country now on what they need to be informed on to make good, honest decisions about what direction the country is going to go for the long term," he told a reporter right after the campaign ended. "At least early in the campaign the media does not do the job it should do in putting forward the issues and the things that are important as opposed to just the trivia of the campaign . . . Of course being president is part personality and part personal attributes and all that. But it really comes down to who bangs hardest on the podium and who screams the most in the microphone and who speaks in alliterative phrases.

"The nature of the campaign is such that we discourage a lot of very fine people," he added, "whether they are academicians or labor or management or bankers or academicians or philosophers or whatever. We have a lot of people [that] should be running for high political office that just won't because of that kind of a demand on their life."

Although he too had now become discouraged by the primary process, Glenn owned the campaign's failure. Those closest to him saw a side of Glenn they had never seen before. One aide recalled him just "staring out the window for a while."

"I guess, in my whole career, that's the biggest thing I ever attempted and was not successful at," he said a few years later. "Is it somewhat bitter to be turned down? Yes it is.

"You don't just lay down an effort like that because I poured my heart and soul and the family's efforts and everybody's. There's a self-criticism you go through. . . . You can't help but feel: Had I only made some different decisions, I would not have let all those people down. And that was the hard part."

Glenn turned his attention back to his duties as a United States senator and an advocate for Ohioans, a strong national defense, and military veterans. The following summer, one of his passion projects started to take form.

America as a whole had never truly appreciated the sacrifices and efforts of those who fought in the Korean War or the importance of that victory. By the closing years of the twentieth century, the Korean War was not romanticized like World War II, or vilified as the Vietnam War had been. It became known as "The Forgotten War." And by 1982, upon completion of the Vietnam Veterans Memorial, the Korean War remained the only major American war not to be formally memorialized in the nation's capital.

In 1985, House Resolution 2205 aimed to change that. Known as the Korean War Memorial Act, the bipartisan House of Representatives bill was sponsored by New Jersey Democrat James Florio and cosponsored by Mississippi Democrat Sonny Montgomery and Arkansas Republican John Paul Hammerschmidt. In July, a House task force conducted hearings on the proposed legislation. Following his opening statement, Florio submitted to the *Congressional Record* several letters he had received from Korean War veterans, including one from Ted Williams.

Before leaving Korea in June 1953, Williams had told International News Service correspondent John Casserly that the citizens back home in America who did not volunteer to fight "ought to be ashamed." But in support of the memorial more than thirty years later, Williams wrote, "Too often, I think, we are concerned with those who actually fought in combat and the need to honor their courage and bravery. There was no shortage of heroes in Korea. But we can't forget those at home either. We as a country were fighting in Korea—and we as a country suffered in Korea. By honoring those who fought in Korea we honor this entire country which did in fact preserve freedom in those years."

Once the task force introduced the bill, the committee heard in-person testimony. The fourth witness—the "cleanup hitter," according to chairwoman Representative Mary Rose Oakar—was John Glenn. On the other side of congressional testimony for the first time in years, he opened with a customary checklist of Korean War stats and figures—number of service members, planes shot down, casualties, deaths—but then shared several personal experiences from his time in VMF-311 and 25th Fighter-Interceptor Squadron.

"I guess I already have my own memorial, because my own memorial is in memories, it's in my mind already," he told the committee. "My own mental memorial, I remember seeing planes on fire. And most people here in the room probably have never seen a plane crash, and know that someone was in it that you knew was a friend."

He also spoke of Lieutenant Colonel John Giraudo being shot down near the Yalu River and his own encounters with anti-aircraft fire. And while praising the heroic efforts of Marine Corps forces on the ground near the Chosin Reservoir, he recalled a friend, a forward air controller, whose job was to call in air strikes.

"While he was standing on this ridge, he was shot right through the neck," Glenn said. "And he fell down, got up again—the story went from people that were with him—and was trying to still give directions . . . gurgling through his own blood. And he died."

Glenn struggled to finish the story as he began to cry, something he had vowed not to do earlier that morning.

"I can't pass along those memories, vivid though they may be," he concluded, still fighting back tears. "And they are vivid. I can still almost feel the stick in my hands, and what it's like to make a run and do the things that had to be done out there. So I hope we do have this memorial, if for nothing else then to help to pass on to our kids and grandchildren an appreciation for this heritage—the heritage of freedom that is not free."

Fifteen months later, President Ronald Reagan signed legislation—approved by both the House and Senate—authorizing the creation of a Korean War Veterans Memorial. The next week, Glenn won re-election with more than 63 percent of the vote as the Democrats reclaimed control of the Senate for the first time in three election cycles.

Despite his lackluster presidential campaign, Glenn started to rise within the hierarchy of the Senate and the Democratic Party. When the 100th United States Congress opened session in January 1987, he took over as chairman of the Governmental Affairs Committee. He embraced the committee's highly nuanced agenda, which focused on matters such as changes to the federal government's cataloging system for Department of Defense hardware and the Nuclear Regulatory Commission's need for an inspector general. And from the chairman's seat, he also found opportunities to criticize the Reagan administration for making too many political appointments to critical government jobs.

By June 1988, with the Democratic Party already aligned behind their presidential nominee, Massachusetts governor Michael Dukakis, Glenn emerged as a popular choice for vice president.

"He's on everybody's short list and ought to be," Democratic National Committee chairman Paul Kirk said a month before the party's convention.

While Dukakis and national party advisors deliberated over the bottom half of their ticket, Republican leaders and their nominee, George H. W. Bush, did the same.

Ronald Reagan's vice president, Bush had finished a distant third at the Iowa caucuses in early February 1988. After turning out an embarrassing showing for the long-presumed front-runner, the Bush campaign needed a boost in the upcoming New Hampshire primary. With an introduction from Sam Tamposi, New Hampshire's Republican governor and key Bush ally John H. Sununu asked Ted Williams to help.

Bush and Williams had much in common, aside from simply the Republican Party. Before captaining the Yale College baseball team in 1948, Lieutenant (JG) Bush had served as a Navy aviator in the Pacific during World War II. Williams, who had never before met Bush, agreed to participate in the campaign.

For over a week, he appeared at several Bush campaign stops in New Hampshire. More often than not—at a rally in Wolfeboro, a shopping mall in Nashua, a fishing and outdoor show in Manchester, even Bush's campaign headquarters in Bedford—Williams far outshone the sitting vice president. While they met with voters during a dogsled race at Opechee Park in Laconia, Williams signed multiple autographs for fans using Bush's back as a desk.

"We tried to take advantage of Ted wherever we could, to be blunt," Sununu later said. "I kept saying to the VP, 'Don't worry, we're gonna get a big crowd: Ted's here.' Afterwards I said to Bush, 'They came to see him and not you, so don't get a big head.' He knew that."

Bush edged out Kansas Senator Bob Dole in New Hampshire, then won sixteen of seventeen states on Super Tuesday, and locked up the Republican nomination in early May.

That summer, well before each party held their nominating convention, Democratic mainstay and seventeen-term Massachusetts congressman Thomas F. "Tip" O'Neill spoke with Williams. Although the recently retired speaker of the House of Representatives had been a diehard Red Sox fan since the 1920s, he had never met the Splendid Splinter. So he was both surprised and thrilled to receive an invitation to the Jimmy Fund's celebration of Williams later that year.

At some point in their discussion about the event in the fall, the conversation turned to politics and both parties' impending choice for a running mate.

"Tip, if Glenn's on the ticket," Williams told O'Neill, "I don't know what I'll do."

"Ted, what do you mean, you're a Republican, aren't you?" O'Neill answered.

Williams then told O'Neill that "when his plane got shot up in Korea, John Glenn was on his wing and guided him back to base."

Fortunately for Williams, Dukakis chose a different senator and military veteran—Lloyd Bentsen of Texas—to join his ticket. (Glenn just as easily could have delivered the famous "Senator, you're no Jack Kennedy" line to Dan Quayle in that year's vice presidential debate.)

With a sigh of relief, Williams voted for Bush, who handily won on Election Day 1988. The next day, John Glenn flew to Boston.

In a tradition that dates back to the 1920s, the United States Marine Corps observes its birthday on November 10. Although the most prestigious festivities take place at the commandant's annual Birthday Ball in Washington, D.C., active and retired Marines alike celebrate the holiday within Marine bases, academies, Veterans of Foreign Wars posts, civic centers, and hotel ballrooms across the world.

Ted Williams and John Glenn celebrated the Marine Corps birthday together for the first time in 1988, during "An Evening With #9: Ted Williams and Friends."

"This is the Marine Corps birthday," Glenn said that night. "Wherever two Marines will be gathered together there will be a cake cut sometime today."

There would hardly be enough cake for everyone. More than four thousand people paid to enter the Wang Center that Thursday evening. The ticket sales raked in more than $250,000 for the Jimmy Fund. Some came to support the nationally known children's charity. Others came to see the baseball royalty billed as headliners: Joe DiMaggio, Bob Feller, Reggie Jackson, and Tommy Lasorda, manager of the recent World Series champion Los Angeles Dodgers. But they all came to see Ted Williams.

After an introduction, an overview of the Jimmy Fund's purpose from head physician Dr. Stephen A. Sallan, and Suzyn Waldman's performance of "A Tribute to #9," sung to the tune of "Take Me Out to the Ballgame," the program began.

The format was a quasi celebrity roast of Williams, minus the roasting. Brought in front of the crowd in shifts, Williams's friends were interviewed one at a time by David Hartman. Each sat in a wicker chair, on a stage that had been made up to look like a cozy fishing cabin, complete with a bar, stools, and a fireplace.

Williams's former teammates and rivals gushed over his baseball skills and made jokes about his disdain for reporters. Longtime Red Sox team-mate Dom DiMaggio refused to answer a pointed question that asked him to name the better hitter: Williams or Dom's brother Joe, who was sitting backstage. Two local media legends, broadcaster Curt Gowdy and *Bangor (ME) Daily News* editor Bud Leavitt, shared their memories of covering Williams's playing days. And upon the close of all the interviews, a five-year-old boy named Joey Raymundo, who was being treated for leukemia at the Jimmy Fund Clinic, presented Williams with an oil painting of the baseball star known as The Kid.

One of the program's highlights, however, came from John Glenn. At least for one evening, the failed presidential candidate erased his recent track record of tedious public appearances from the moment he sat down.

Stories about Williams's prowess as a kroindyker and his contradictory nickname, "Bush," incited a rise from the audience. Stories about Williams's crash-landing at K-13 and the mission in which a hole blew through his Panther's tip-tank provided the audience with details that most had never before heard.

Concerned that it might embarrass the man of the hour, he chose not to share the events of Mission Number Acme 33, the early-early road recce that Glenn thought had ended his military career with a court-martial. Instead, he closed with a tribute to his friend.

"As far as I'm concerned, Ted *only* batted .406 for the Red Sox [in 1941]. He batted 1.000 for the Marine Corps and the United States."

Glenn then stood up and, with "The Marines' Hymn" playing him off, walked to the side of the stage to join the other interviewees.

The program then continued with additional speakers until Williams finally came out for a much lengthier interview with Hartman.

To the fans who still viewed the youthful, svelte slugger through their memories—or had just watched the video highlights of his playing career that preceded his entrance—Williams appeared much different. Well above his playing weight, he even pulled a pair of glasses from his jacket pocket, acknowledging that the man with mythical eyesight now needed readers to see his prepared remarks.

Reiterating his unworthiness for such an honor, Williams thanked the Jimmy Fund's founders, leaders, and supporters, then did the same for the friends that had joined him on the dais. And in another display of his newfound softness, Williams thanked the fans of New England as well.

At a few points during his questions Hartman paused to introduce additional dignitaries who wanted to congratulate Williams but could not attend in person. The first prerecorded video shown was of President Ronald Reagan, who praised Williams for his service to the nation and particularly his "ability to be strong and independent, and yet compassionate and giving."

Immediately after Reagan's message ended, as the lights returned to the stage, Williams paused for a moment, then spoke.

"It's hard to beat that," he said, a little choked up. "But I'd like to tell you one story about somebody here tonight, because I know how lucky I've been in my life. One of the luckiest things that ever happened to me was when I was with John Glenn on one of our missions one morning."

Williams then shared the events of Mission Number Acme 33, leaving out no details about that predawn flight near the Rimjin River on April 22, 1953. A highly demonstrative Williams shook in his seat as he mimicked the movements of the F9F Panther, the firing of his GP at a presumed collection of Allied troops, and a nervous, sweat-covered John Glenn chewing him out.

"And all I could see [was]: 'Williams Bombs U.S. Troops,' or something!" he said.

As laughter from the crowd died down, Williams became serious.

"That man right there, I'm telling ya," Williams said, pointing to Glenn. "Nobody admires you more than I do, John. Nobody. . . . So when he made his trip around the Earth, boy, I was proud to know you, John, I can tell you that.

"And I wish you all the luck in the world," he continued. "My greatest regret is that you're not a Republican."

That was probably as close to an apology—for not endorsing Glenn as a presidential candidate four years earlier—as Williams was ever capable of mustering.

CHAPTER THIRTEEN
No Cure for the Common Birthday

Ted Williams never did marry again following his third divorce. But even well into his seventies his romantic life carried on.

In the summer of 1991, Williams joined Indiana University basketball coach Bobby Knight on an ESPN-sponsored fishing trip to the collapsing Soviet Union. According to biographer Leigh Montville, while there Williams met a Russian woman north of the Arctic Circle, instructed the trip's guide to purchase him condoms, then warned his roommate (Knight) that the room might soon be off-limits.

For years, however, Williams had been steadily dating a divorcee with three adult children. Louise Kaufman, whom he had known for decades and who lived a few houses down the road in Islamorada, had effectively moved in with Williams by the late 1970s. When President George H. W. Bush awarded Williams the Presidential Medal of Freedom in November 1991, Kaufman joined him for a night in the Lincoln Bedroom.

But after roughly thirty years of on-again, off-again residence in Islamorada, Williams had become fed up with the traffic on Route 1 and gradual expansion throughout the Keys. His contract with Sam Tamposi also required that Williams permanently reside within the central Florida development that they had been promoting throughout the East Coast. So in 1987, he left the Keys for a temporary home in Citrus Hills while he awaited construction of a spacious four-bedroom ranch house at the top of a hill cloaked in oak trees and Spanish moss.

Kaufman moved with him.

"Gee, I'm so fuckin' happy about Louise," he told Pulitzer Prize–winning journalist Richard Ben Cramer. "Goddamn, she's a great person. Have more fun with her than . . . Goddamn."

One Christmas, Kaufman's grandchildren gave Williams a puppy that he clearly did not want.

"The last thing we need is a goddamned fucking dog," Williams's daughter Claudia remembered him saying.

In short order Williams warmed to the dog named Slugger. A Dalmatian, Slugger followed Williams around the house, played fetch, sat beside him during Red Sox television broadcasts, and eventually slept in his bed. But he wasn't terribly obedient, which became a problem since Williams preferred to walk him without a leash. He also jumped on visitors who entered through the back door.

"I love this old guy," he said as Slugger climbed into his lap. "When I first got him eight years ago I said, 'What do I need something like this for.' Now, every day of my life, I pray to God that he takes me before he takes Slugger because there is no way I could live without him."

By then, neither was in great shape. Slugger was undergoing extensive treatments for fibrosarcoma, a type of cancer found in dogs. Williams had endured a fall that broke his shoulder, two mild strokes, and a more severe stroke that significantly damaged his eyesight.

"Since I've become somewhat disabled, Slugger has been more protective," he said.

The third stroke, the most serious one, occurred in February 1994, just nine days after the star-studded opening of the Ted Williams Museum and Hitters Hall of Fame. Located two miles from his home, in Hernando, Florida, the 5,200-square foot, diamond-shaped building featured exhibits and memorabilia from all three of Williams's celebrated careers: baseball, fishing, and the Marine Corps. *Boston Globe* sports columnist Dan Shaughnessy called the museum "not unlike a presidential library, but then again, Ted always was a little bit presidential." Fittingly, all five living former United States presidents, Richard Nixon, Gerald Ford, Jimmy Carter, Ronald Reagan, and George H.W. Bush sent messages or pre-recorded videos of congratulations to the grand opening.

Although annual ceremonies, which started the following February, would induct new members into Williams's Hitters Hall of Fame, non-ballplayers were also immortalized within the museum. At the 1997 festivities, John Glenn was honored with a nameplate on the "Legends Walk of Fame." Two years later, he received the annual Ted Williams

Museum Lifetime Achievement award, a beautiful round, bronze-relief plaque of The Kid.

But Glenn could not attend the museum's ribbon-cutting. Earlier that week, as ranking member of the Armed Forces Readiness Subcommittee, he had been in Munich, Germany for the North Atlantic Treaty Organization (NATO) Conference on Security Policy. Part of a small congressional delegation, Glenn urged NATO and newly appointed secretary of defense William J. Perry to act in response to the growing humanitarian crisis during the Bosnian War. He then rushed back to Washington, D.C., to address domestic concerns. While Ted Williams's museum opened in the presence of sports legends such as Muhammad Ali, Joe DiMaggio, and Bobby Orr, Glenn testified before the Senate Finance Committee to endorse fellow Ohioan Mary Ellen Withrow as the next United States treasurer.

Despite missing the celebration in Hernando, Glenn hoped to visit Williams soon. News of his most recent stroke had been covered extensively by the media. Eventually, Glenn's personal business interests gave him the perfect opportunity.

During his NASA years in the early 1960s, Glenn had met a man named Henri Landwirth. A Holocaust survivor originally from Belgium, Landwirth operated the Cocoa Beach Holiday Inn and became friends with the Mercury Seven astronauts. Landwirth eventually asked Glenn to invest in additional Orlando-area Holiday Inn properties, in Kissimmee, Altamonte Springs, and Haines City. With the creation of Walt Disney World, the businesses boomed and by the late 1970s Glenn was a millionaire.

Throughout four terms as a United States senator he kept his interests in the hotels and actively participated in management. When time permitted he visited the area. The Glenns did not have a home in Florida, but with Lieutenant General Tom Miller they did co-own a sixty-three-foot Bertram Cabin Cruiser that was docked off the coast of Maryland. Miller and Glenn had christened it the *Seniram II*, or *2 Marines* spelled backward. The $400,000 motor-powered yacht employed a full-time captain and was often leased out for VIP charters, but in the winter the Glenns and Millers occasionally took their "mobile condo" down the Atlantic.

In October 1995, Annie and John traveled to Florida, met up with their daughter Lyn, then decided to call Ted Williams, who now lived less than a hundred miles from Orlando. Eager to see his friend, Williams invited them over then put on his best USMC polo shirt.

The Glenns drove into central Florida, hit County Road 486, and by seeing the names of the side streets, they knew they were getting close. From W. Fenway Dr. they turned onto N. Blue Jay Ter., then Ted Williams Ct., and approached the wrought-iron gate with baseballs on the posts and the number "9" in Red Sox script letters.

Along with his twenty-seven-year-old son John-Henry, Williams welcomed John, Annie, and Lyn. They sat for a few hours, ate lunch, took photos, and absolutely steered clear of politics as a topic of discussion.

"Dad asked Ted about his fishing," Lyn recalled. "That led to lots of stories on Ted's part . . . about the tournaments and where he'd been traveling. I think John-Henry might have gotten some of the magazines about that."

They also talked about their military service while they studied scale models of the F4U-1 Corsair fighter-bomber that they had both flown during World War II.

As different as they were, as much as they disagreed on so many issues, especially politics, Ted Williams and John Glenn enjoyed each other's company. That held true as young Marine pilots sitting around the mess hall at K-3 in between combat missions and as graying senior citizens sitting around the dining room table in a Florida retirement community.

And despite forty years having passed since they flew Panthers side-by-side over Nampo, Sinchon, and Yongp'o-ri, Williams and Glenn still shared a connection unbroken by time.

"When you fly in combat with somebody, there's a bond than runs so deep you cannot describe it," Glenn said later.

The bond ran deep enough that Glenn—never one to take the Lord's name in vain—usually looked past the short-tempered Williams's casual and liberal use of swear words. Annie, however, not as accepting of the crude language found on a Marine base, admonished Williams at each (frequent) use of a profanity.

"Now, Theodore, stop that," she said.

Williams repented, then went right back to cursing.

Although Williams was "the most profane man she ever met" Annie returned to Citrus Hills with John in the winter of 1998. Again, Glenn was in Florida on business. But this time, his business had nothing to do with Holiday Inns. He was sitting on big news that he just could not yet share.

"Here it was, two weeks before the announcement and he never said a word about going back up again," Williams later said. "I thought, 'Jeez, he's a helluva pal.'"

———

On February 20, 1997, in front of five hundred supporters, John Glenn stepped to a podium on the stage of Muskingum College's Brown Chapel. Exactly thirty-five years had passed since large crowds gathered around televisions throughout his alma mater—as well as the rest of the world—to watch *Friendship 7* orbit the Earth three times.

While in many ways that day in 1962 marked the beginning of Glenn's rise to national stardom, this day signified the end. Or at least the beginning of the end. Now seventy-five years old, Glenn was announcing that he would not seek a fifth term in the United States Senate.

"For all the advances in science and medicine that I have supported and that have occurred in the 35 years since my orbital flight, one immutable fact remains: There is no cure for the common birthday," he told the audience. "Although my health remains excellent, and my passion for the job burns as brightly as ever, another term would take me to the age of 83. For that reason—and that reason alone—I have decided that I will not be a candidate for re-election to the Senate in 1998."

Just a few hours after Glenn's press conference ended, at 3:32 a.m. Eastern Standard Time, NASA's space shuttle *Discovery* touched down on the runway of Cape Canaveral. A ten-person crew had spent nine days in orbit on a mission to service the much-maligned Hubble Space Telescope. Launched to great fanfare seven years earlier, the $1.5 billion dollar telescope had become a public relations disaster. For several years, the images sent back to Earth were significantly out of focus due to flaws in the telescope's mirrors.

A repair crew corrected the problem three years later, enabling the telescope to deliver majestic, never-before-seen images that gave humanity a much greater understanding of the cosmos. But between the Hubble fiasco, the tragedy of the 1986 space shuttle *Challenger* explosion, the disappearance and loss of contact with the $900 million Mars Observer probe in 1993, and a budget of more than $13 billion annually, NASA had squandered much of the public's goodwill first earned by John Glenn and the Mercury Seven astronauts.

"I think some of the romance has gone out of the [space program]," Laurence Peterson, director of the Center for Astrophysics and Space Sciences at the University of California at San Diego, said in December 1993. "It's still there, but people are beginning to ask, 'At what cost?' That's a question that doesn't get asked in boom times."

Although frustration, at being privately and permanently grounded by President Kennedy, had caused Glenn to resign from the space program in 1964, NASA always remained on his mind. During his decades in the Senate, he was one of NASA's most passionate supporters. Several times in the 1980s, when the Reagan administration sought to cut NASA's budget by hundreds of millions of dollars, Glenn chastised those efforts as shortsighted and dangerous.

"The mind set of a few people in key positions at NASA has gone from an optimistic and super-safety conscious 'can do' attitude when I was in the program to an arrogant 'can't fail' attitude on the day the *Challenger* exploded," Glenn said in the summer of 1986.

In the hopes of securing better leadership and proper funding, and while still chairman of the Governmental Affairs Committee, Glenn scrutinized the annual NASA budget proposals with great interest. In the early 1990s, one of those proposals caught his attention.

Also a longtime member of the Senate's Special Committee on Aging, he became intrigued by research that NASA had conducted on the parallels between age and the physiological effects of space travel. Still longing for another trip to space, he saw an opening. If NASA didn't want to risk the life of a forty-something-year-old American hero, perhaps they wouldn't mind risking the life of a seventy-something soon-to-be-retiree. In a case of trademark John Glenn sniveling, he concocted a proposal of his own. A comparison of the data collected on his body before, during, and after the *Friendship 7* flight, with data collected before, during, and after another space flight, decades later, might reveal a link between aging and space travel.

Glenn presented his idea to NASA officials at least fifty times.

"I'd like to go up again," he told reporters as early as 1992. "I already told them, and I was only half joking, that when they get around to doing a geriatric study, they've already got a baseline on me. I'm available."

After more than four years, Administrator Dan Goldin finally caved to Glenn's badgering, but on two conditions. First, Glenn had to pass all the physical requirements and medical examinations. Second, he must join the mission as an active crew member, not a tourist on a space cruise. Glenn wouldn't have it any other way.

"I believed that America is aging, and I thought it would really be good for the American population to not put people into age groups," Goldin later said. "And it would be good for the soul of America because NASA does things that are important technically, but we fly *people* to space, so they could live vicariously through those that go there, because everyone can't go to space. I just thought it would be really, really good for the American psyche."

Glenn breezed through a series of extensive medical examinations, particularly on his heart, and was deemed in excellent health by several different physicians.

"[They] put me through more physical tests than any other astronaut ever selected," he later said. "But I'm in fairly good shape and passed all of their examinations."

An impressive bill of health for a seventy-five-year-old, coupled with the formation of thoughtful, scientific objectives, led NASA physicians and administrators to give Glenn's participation in the mission their approval. Annie, Lyn, and David took far more convincing.

"I was really, really angry," David Glenn said years later. "Because I just thought after everything we'd been through with him in his life, for him to go back and go on another space flight . . . I thought 'Can't you just damn well be done with that?' So I was really angry, maybe more so than my mother and my sister, but I think we were all upset.

"I remember we were out at this condo that the family had in Vail [Colorado] and we were all together, we'd go out there to ski every year, meet up," David continued. "And he was talking about [returning to space] again. And he was just like a little boy, I could see how excited he was. And I just gave up. I told him that at the time, 'I give up.' And we all felt the same way. And we just thought, 'OK, hope for the best here,' because it just made him just joyful to think about, he was just so excited about it. You just couldn't be against and deny him that passion for doing this kind of stuff."

With dedication reminiscent of a Mercury astronaut intent on becoming the first American in space, Glenn spent eight months training his body and his mind. In preparation for Space Transportation System Mission 95 (STS-95), he spun in the centrifuge at 3 g's, rode in NASA's T-38 space training jet to simulate the shuttle's runway landing, and learned the finer points of eating, sleeping, and going to the bathroom in space. He also diligently prepared for his role as a payload specialist. And like Ted Williams arriving at K-3 decades earlier, Glenn just hoped to blend in as a member of the team and not draw celebrity attention.

"He came down for his first mission training period," recalled Dr. Scott Parazynski, the mission's flight engineer. "He walked into our crew office and he said 'All right, any of you guys call me *Senator Glenn*, I'm just going to ignore you. Call me *John* or *Payload Specialist Number 2*. That's it.'

"He just wanted to be a contributor. He didn't want any special treatment."

Training sessions took place at the Johnson Space Center in Houston, Texas, as well as Cape Canaveral, the actual launch site for space shuttle *Discovery*. On one of those trips to Florida, Glenn again stopped by Citrus Hills to see Ted Williams.

"Hell, he's in excellent shape, he looks like he's about 57," Williams told the *New York Daily News* in early October. "We just started talking, you know, about the weight of [the shuttle] and the pressure and all. I've seen him excited and enthusiastic [before], but he was really excited about this trip."

With the mission date set for October 29, 1998, Glenn personally invited Williams to attend the launch at the Kennedy Space Center. Although he told Glenn, "You bet I'll be there!," Williams knew showing up would be a challenge.

In December 1996, Williams had tripped over Slugger, fallen, and broken his hip and a bone in his leg.

"I stepped on him. I mean, when he made a big yelp, I did everything and I fell," he said. "Well, that hip hurt to hell."

Doctors put a pin in his leg and prescribed months of rehabilitation and physical therapy. Inside his home, he needed a walker just to move from room to room. Outside of the home Williams could only get around with a wheelchair, which he hated. Travel of any kind was painful and exhausting for the eighty-year-old. But there was no way he would miss Glenn's big day.

"Bring the damned wheelchair and the walker," he told his children, John-Henry and Claudia, "and make sure I have my good binoculars!"

On the morning of the *Discovery* launch, the Williams family arrived at the Saturn V Center. Beneath a nearby tent, they joined a collection of six-hundred-some VIPs that included seventy-eight members of Congress, World Heavyweight Champion Evander Holyfield, and actors Leonardo DiCaprio and Tom Hanks. Steven Tyler, the lead singer of the band Aerosmith, was also there, but among all those celebrities Williams was the rock star. Everyone wanted to take a photo with him or shake his hand. Scattered military dignitaries also on hand were just as awed by his presence. One was Secretary of the Navy John Dalton.

"He was only 10 feet away, very close," recalled Marine Corps Major General Larry S. Taylor. "He had not seen Ted previously, [Dalton's aide] whispers something in his ear and I see the Secretary of the Navy start hurrying, he was like a 12-year-old, dodging people as fast as possible so he can get down to talk to Ted Williams. He was just like a kid. It was great. And they talked a little away. That was the effect Ted had on any number of [people], especially older guys."

The launch was also carried live by the national media. ABC, NBC, CBS, and CNN each reported all day long from Cape Canaveral and Muskingum College. Tom Brokaw anchored NBC's coverage for three hours (plus two brief delays totaling nineteen minutes) prior to the launch. The Emmy award–winning journalist interviewed Vice President Al Gore about the future of the space program, checked in with NBC correspondent Robert Hager for technological details on the mission, and asked astronauts Scott Carpenter and Michael López-Alegría to speculate on the mindset of the men and women sitting aboard *Discovery* as they awaited blastoff.

But with so much airtime to fill, there were spots for a few profiles on the individual astronauts. More than two hours from the scheduled launch time, NBC cut from live images of Glenn and the other astronauts being strapped in to their seats, back to Brokaw. Beside him was Ted Williams, wearing his red VMF-311 baseball cap.

"I am privileged beyond my ability to describe it," Brokaw told the viewers, "to introduce to you another hero, who has as his hero, John Glenn. This is a man who defines hero in the American sporting life: it's Ted Williams."

Fidgeting in his seat, speaking slower and with the subtle hints of three recent strokes, Williams shared his memories of Glenn from Korea and the ensuing years. He even called the Democrat "a great senator." Following a commercial break, Brokaw surprised Williams with a video clip from an interview he had conducted with Glenn earlier that month in Washington, D.C. After repeating the exaggeration that half the missions Williams flew were on his wing, Glenn told Brokaw, "Ted was great, he was a good pilot and no one would ever question his hand-eye coordination."

"Those were dangerous times when you were flying in Korea together?" Brokaw asked Williams, back on air.

"I want to tell you the flights that I went with John Glenn, I still marvel at how smooth and easy everything came out when I was with him. He is tremendous in every way that I know of."

Williams soon returned with his children to the VIP Center and awaited the launch. At 2:19 p.m., with no further delays, main engines were given "a go" and the shuttle lifted off. Under the power of twin solid rocket boosters—capable of nearly twenty times the thrust of the Atlas rocket that powered *Friendship 7*—it broke free from Launchpad 39B. As *Discovery* rose up in the air, Ted Williams rose up in his wheelchair and shouted "That's my friend!" over the thunderous blast.

"I never admired anybody more than John Glenn," he told the *Boston Globe* that day. "He's terrific in every way. He is a sensational American hero."

As the crew reached an altitude several hundred miles above the Earth, Glenn unstrapped himself and shed his bulky orange launch-entry spacesuit and helmet. Aboard *Friendship 7* he had been strapped into the tiny, cramped capsule for the duration of his nearly five-hour journey. The *Discovery* shuttle's cargo bay alone was eighteen times bigger than the entire *Friendship 7* capsule. Inside the cargo bay, Glenn was free to move around the spacecraft, his sparse, white hair still as he floated in weightlessness, his large, thick glasses atop his smiling face.

"When he got up into space on *Friendship 7*, all he could really do was loosen up his shoulder straps a little bit, he wasn't freely floating—as we shuttle astronauts enjoy doing—so we shuttle guys would tease him that he was actually a 'space rookie.' He played along with it," Dr. Scott Parazynski recalled. "When he first floated up to the flight deck . . . he floated up through the inter-deck access hatch and gave me a little high five, and then floated up to the overhead windows and he was just mesmerized. He was just in awe. It was a really special moment to share with him."

Glenn then went to work. He assisted in readying the shuttle's Space-hab pressurized laboratory and sat for the first of hundreds of examinations conducted by the onboard physicians. A focus of the research on Glenn and aging was the impact that the effects of the microgravity of space would have on the human body. In addition to monitoring Glenn's heartbeat, blood pressure, coordination, balance, and sleep, Drs. Chiaki Mukai and Scott Parazynski collected blood and urine samples from the seventy-seven-year-old. Parazynski took blood from Glenn so often that he began calling the medical doctor and former emergency room physician "Count Dracula."

In between each "bloodletting," as he called it, Glenn reflected on the images he saw through the shuttle windows. Thirty-six years earlier, he had been too busy to pray while aboard his space capsule. This time, he did.

"I pray every day," he told reporters during a remote interview from the shuttle. "To look out at this kind of creation out here and not believe in God to me is impossible. It just strengthens my faith."

Within nine days, the crew had completed its technological and scientific objectives. They successfully launched a probe that measured extreme ultraviolet light emissions, deployed the Spartan free-flyer payload probe to gather data on solar coronas and solar winds, and tested upgrades that would eventually be installed on the Hubble Space Telescope.

The shuttle touched down safely on the morning of November 7, but Glenn's mission was not yet complete. For weeks NASA doctors continued to monitor his heart, balance, and sleep, and of course collected more blood and urine. By Thanksgiving, his experience as a human guinea pig was mostly finished, although he still sat for several MRIs over the next few months.

Deemed to be in perfect health, Glenn reunited with the rest of the *Discovery* crew in early December for an extremely short parade through raindrops along Florida's A1A Highway. More than twenty-five hundred people cheered as Glenn coasted by in a silver 1998 Chevrolet Corvette convertible that headed toward a celebration at the Cocoa Beach Doubletree Hotel.

On his way inside roughly one hundred overzealous fans blew past the plastic ribbon barriers to shoot photographs and video with the American hero. Police threatened to arrest each unless they did not stop. Inside the hotel's ballroom he was again crowded by fans (invited, credentialed fans), who gave him handshakes, hugs, and from the local mayors, keys to the cities of Cape Canaveral and Cocoa Beach.

And from Ted Williams—tired after traveling across the state again, struggling to stand up—he received a welcome home and a pat on the back.

———

More than forty years after his unexpected and—in his mind—unfair recall to active military service Ted Williams had let go of his anger toward the United States Marine Corps. In fact, he came to embrace his status as a veteran much like he embraced his status as one of baseball's elder statesmen.

The annual ceremonies for the Ted Williams Museum and Hitters Hall of Fame often resembled a Marine Corps Birthday Ball as much as a celebration of sports history. The festivities sometimes featured a Marine Corps band, color guard, and, during an awards ceremony in 1995, a fly-over by two Harrier AV-8B jets. The Harriers were based out of the Marine Corps air station in Yuma, Arizona, home to Marine Attack Squadron 311, formerly known as VMF-311.

Williams, who wore his VMF-311 cap to most public events, also encouraged active and retired Marines to attend the ceremonies. For the grand opening in 1994, Williams invited the commandant of the Marine Corps, Carl E. Mundy, Jr., but the four-star general was unavailable. General Mundy directed a colleague, Major General Larry S. Taylor, to go in his place. A baseball history fanatic, Taylor jumped at the chance to rub elbows with several of the game's greatest living legends.

Williams spotted Taylor in his Marine uniform from across the room that was littered with sports celebrities, politicians, and a few wealthy fans.

"He grabbed me by the sleeve of my uniform," Taylor recalled. "He said, 'I care more about these guys than I do about all the presidents, all the ballplayers, and all you assholes.'"

Although they only spoke briefly, Williams immediately liked Taylor. Now the commanding general of the Fourth Marine Aircraft Wing, Taylor had flown missions in the Sikorsky H-34 helicopter in Laos during the Vietnam War. A week later Williams asked him to visit Citrus Hills, and he soon began regularly inviting Taylor to his public appearances. He was with the Williams family at John Glenn's *Discovery* launch.

"We hit it off," Taylor said. "There's nothing he preferred to talk about more than flying an airplane and there's nothing I'd rather talk about than baseball."

For his friend, Taylor asked the new Marine Corps commandant, Charles C. Krulak, to call Williams on his birthday. Upon hearing who was on the phone, Williams tried to stand up from his wheelchair and salute the four-star general.

The Marine Corps believed that Williams's many public displays of support aided their recruitment numbers. Krulak, who had followed the tail end of his Red Sox career as a student at Phillips Exeter Academy in New Hampshire, wanted to show Williams his appreciation. He devised a unique way to pay homage to the man who already had a Presidential Medal of Freedom, membership in the baseball Hall of Fame, and enough plaques, certificates, and awards to fill a museum. He promoted Captain T. S. Williams to the rank of colonel.

Although just a ceremonial honor—Williams had both been discharged by the Marine Corps and never reached the preceding ranks of major or lieutenant colonel—the paperwork had all the signatures and official markings.

A year later, Williams attended the annual National Baseball Hall of Fame Veterans Committee meetings in nearby Tampa, where seventeen sportswriters and retired stars voted on the candidacy of eligible alumni. Williams had not been tight-lipped or modest about the promotion: his baseball friends knew that he liked being addressed as "Colonel." So as Williams was wheeled into the Airport Marriott conference room, Stan Musial pulled from his jacket pocket a harmonica and played "The Marines' Hymn."

"As I told John Glenn, who maneuvered me out a tough situation in Korea, 'they've promoted me to Colonel, and, hell, they haven't even made you a General yet,'" he informed his fellow committee members.

Into his eighties, Colonel Williams's health remained fairly poor. He no longer had the stamina or eyesight to fish and begrudgingly sold his cherished cabin on the Miramichi River in New Brunswick, Canada. But he continued to travel, usually requiring a wheelchair.

A week before Glenn's *Discovery* launch, Williams was in New Jersey. A longtime New York Yankees rival had promised to attended Williams's museum ceremonies if Williams attended the opening of the Yogi Berra Museum at Montclair State University.

"Normally you have to be dead to get a museum and neither of us is dead," Berra said.

The following spring, Williams made a second trip to Cape Canaveral. He had been so amazed by the spectacle of Glenn's voyage the previous fall—"I had never in my life even comprehended the monstrous power that thing went up into the air with"—that he vowed to witness the launch of the next *Discovery* mission, STS-96. Despite the predawn schedule that meant a 3:30 a.m. wakeup call, Williams again drove across the state to see another blastoff, even if John Glenn was not aboard.

"What a man [Glenn] is," Williams told the reporter who asked why he was there. "He's my idol."

And that June he flew to New York City in the hopes of meeting with Major League Baseball commissioner Bud Selig. For several years, Williams had championed the reinstatement of Shoeless Joe Jackson, the baseball folk hero permanently banned from the Hall of Fame for allegedly helping throw the 1919 World Series. According to famed *Atlanta Constitution* sportswriter Furman Bisher, Williams had "recruited" Glenn to the cause during his final months as a senator.

During the trip to New York, he also visited Shea Stadium to toss out the ceremonial first pitch prior to a Red Sox game against the Mets. To mark sixty years since his rookie season, the interleague showdown had been billed as "Ted Williams Night," a rare treat for baseball fans. But the Splendid Splinter had actually made several appearances at big-league stadiums in the past few years. He threw out the first ball before the Tampa Bay Devil Rays inaugural game in 1998, attended recent All-Star Games in Pittsburgh and Toronto, and made multiple visits to games at Jack Murphy Stadium in his hometown of San Diego.

He had not set foot in Fenway Park, however, since tipping his cap to the crowd on Ted Williams Day in May 1991, six months before suffering his first stroke. Major League Baseball, Fox television affiliates, and millions of baseball fans across the world were elated to learn that Williams had agreed to attend the 1999 All-Star Game at Fenway Park. Throughout the summer, Boston's general manager Dan Duquette had been hounding Williams to show.

"He wasn't sure if he could come because of his health," Duquette later said. "I kept talking to him. I said we'd get him a private plane. All of his friends would be there. The fans wanted to see him. He had to come."

Months earlier, to celebrate the close of the century, a panel of experts led by baseball's official historian Jerome Holtzman selected a list of the Top 100 players in the game's history. Throughout that summer, fans would whittle down the choices and name twenty-five members to the All-Century Team. Kevin Costner, star of the movie *Field of Dreams*, announced thirty-five of the nominees in attendance during an elaborate pre-All-Star-Game cere- mony at Fenway Park. After the singing of the national anthem and intro- duction of the All-Star Game rosters, Williams toured the playing field in a golf cart while tipping his cap to the adoring crowd of 34,187. The cart stopped near the pitcher's mound, where Williams was supposed to throw out the ceremonial first pitch. But the all-stars and the All-Century nomi- nees engulfed him for nearly ten minutes, hanging on his every word.

"We were all in awe of the reverence that all those all-stars had for Ted. The way they surrounded him . . . that was a magical moment," remem- bered Red Sox and CBS Sports television broadcaster Sean McDonough. "The response that he got, and all those all-stars, present and past, who seemed like they were extraordinarily grateful just to have to the opportu- nity to be close to him."

Barely able to see, Williams needed help from John-Henry just to stand up. San Diego Padres outfielder Tony Gwynn, one of the All-Century nominees, propped Williams up to toss out the first pitch to Red Sox Hall of Fame catcher Carlton Fisk.

One of the most entertaining All-Star Games in recent memory followed the nostalgic scene. Red Sox ace Pedro Martinez opened the game by strik- ing out the first four batters he faced, including two future Hall of Famers and the reigning National League Most Valuable Player. But that eve- ning, and throughout his five-day trip, Williams was the main attraction across New England, not just among the fifty-one Hall of Famers and future Hall of Famers that basked in his presence before the first pitch.

In a private, left field luxury box, Williams received a visit during the game from Matt Damon, the Boston native and one of the stars of the recent World War II film *Saving Private Ryan*. Outside the box, Marines from the local recruiting office and the Navy aviators who had streaked over the sta- dium in a pregame F-14 Tomcat flyover stood at attention before Colonel Williams. And of course reporters pressed him whenever possible.

Everyone wanted to discuss with Williams their own topics of interest. Reporters searched for quotes on modern home run heroes Mark McGwire and Sammy Sosa and the rumor that Red Sox ownership planned to replace Fenway Park. The Marines asked about a statement he often made: "The Marine Corps was the best team I ever played on." Matt Damon wanted to discuss Williams's book *The Science of Hitting.* They all got their wish. But Williams wanted to talk about watching his friend John Glenn once again ride the rocket.

"For months afterward he would attempt to describe it over and over to anybody who would listen," Claudia Williams remembered.

In an odd moment of sports cross-breeding prior to the All-Star Game, Williams attended two days of stock car racing at the New Hampshire International Speedway in Loudon. Through his friend Dave McCarthy, a New Hampshire state trooper, Williams had come to sponsor sixteen-year-old Kenny "The Kid" White, Jr., in the Busch North series, a regional racing circuit. On Saturday, he watched White's Chevy Monte Carlo, emblazoned with the number "9," a pair of crossed wooden baseball bats, and the Jimmy Fund logo, compete in the Pennzoil/Replacement Auto Parts 100 qualifier.

The next day, Williams returned to the "Magic Mile" to serve as the grand marshal and starter for the Jiffy Lube 300, a NASCAR Winston Cup Series tour stop. In front of more than ninety-three thousand raucous fans Williams announced, "Gentlemen, start your engines," then exited the track. Even with his diminished hearing, Williams couldn't tolerate the intense sound and thrust of forty-three high-powered race cars.

"I've watched them on television, but being right there when they're . . . Vrooommmm . . . Boy. It reminds me of when I saw John Glenn go up on his shot, and when you're there and you see that go, you say, 'I've never seen anything like this.'"

Williams also stopped by the Jimmy Fund Clinic on Binney Street, the same place where he'd visited dozens of cancer patients prior to the "Ted Williams Welcome Home" banquet in August 1953. He chatted and joked with a handful of bald children wearing protective masks and hospital gowns. He even met, for the first time, Einar Gustafson, the original "Jimmy," now a sixty-three-year-old Maine truck driver.

During his visit to the clinic, Williams was asked about his recent trip to see John Glenn's return to space.

"His eyes lit up," recalled Saul Wisnia, a senior publications editor for the Dana-Farber Cancer Institute. "He just got really demonstrative: 'You could feel the ground shake and it took off and, boy, that was something!' Then we asked about being Glenn's wingman. And he said, 'That was my greatest honor.'"

"I just remember feeling I was in a very special moment," Wisnia said. "Just one legend describing another."

CHAPTER FOURTEEN
Losing a Great Friend

Slugger the dog died from kidney failure a few months after the 1999 All-Star Game at Fenway Park.

"[Williams] was very stoic but quite verbal about his attachment to the dog," said Charles Magill, the veterinarian who put Slugger down. "'Dogs are a lot more loyal than people and a lot nicer,' he said."

A grieving Williams found comfort in framed photographs, a painting of Slugger that he'd commissioned from New Jersey artist Karen O'Neil Ganci, and the belief that eventually "we're gonna be together." For years, Williams had told friends and family that when he died he wanted to be cremated and have his "ashes mixed with Slugger's ashes and spread over the deep waters off of Islamorada, down in the Keys."

"Ted loved Slugger so much," Magill said. "I think John-Henry may have been a little jealous of the dog."

Williams's relationships with all three of his children had always been complicated. Bobby-Jo, the eldest and the product of his first marriage, to Doris Soule, mostly lived with her mother, but she visited him in Boston for summers. They quarreled as Bobby-Jo grew up during the tumultuous 1960s. She battled drugs and alcohol, attempted suicide after receiving an abortion, then spent a brief period in a psychiatric facility. But they eventually reconciled. In the late 1990s, she and her husband Mark Ferrell moved to Citrus Hills to be near Williams.

John-Henry and Claudia, the children from his third marriage, also weaved in and out of their father's life for many years. Both were raised by their mother, Dolores Wettach, in rural Vermont, but they joined him for vacations in Islamorada and New Brunswick. At thirteen years old John-Henry was the Red Sox batboy in spring training and for the team's Old Timers' Game. He also accompanied his father on fishing trips across the Keys.

"John-Henry would come down and Ted was pretty hard on him," remembered Rick Ruoff, a fishing guide in the Keys whom Williams befriended. "I think it was hard being Ted Williams's son. Ted was a perfectionist and he wanted everybody around him to adhere to that. . . . He was a hard guy."

In December 1991, John-Henry, who played semipro baseball but did not make his college team, graduated from the University of Maine with a degree in finance. While with his father in Florida, he slowly became involved in the family business: selling Ted Williams souvenirs.

Williams had recently lost $37,800 in a baseball card deal with a local memorabilia dealer that went sideways and eventually led to his partner's imprisonment on second-degree felony charges. Believing his father had been swindled, John-Henry assumed command of the autograph operation.

"It's almost a bittersweet situation, that he got sick," John-Henry said a few years later. "Because of that, that really formed a relationship. He really wouldn't be alive today I'm sure, if I hadn't. I do a lot of dirty work that needs to get done, a lot of things that he doesn't need to know about.

"I think Dad will be the first person to tell anybody that he is not the smartest businessman in the world," he added. "He's very kindhearted and he's an easy person for people to take advantage of. . . . When I was getting out of school, I had a revelation—there's one person that I can make sure of that won't take advantage of him and will protect him, and that was me."

Williams had previously signed a $2 million agreement with Upper Deck, a baseball trading card company that required him to autograph merchandise and appear at public signing events. But through Grand Slam Marketing, a business started by John-Henry, he encouraged his father to sign additional items, which he sold separately. John-Henry also created the Ted Williams Card Company, which directly competed with Upper Deck. Given Williams's strokes and falls, many people believed that John-Henry was using his ailing father as a cash cow.

"His son would come up and bring a ton of memorabilia up, and really exhaust his father by having him sign quite a bit of stuff," recalled Robert Hogerheide, a retired Navy chef who personally cooked Williams meals in his home toward the end of the 1990s.

"Sign, sign, sign. They would do it for hours at a time until the man was so tired he couldn't write anymore," said Kay Munday, an in-home assistant to Williams. "He pushed and pushed his dad to do all this stuff and of course it was for money. The ultimate thing was money."

In addition to retail sales of memorabilia, John-Henry encouraged Williams to appear at public autograph sessions, which usually charged several hundred dollars per item. For a weekend signing show at Atlantic City's Tropicana Hotel in November 1996, Williams was reportedly paid $500,000. John-Henry also worked tirelessly to rid the market of stolen memorabilia or forgeries of his father's signature. The more signed photographs, bats, and cards that reached the public, the less valuable each autograph was and the less Grand Slam Marketing could charge per appearance. John-Henry carefully scrutinized the people to whom his father gave autographs and memorabilia, even Williams's old friends, such as John Glenn.

"Dad wanted to get autographs for my nephews," Lyn Glenn recalled about her visit to Citrus Hills in 1995. "And I think Ted refused to give it to Dad because he only sold his autographs. . . . Dad was surprised that for somebody who had known him so long that there would be any question about that. But then Dad's also one of the people that his views about autographs and all of that was that 'If you want it, of course, and I'll give it to you and I'll stop and give you my time.' Because that's part of his responsibility for the work that he did.

"Dad never sold his name for anything," Lyn Glenn continued. "He never made advertisements. He was a government employee doing a job as a Marine and he would never take money for something that he did."

The most notorious example of John-Henry's business ventures occurred during the 1999 All-Star Game. Two years earlier, he had formed an internet service provider (ISP) called Hitter Communications. Branded as "Hitter.net," the business struggled to handle the requirements of a dial-up-era internet company. John-Henry took to borrowing large sums of money from his father's friends, as well as hosting pornographic websites on the Hitter.net ISP, to stay afloat.

Ted Williams, who knew nothing about the business or its practices, actively and willingly participated in the company's promotion. Tom Brokaw even helped draw traffic to the business during the countdown to John Glenn's STS-95 launch in October 1998. He kept Williams on set following a commercial break to tell the NBC audience, "Ted Williams is a very modern American hero: he's got his own website, www.tedwilliams. com, and you can learn a lot more about him there." Before the interview, Brokaw agreed to John-Henry's request to plug the website, one of the largest traffic sources and an advertiser for Hitter.net.

Although he wore the cherished VMF-311 hat on his head that day at Cape Canaveral, Williams also wore a "Hitter" polo shirt, which had become his unofficial uniform for public events. For his sentimental return to New England the following summer for the All-Star Game he wore a Hitter.net polo everywhere, even to his visit to the Jimmy Fund Clinic. According to a family attorney, Peter Sutton, Williams and his son handed out Hitter.net promotional merchandise throughout the entire All-Star festivities. The Busch North Series stock car that Williams sponsored and watched race that weekend carried the Hitter.net logo on the sides and hood.

And at the All-Star Game, while all the other All-Century Team nominees donned their familiar baseball caps—Stan Musial in a St. Louis Cardinals hat, Willie Mays in a San Francisco Giants hat, Hank Aaron in an Atlanta Braves hat—Williams tipped to the Fenway crowd a cheap-looking, white cap bearing only a large, plain "Hitter.net" logo.

Even more than the unabashed peddling, many members of the media, and those close to Williams, hated the message the Hitter.net hat sent.

"It was disgusting," Jack Gard, one of Williams's caretakers at the time, later said. "That really made a lot of Ted's friends back away because they could see [John-Henry] was exploiting him."

The Hitter.net drama eventually blew over, and Williams made another high-profile appearance that fall. Selected by the fans to the All-Century Team's twenty-five-man roster, Williams attended Game Two of the 1999 World Series in Atlanta. During another gaudy presentation on the field, in front of the crowd and television cameras Willie Mays and Ken Griffey, Jr., practically carried Williams across the stage to his seat. This time, he wore a Red Sox hat.

Despite persistent problems with walking and even seeing, he continued to make public appearances.

Williams's friend Tommy Lasorda noticed on at least one such occasion that John-Henry was "demanding that his father be compensated" for public celebrations.

In the early months of 2000, Williams attended his induction to the

International Game Fish Association Hall of Fame, addressed the crowd at the Hitters Hall of Fame induction ceremony, and stopped by Los Angeles Dodgers spring training in Vero Beach, Florida, to talk with Lasorda and interrogate right fielder Shawn Green about his bat's weight. And at the annual New Hampshire Baseball Dinner in Manchester he took the stage with Republican presidential candidate George W. Bush. Earlier that afternoon he had publicly endorsed the governor of Texas for president, twelve years after doing the same for Bush's father.

On his way up to New Hampshire, Williams stopped at the Yogi Berra Museum in Little Falls, New Jersey, to attend the first screening of a documentary on baseball great Hank Greenberg, a player Williams had admired early in his career. The night before the premiere, Williams went to a dinner party at an upscale hotel on Manhattan's East Side. The collection of prominent sportswriters also in attendance seized the opportunity to interview the eighty-one-year-old legend about the future.

"I've never been very religious, so I don't know what's going to happen, if anything when I'm dead," he said. "I'll tell you this, though, I'm not afraid to die."

In October Williams was admitted to Shands Hospital in Gainesville, Florida, for breathing problems. Surgeons implanted a pacemaker to improve the congestive heart failure that doctors had discovered. Two months later he underwent major open heart surgery at the New York Weill Cornell Medical Center. The nine-and-a-half-hour procedure conducted by fourteen doctors, nurses, and technicians, repaired a leak in his mitral valve. Children at the Jimmy Fund Clinic sent him a huge, crayon-colored get well card.

John Glenn called regularly to check on his friend, but he only spoke with John-Henry. Williams required a respirator to breathe and a tracheotomy tube remained in his throat. Published reports also indicated that Williams had suffered some neurological impairment from the surgery. Following the procedure he was flown cross-country to San Diego for a lengthy rehabilitation stay at Sharp Memorial Hospital, a few miles north of his alma mater, Herbert Hoover High School.

Williams slowly regained cognizance, but not the ability to speak. Until he overheard John-Henry mention that Glenn had called again. Weakly, Williams asked "How is he?"

"It meant that right at that moment he knew what I was saying, he knew who John Glenn was, and he knew how to put together the words to ask a question about it," John-Henry said. "We all felt this was a big positive step."

Later that winter, Glenn and Annie visited Williams at Sharp Hospital. In his hospital bed, hooked up to monitors and machines, Williams was the same as always.

"He had some salty language, of course," Glenn remembered. "But Ted would say, 'OK, clean it up! Annie's here.'"

Glenn had been in San Diego at the time to deliver a keynote address to the annual National School Board Association (NSBA). Robert Gass, president of the Massachusetts chapter of the NSBA, attended the convention and at a reception got in a long line to shake Glenn's hand and take a photo with the now-retired senator and astronaut. Gass, a Red Sox season ticket holder, asked about the health of Boston's greatest slugger. Glenn gave him an update then spoke at length about his friendship with Williams. While the line behind him grew restless, Gass soaked up Glenn's memories. One story told of Williams being asked about post-traumatic stress disorder in military veterans and if he ever had nightmares or difficulty sleeping as a result of the war. Williams answered, "I had a lot of nightmares, and Bob Feller was in every one of them."

"John Glenn only wanted to talk about Ted Williams," Gass told his local newspaper.

Williams's condition, however, only worsened. Aside from several infections, his kidneys began to fail, requiring frequent dialysis. Still, his doctors approved a transfer to rehabilitation in a Florida hospital, and for his eighty-third birthday, Williams was sent back home to Citrus Hills.

"I'm feeling pretty good," he whispered over the phone to Dan Shaughnessy of the *Boston Globe*. "But my whole life has been knocked out of joint. Oh, boy. I've never been through years like I've been through in the last four years. There's nothing I can compare it to in my life. I really have been through hell."

With occupational and physical therapy his mobility improved and his appetite returned—he still ate double orders of bacon at each breakfast—but his spirits were lifted mostly by phone calls from friends such as John Glenn.

"The first thing he wanted to talk about was Korea," Glenn later said.

In 2002, July 4 fell on a Thursday, but with the traditionally slow summer schedule, many people used the national holiday as an excuse for a four-day weekend. John and Annie Glenn celebrated America's 226th birthday by vacationing on Chesapeake Bay. The following afternoon Glenn learned that Ted Williams had passed away at the age of eighty-three.

"I was very encouraged last time I talked to him about four or five weeks ago," Glenn told the *Boston Herald*. "He was upbeat and speaking. His speech was not slurred . . . [he] had been walking and was in far better shape than he was previously. It was a real shock when I heard he finally passed on."

Flags across Boston flew at half-staff. The Red Sox, hosting the Detroit Tigers at Fenway, held a lengthy moment of silence before the first pitch. All the players wore a number "9" sewn into their sleeves. John-Henry insisted that his father did not want a funeral, but rather a "celebration of his life," which the Red Sox planned later that month.

Monday, July 22, was an off day for the second-place Red Sox. But between the hours of 9 a.m. and 9 p.m. more than thirty thousand fans came to Fenway Park for an all-day memorial. Tickets to attend cost multiples of nine ($9, $18, and $27) and all the proceeds went to the Jimmy Fund. Along the Green Monster hung three mural-sized photographs of Williams: completing his graceful swing, greeting a group of young Jimmy Fund patients, and sitting in the cockpit of an F9F Panther. Atop the grass in left field lay a seventy-seven-foot-long garland of white carnations arranged in the shape of a number "9."

A Marine Corps jet flyover and singing of the national anthem opened the program, which resembled the 1988 Jimmy Fund event at Boston's Wang Center. A revolving collection of friends, admirers, and former teammates sat in chairs by home plate, alongside one of the program's two moderators, ESPN's Peter Gammons and Red Sox play-by-play voice Sean McDonough. Each guest discussed fond memories of Williams, as a person, a ballplayer, or a servant of the Jimmy Fund.

When the testimonials were finished, current and retired Red Sox players walked to left field, surrounded the number "9" made of carnations, and placed their caps over their heads. A lone Marine Corps bugler played the customarily somber rendition of taps, followed by a booming, upbeat, inspirational performance of "God Bless America" from a twenty-two-piece Marine Corps band and former Marine Corps sergeant and Massachusetts state trooper Dan Clark.

Halfway through the program, John Glenn and Jerry Coleman took the field to give fans perspective on Williams's fabled military career.

"I got to know Ted very, very well and the bonds of shared combat do, indeed, run deep," Glenn said. "Baseball excellence may be what Ted will be remembered for by most people. But his dedication to another kind of excellence, as a Marine jet fighter pilot, will be my greatest memory of him."

Like Coleman, Glenn spoke of Williams's near-death experience in crash-landing at K-13, the most famous tale from his service. Glenn also shared his memory of escorting to safety Williams's flaming Panther, its fuel tip-tank pierced by a rock. Far fewer people knew that story. Almost none knew the next story that he told, about pitching shadow batting practice to a group of children in Kyoto, Japan.

"Baseball may have lost one of its greatest, the greatest hitter ever," Glenn concluded. "But our nation lost one of its most dedicated patriots. And Annie and I lost a great friend."

Conspicuously absent from the poignant, heartwarming service at Fenway Park were Claudia, Bobby-Jo, and John-Henry. By that point, seventeen days removed from Williams's death, the public had already seen enough of and heard enough about his children.

The evening of Williams's death the *Boston Globe* received a phone call from an Ohio attorney named John Heer. He had an unbelievable story to tell: Ted Williams's daughter believed that Ted Williams's son had ordered their father's dead body frozen.

Globe science reporter Beth Daley, who had recently returned from reporting in post-9/11 Afghanistan and Pakistan, reluctantly took the assignment. Her first step was to call Bobby-Jo Ferrell. Within a few hours she uncovered a family squabble only complicated by a father's enormous legacy.

"She was both upset about her father dying, her estrangement from him, as well as what she perceived to be her half brother's attempt to kind of steal everything, get everything monetarily, and doing something to her father's body that I think she truly believed shouldn't be done. She was crying half the time," Daley remembered.

Several years earlier John-Henry had become curious about cryonics, the process of freezing human tissue with the purpose of being reanimated at a later date. In time, he and Claudia approached their father about a family pact in which all three of them agreed to be cryogenically frozen upon their deaths, in the hopes that one day they could be together again. The freezing facility John-Henry had chosen was called Alcor Life Extension Foundation, located in Scottsdale, Arizona.

Twice in recent years Williams had unequivocally and formally stated his wishes following his death. In December 1991, just a few weeks after suffering his first stroke, he wrote a letter to his attorney, Robert E. McWalter. He stated that he wanted no funeral, his body to be cremated, and his ashes "sprinkled at sea off the coast of Florida where the water is very deep." An updated last will and testament, signed by Williams five years later, repeated the exact same final request. But after his father's death, John-Henry produced a signed, handwritten, motor oil–stained half sheet of paper, outlining an agreement to be "put in bio-stasis after we die." It was dated November 2, 2000, the same week that Williams rested in Shands Hospital awaiting pacemaker surgery.

The authenticity of Ted Williams's signature and the timing of all three signatures became the source of much speculation.

"There's no way that was done in that hospital room that day," said Frank Brothers, a caretaker present throughout Williams's stay at Shands Hospital. "[Months later] I asked him, 'Ted, if something happens to you, you still want to be cremated and go down to the Keys with Slugger?' And he specifically said, sharp and clear, 'Yes!'"

John-Henry had mentioned the change in plans to several people within his father's inner circle. He told Major General Larry S. Taylor about the pact in San Diego, on their way to visit Williams at Sharp Hospital.

"John-Henry had just come back from his first visit over to Alcor, the freezing facility," Taylor remembered. "He starts telling me about this business. And at first I didn't think he was serious. He started telling me and I realized he's serious about this. I bit my tongue about what I really thought, because if I tell him I think it's nonsense he'll just tune me out altogether. . . . I tried to tell him, if you do this the younger generation won't remember anything about hitting .406 and Hall of Fame, greatest hitter. All they'll remember is that's the old guy that got himself frozen."

Bobby-Jo learned of the Alcor plan from John-Henry in June 2001.

She claimed that he "told me we could sell Daddy's DNA," which greatly disturbed her.

"They thought John-Henry was going to exploit the situation for his own financial gain. That was horrifying to them, just horrifying," John Heer remembered. "I don't think that was a realistic notion, but that's what Bobby-Jo had in her mind from this conversation with John-Henry, that he had apparently said something to the effect of 'Wouldn't it be great to have a bunch of little Ted Williamses running around?'"

According to Heer, John-Henry subsequently shut Bobby-Jo out of her father's life and she never saw him again. In her own 2014 memoirs entitled *Ted Williams, My Father*, Claudia Williams wrote that her father explicitly said that he no longer wanted to see Bobby-Jo. Regardless, in the immediate hours after Williams's death, his eldest child received no information or updates on his status or any arrangements for his remains.

Dr. Richard Kerensky was Williams's cardiologist at the University of Florida. After several years as his physician, Kerensky became close with the Williams family. He accompanied Williams to the 1999 All-Star Game and remained in constant Nextel two-way walkie-talkie contact with John-Henry throughout his father's physical decline. Kerensky saw disaster, but also optimism, within John-Henry's interest in Alcor.

"John-Henry could be difficult but I don't think he was an evil person at all," Kerensky later said. "The whole freezing thing, he showed me that pamphlet when we were eating sushi together a couple years before. And I was like, 'Oh my God, John-Henry, you're gonna be on the cover of *National Enquirer*, you don't want to do this.' I was wrong, he was the lead story on CBS News.

"But there was never any malicious intent there. . . . he felt like every medical condition could be beat with technology. He truly believed that if you're frozen that eventually the technology would get good enough and you could actually rebuild a person with nanotechnology. He was a very smart guy. It's a little bit crazy, but it wasn't anything like trying to make money on it or sell Ted's DNA or all this garbage. I think, in his mind, Ted could get frozen, he could get frozen, and he could have a better childhood than the one he missed out on. That they could have a better father-child relationship than the one they missed out on."

Despite Bobby-Jo's objections, in the minutes following Williams's death on the morning of July 5, 2002, his veins were injected with the anti-clotting drug heparin and his corpse was covered in dry ice. A private jet waiting at Ocala International Airport then flew Williams's body to the Alcor facility in Arizona.

Beth Daley's article in the *Boston Globe* ran the next morning and was picked up by dozens of additional newspapers across the nation, setting off a media firestorm.

"The aftershock was craziness," she recalled. "I remember strongly advocating for it to not be on the front page, because it was so crazy. It was the day he died. . . . From what I recall there were so many freaking phone calls to me, I know I got tons of emails. . . . It really caused a great deal of consternation among all the fans and there's a hell of a lot of them in Boston. People were really up in arms."

In the weeks leading up to the memorial at Fenway Park, the bizarre story of a secret plot to freeze, preserve, and stash away Williams's dead body nearly overshadowed the loving tributes to the sports icon.

Worse yet, the general public lapped up jokes about "Tedsicles." *The Tonight Show with Jay Leno* and *Late Night with David Letterman* poked fun at Williams's frozen status. As part of his trademark segment, Letterman issued a list of "Top Ten Good Things About Being Cryogenically Frozen." Nationally syndicated political cartoonist Jeff Danziger's July 9 sketch featured a man—covered in ice cubes—being wheeled onto the field as the Red Sox "secret weapon" in the final game of the 2015 World Series: "It's Ted Williams, whose [*sic*] been thawing out in a secret Fenway Park basement!" And in the streets of Boston, outside Red Sox home games, vendors sold "Defrost Ted" hats, shirts, and bumper stickers.

Four days after Williams died, with his body already located inside the Alcor facility, Bobby-Jo posted an open letter to a new website (www.TedWilliamsLastWish.org) that she had created for raising funds to stop her half siblings' plan. She asked her father's friends, those who had "knowledge about my daddy's wishes to be cremated, to stand up and be heard at this time."

She also made two direct appeals, one to the President of the United States, George W. Bush, and another to a retired United States senator.

"John Glenn appreciated my Daddy's being his wingman," she wrote. "I want John Glenn to come forward now, and come to his friend's aid. John Glenn, my Daddy desperately needs a wingman right now!"

From his home in Maryland, Glenn steered clear of the controversy by explaining that he had never discussed end-of-life planning with Williams.

"In my visits and conversations with my friend, Ted Williams, we discussed his recovery and living," Glenn said via press release. "We had no conversations regarding his wishes for the handling of his remains. Annie and I continue to grieve the loss of our friend, a friendship that spanned over forty years. Ted Williams above all else loved his family and they loved him as well. I am confident that the bonds of family will guide them to a resolution of this very painful issue."

Even at the Fenway Park memorial, Glenn insisted, "I'm sure they're going to get it worked out. . . . That's up to them, not me."

But a few years later, once the heat of the scandal subsided, Glenn shared his thoughts on the fate of his friend.

"I was surprised at that," he told Ben Bradlee, Jr., in 2004. "But once the life has gone out of the body, I don't care what they do, whether its cremating, freezing or whatever.

"I suppose people will remember that more than baseball or Jimmy Fund," he added. "It might interfere because it's so unusual. . . . Used to be they look down on cremations but now it's a very high number. That's more accepted. Who knows? The likelihood that people will be restored to life doesn't seem high, but does that lessen my admiration for Ted? Not one bit. Who knows what happens in that area (the afterlife) anyway."

———————

The morbid tug-of-war pitting Bobby-Jo against John-Henry and Claudia over their father's remains persisted across months of court filings and hearings. By October, Bobby-Jo could no longer afford the necessary legal fees and she effectively abandoned her challenge of the cryogenics plan. In exchange, Williams's estate fast-tracked her share of the irrevocable trust that her father had established in 1986. She received roughly $200,000 and left Citrus Hills for good.

But the controversy surrounding Ted Williams's final resting place did not end with her signature of that settlement agreement. It only became more gruesome.

In the summer of 2003, *Sports Illustrated* published an exclusive investigation into Alcor's custody of Williams. In his reporting, Tom Verducci, the article's author, discovered that Williams's body "is not resting upside down in a liquid-nitrogen-tank at Alcor, as has been reported. Instead his head is stored in a liquid-nitrogen filled steel can that resembles a lobster pot. . . . His head has been shaved, drilled with holes, accidentally cracked as many as 10 times and moved among three receptacles."

On the evening that his body arrived to Alcor, roughly fifteen hours after his death, Williams's head was detached from his torso as part of the freezing program's "neuroseparation" option. Next, two holes were drilled into the head where sensors were inserted into the brain to detect if any cracks would occur during freezing. The frozen head and frozen torso remained in the Scottsdale facility over the next several months, but Alcor claimed John-Henry Williams had not paid his bill's outstanding balance of $111,000. In Verducci's investigation, he learned that Larry Johnson, Alcor's chief operating officer at the time, taped several discussions with his colleagues, including one in which a board member "joked about 'throwing [Williams's] body away,' posting it on eBay or sending it in a 'frosted cardboard box' C.O.D. to John-Henry's doorstep, to persuade him to pay the bill."

At the same time, Johnson also intended to release via website photographs of Williams's decapitated, drilled, and mangled head, but only for a price. He told *Florida Today* reporter Peter Kerasotis that he needed the money to cover his legal fees. Having resigned from Alcor, Johnson expected his former employer to take legal action against him.

Johnson took the website down after just a few days, then later released his own tell-all about his experiences at Alcor. In the book, Johnson claims that in addition to the Alcor technicians' careless treatment of the body, they took photographs with Williams's head. One employee also allegedly used Williams's head for "batting practice." As Johnson described, the decapitated head had been placed on top of an empty Bumble Bee tuna can so that it would not stick to the bottom of the case. In his attempt to separate the tuna can from the head, Johnson says that the technician bashed it with a monkey wrench.

Even before the publication of Johnson's claims to *Sports Illustrated*, Arthur "Buzz" Hamon went public with horror stories of Alcor.

Hamon had been a close friend as well as the former executive director of the Ted Williams Museum and Hitters Hall of Fame. In February 2003, he told the *New York Daily News* that the final time he spoke with

Williams, he asked for his help in finding a lawyer, claiming "I've made a mistake."

According to Hamon, after Williams's death, he and a friend (a former Phoenix-area mortician) managed to sneak into Alcor. He claimed to have seen very disorganized, unsanitary conditions throughout the facility, before entering a crowded room of cylinders, one of which contained Williams's body.

"All I could think of was Ted and what he would have thought if he'd known what John-Henry had done to him," Hamon said. "It was bad enough knowing that somewhere in one of these cylinders, Ted was hanging suspended, upside down, with his head in a bucket. But he was in there with four or five other bodies and assorted heads."

A day after his piece ran in the print and online editions of *Sports Illustrated*, Tom Verducci appeared on CNN's *American Morning*. After answering questions from host Bill Hemmer about Alcor, Larry Johnson, and cryonics, Verducci offered the final word on his investigation.

"I think you're talking about a diminished legacy," Verducci said. "I think there are generations of kids and young adults who are growing up who now will associate Ted Williams not with baseball, not with the service to his country as a fighter pilot in two wars, but as the guy who was suspended and frozen in time, if you will."

CHAPTER FIFTEEN

Fighter Pilot, Astronaut, US Senator

"I'd rather burn out than rust out."

—eighty-nine-year-old JOHN GLENN

On August 26, 2012, the Cleveland Indians hosted the first-place New York Yankees beneath a beautiful light blue sky at Progressive Field. In the center field bullpen, as he prepared to face a roster that led all of Major League Baseball in home runs that year, Indians starter Ubaldo Jiménez threw dozens of warm-up pitches. A few hundred feet away, in a tunnel beneath the stadium, John Glenn did the same.

To mark half a century since the *Friendship 7* orbital journey, the Indians organization had invited Glenn to throw out the game's ceremonial first pitch. An hour before the 1 p.m. start time Glenn practiced his windup and release by tossing a ball to Ray Lugo, director of the John H. Glenn Research Center. Renamed to honor Glenn in March 1999, the NASA facility stood across the street from the runway at Cleveland's Hopkins International Airport.

His ninety-one-year-old muscles loosened, Glenn rested in the home team dugout, where a collection of baseball writers sat with him.

"There were a number of people who wanted to talk to him," remembered Sweeny Murti, a forty-two-year-old New York reporter covering the Yankees. "I just remember the awe of *'that's John Glenn.'* It's hard for me to get starstruck in the job that I do. I spent fourteen years around Derek Jeter and Mariano Rivera. People walk in and out of Yankee Stadium all the time and I've been around plenty of famous sports stars. This was just something different. It was Beatle-esque to me. I was in *his* orbit."

One of the reporters naturally asked Glenn about the baseball hero who had now been gone more than ten years.

"Ted was a good friend," Glenn said. "I got to know Ted pretty well and we had a great time. After we came back [from Korea] we kept in touch. And when he was sick and got in trouble, we visited several times in the hospital and at his home in Florida."

With game time approaching, Glenn walked toward the mound. From just in front of the rubber, he set and reared back. Throwing underhand, much like he had decades earlier during a March softball game at K-3, he landed the ball just a few feet short of home plate. Indians first base coach Sandy Alomar, Jr., caught the pitch, gave the ball back to Glenn, then the two posed for a photograph.

"That was a thrill for me," said Alomar. "He said 'Can you sign me the baseball?' I was thinking, 'Maybe you should sign it for me.' I can't wait to get that picture."

Although he had long since left the Senate, and did not have any schemes for a third space mission, Glenn kept exceedingly busy in retirement.

He attended NASA and military celebrations, such as the retirement of the space shuttle *Discovery* and the christening of the USNS *John Glenn*, a 785-foot Navy mobile landing platform ship moored in Southern California.

Closer to his Ohio home, Glenn worked with the political school that he helped establish at nearby Ohio State University in 2006. The John Glenn Institute for Public Service and Public Policy, he insisted, would not be "a Republican college or a Democratic college. Quite the opposite of that. It's going to be what we hope will be the best college of studies of government and policy of any place in the country."

And although he detested personal attacks and negative campaign advertisements—"People intend to believe the worst and not the better, unfortunately"—Glenn continued to engage in politics. He campaigned for Democrats such as Senate candidate Sherrod Brown and gubernatorial candidate Ted Strickland and attended the party's national convention every four years. When Democratic candidates for president, such as Senator John Kerry in 2004 and Senators Hillary Clinton and Barack Obama in 2008, came through Ohio, he traveled with them. In the final month of the 2008 election cycle, Glenn spoke at an Obama-sponsored voter registration drive at Ohio State University, then yielded the stage to the event's entertainment, rock star Bruce Springsteen.

"It's not every day you get introduced by John Glenn," said Springsteen, who broke into a guitar riff of the Byrds' 1966 hit "Mr. Spaceman."

As president, Obama met with Glenn on several occasions, most notably during a May 2012 ceremony in the East Room. Twenty-one years after Ted Williams received the Presidential Medal of Freedom from George H. W. Bush—the Republican primary candidate he endorsed at events across New Hampshire—Glenn received the same honor from a candidate for whom he had once stumped.

Despite such a packed post-retirement schedule, he and Annie made time to travel together. Without any specific destination or hotel reservations, they took a cross-country trip in his green Cadillac, covering more than eight thousand miles before returning home. And even into his late eighties, Glenn still piloted his Beechcraft Baron. Annie sat next to him on flights between their homes in Maryland and Ohio, to skiing trips in Vail, and to visit family and friends.

But given his age, his pilot's insurance carrier required Glenn to receive annual recertification training. During Bonanza Pilot Proficiency Program weekend seminars at Port Columbus Airport, retired Navy Captain Kent Ewing served as his instructor each time. Annie also took the program's "companion" course.

On their lengthy flights together, Glenn entertained Captain Ewing with tales of early NASA experiments in the centrifuge, test pilot work at Patuxent River, and hunting MiGs over the Yalu River. And he told Ewing about flying with Ted Williams.

"He said he was probably one of the best stick-and-throttles he's ever flown with, a guy who could do anything with the airplane," Ewing recalled. "He did say Ted Williams was one of the best pilots he'd ever known, but he was constantly trying to get him in trouble. . . . He said he almost got him court-martialed once."

There remained, however, no cure for the common birthday. Not long after turning ninety, Glenn finally sold the thirty-year-old Baron and permanently gave up flying. A few years later, he suffered a stroke and also needed surgery to replace a heart valve. The stroke, coupled with macular degeneration, cost him much of his eyesight and he could no longer read.

"Annie was a severe stutterer until she was in her 60s and got some therapy that corrected that, so I used to have to read to her," he said.

"So now I can read to him," Annie interjected. "It's wonderful."

"It's not so wonderful to me," he said, laughing.

Despite his declining health, Glenn kept making public appearances.

In late June 2016, he attended a renaming ceremony inside Port Columbus Airport. The place from where he said goodbye to Annie, Lyn, and David before leaving for the Korean War would soon be called John Glenn Columbus International Airport.

"It's quite a thing to have a big-city airport named after you," he said from a podium with his cane hanging from it.

In early December of that year, he was admitted to the James Cancer Hospital at Ohio State University. For weeks, Glenn had been planning to attend a day-after-Pearl-Harbor commemoration at Muskingum University. The ceremony, entitled "A Call to Service: A Remembrance," was held within Brown Chapel, the exact place he and Annie had been driving to seventy-five years earlier when they learned of the Japanese attack. But on December 8, 2016, John Hershel Glenn, Jr., the last surviving member of the Mercury Seven, passed away at the age of ninety-five.

There was a public ceremony to honor him at Ohio State University, but his body would not be buried just yet, and not in his beloved home state. Glenn belonged to the entire nation.

On the morning of April 6, 2017, through a steady downpour, seven wet horses slowly pulled a black wooden caisson decorated with silver stars and golden wheel hubs. Atop it sat a simple, unadorned casket carrying the body of Colonel Glenn dressed in his traditional Marine Service Alpha uniform. Led by the Caisson Platoon of the Old Guard and six soaking members of the Marine Corps' Body Bearers Unit, a few dozen friends with umbrellas trailed behind the caisson, as did a black stretch limousine. They all proceeded toward Glenn's final resting place at Arlington National Cemetery in Virginia.

Before the graveside service, the small crowd, including ninety-seven-year-old Annie, sat in Old Post Chapel for a brief ceremony. Marine Corps Commandant General Robert B. Neller spoke in depth of Glenn's military service during World War II and Korea. That prompted Senator Rob Portman, the Republican occupying the seat that Glenn had once held, to remark, "He was a hero long before he orbited the Earth."

The United States Navy Band Sea Chanters quartet closed the service with "Amazing Grace" and "The Lord's Prayer," followed by a lone Marine Corps bugler's customary rendition of taps. But prior to his death, Glenn had requested his funeral not end on such a somber note.

Instead, the bugler surprised the mourners by belting out reveille, the booming, upbeat, inspirational tune that awakens soldiers, sailors, and pilots every morning.

"[That was] so like John," said Connie Shultz, a close friend in attendance. "He was such a curious man, such an optimist. He would greet the ending of his life—which he knew was coming—with that optimism. He couldn't wait to see what would come next."

Epilogue

"He liked him, he trusted him, and he cared for him because they were buddies over there, trusting each other. . . . They were very different, but that may be part of what makes friendships."

—Dr. David Glenn

John Glenn was modest, measured, and above all loyal, loyal to his Presbyterian faith, his nation, the Democratic Party, his children, and his wife of seventy-three years, Annie. Ted Williams was a cocky, moody, foulmouthed agnostic, an unwavering Republican who had three ex-wives, multiple mistresses, and three children whom he only saw when it was convenient.

The two also sounded and looked totally different.

Williams spoke in a loud, boisterous twang that echoed John Wayne, or as Williams said, John Wayne echoed him. The monotone, soft-spoken Glenn rarely raised his voice above library decibels.

In their youths, Williams—tall, lean, and handsome with wavy black hair—towered over the much shorter Glenn, whose pug face and fading, reddish crew cut screamed "Marine." And while Glenn, still in exceptional health, spent a portion of his late seventies training for a second NASA mission in outer space, three strokes left Williams frail and dependent on caretakers at roughly the same age.

Even their deaths reflected two discordant fates.

Regardless of the legal, moral, and ethical questions surrounding his last wishes for his remains, the perpetual controversy following Ted Williams's death cheated him out of a dignified end. Instead, Williams's farewell was marred by family turmoil, lawsuits, and court hearings, greed and deception, and macabre, unthinkable rumors of mutilation. John Glenn, on the other hand, received in death a solemn yet hopeful sendoff at his country's most hallowed resting place, Arlington National Cemetery.

But Glenn and Williams were not quite as different as they seemed. Sure, they had polar opposite paths to K-3 in February 1953: Glenn desperate to serve, Williams desperate to avoid service. They also had divergent paths away from K-3 five months later: Glenn leaving to battle head-to-head with Communist MiGs as part of the Air Force, Williams returning to the U.S. to battle American League pitchers. Still, both were good-hearted patriots who served their country and genuinely cared about others, be they life-long friends or perfect strangers. Despite the scandals following his death in 2002, that part of Ted Williams's legacy remains intact. John Glenn's was never in question.

Each was also fixated on the intricate—and, to outsiders, trivial—details of their passions. For Williams, that applied to hitting a curveball, eyeing mallards soaring above a rice paddy, and tying the perfect fly to his fishing rod. To Glenn, that applied to piloting an aircraft, at either twenty thousand feet above the ground or from within the Earth's orbit, and negotiating a nuclear non-proliferation treaty.

After his retirement from baseball, Williams visited Red Sox spring training at a time when space race news routinely plastered front pages. On the field at Scottsdale Stadium in Arizona, he repeatedly talked his former colleagues' ears off about the astronaut he personally knew.

"Williams called Glenn 'the most dedicated man I've ever met,'" Red Sox scout Charlie Wagner remembered. "He used to say to me, 'you know how baseball people talk baseball, Charlie—well, Glenn talked flying the same way. With him it was a 24-hour a day job.'"

The man who literally wrote the book on *The Science of Hitting* could appreciate Glenn's obsessive nature.

For both men, those obsessions also had a habit of getting in the way, despite all they achieved. Glenn squandered a good shot at his party's presidential nomination due to a stubborn fixation with nuance and minutiae, something that also cost Williams dearly in his relationships with those closest to him.

"He put family life aside," Williams biographer Ben Bradlee, Jr., noted. "Anything he undertook he wanted to do right. He was a perfectionist and he had no tolerance for those who did things in what he felt were a shoddy manner. And he was in a zone, really, his entire life. And when you're in a zone like that you can break a lot of china along the way."

Williams ducked the media throughout his entire baseball career. He disliked almost every local sportswriter and, after fans booed him during his rookie season, refused (for half a century) to address the crowd's cheers with a tip of his cap. But Williams repeatedly said, "All I want out of life is that when I walk down the street folks will say 'There goes the greatest hitter who ever lived.'" Williams accepted and encouraged the recognition of his talents and hard work, even if he wouldn't acknowledge it.

So from the moment John Glenn's *Friendship 7* space capsule safely fell from orbit, splashing down in the Atlantic Ocean, he and Ted Williams also shared the crushing weight and unceasing burden of celebrity. Not many people whom Williams or Glenn ever encountered could appreciate being so compelled, so accomplished, so exceptional that they were on a first-name basis with an entire country, let alone much of the civilized world.

It was only natural for the man celebrated by millions as the greatest hitter who ever lived to sense a connection to the greatest aviator who ever lived and the standard bearer for space exploration. And vice-versa. They both understood that their gifts and rabid pursuit of excellence came with a price: fame. How they handled that fame was a different story.

The intersection of John Glenn and Ted Williams did not alter the course of world history. It did not even change the military, baseball, politics, space travel, or any of the avenues that either pursued. But it did change two men who, in a way, changed the world.

Glenn's relationship with Williams did not influence his path to NASA, the Senate, or a permanent place in the pantheon of American heroes. Likewise, Glenn's presence in Williams's life did not make him a great ballplayer or icon of professional sports. He was already both by the time the two met. But they weren't just friends, and they certainly weren't just two ships passing in the night.

They truly admired each other. There's something to be said about a titan who reveres another titan.

Several generations have worshipped Ted Williams. Young kids, Hall of Fame ballplayers, the secretary of the Navy, an Air Force colonel on an active military runway in a foreign country less than fifty miles from a hostile enemy, all idolized Ted Williams. Ted Williams idolized John Glenn, in 1953, in 1962, in 1988, in 1998, and prior to his death in 2002.

John Glenn did not *idolize* Ted Williams, but there is a uniqueness about his affection for the man he called "an excellent combat pilot, a great patriot, and a close friend." Glenn often sat with presidents, foreign heads of state, corporate CEOs, generals and admirals, and intrepid, death-defying explorers. And he befriended the greatest hitter of all time, but that title is not why he liked and respected Williams. "Ted only batted .406 in 1941," Glenn told the crowd at Boston's Wang Center in 1988. "He batted 1.000 for the Marines and the United States of America." Other than his family and close friends, the Marine Corps and the United States of America were most near and dear to Glenn's heart. For all the personality conflicts—moral, political, social—he may have had with Williams, because of that 1.000 batting average Williams would always occupy a special place in Glenn's memory.

The day after John Glenn died in December 2016, politicians, service members, astronomers, celebrities, journalists, and ordinary fans all offered recollections of and praise for the legendary American. Most of them included the phrase "Godspeed, John Glenn," a throwback to the famous words fellow Mercury astronaut Scott Carpenter told his friend ten seconds before *Friendship 7* lifted off the ground at Cape Canaveral.

On his blog, award-winning columnist and author Joe Posnanski shared a different kind of tribute.

Prefaced with "[I] don't know if it's true. I want it to be true. The basics of the story seem to be true," Posnanski painted a vivid portrait of an anecdote he once heard about John Glenn and Ted Williams.

> "Supposedly they were once at an event of some sort, and Williams was off after a while ranting about something or other. When Ted got ranting about whatever the topic— whether it was baseball, fishing or the decline of the United States of America—there was no stopping him, no slowing him down. He was a runaway freight train, and whatever or whoever got in his way just got run over. That's because Ted Williams was the biggest man in every room he ever entered. . . .

"'Ted,' John Glenn said at some point as the conversation grew a bit too loud and profane and fierce.

"'Listen here I'm trying to finish this,' Williams said. 'When I . . .'

"'Ted,' John Glenn said again, this time with a little bit of bite in his voice.

"And Ted Williams looked at his old friend. John Glenn was a few inches shorter than Williams, and his voice was considerably softer, and if he ever swore it sure as heck wasn't in public. He was a square guy from Ohio who married his high school sweetheart, who once told the Mercury Astronauts to stop messing around on their wives, who once said after flying 'To look out at this creation and not believe in God is, to me, impossible.'

"Ted Williams looked at ol' Magnet Ass, and he just stopped. He understood. For once, he was looking at the biggest man in the room.

"'Awright,' he said quietly as he settled down. 'I can't compete with a bleeping American hero.'"

If anyone could humble Ted Williams, it was John Glenn. Although it's a safe bet that Williams used a more colorful word than "bleeping."

Appendix

United States Marine Corps VMF-311,
Based at K-3, Pohang, South Korea
February through July 1953

Commanding Officer (Feb. 1 to Apr. 20)
Coss, Lt. Col. Francis K.

Commanding Officer (Apr. 21 to May 31)
Executive Officer (Jan. 20 to Apr. 20)
Moran, Lt. Col. Arthur M.

Commanding Officer (June 1 to July 27)
McShane, Lt. Col. Bernard

Executive Officer (June 1 to July 2)
Skinner, Maj. John, Jr.

Executive Officer (July 3 to July 27)
Heier, Maj. William D.

Officers:
Armagost, Capt. William I.
Austin, Capt. Marshall S.
Bailes, Capt. Joe D.
Bruce, Maj. Ronald L.
Brothers, 2nd Lt. William Q., Jr.
Brown, Capt. Rowland C.W.
Brown, Capt. William P.
Campbell, Capt. Jack W., Jr.

Canan, Maj. Christopher M.

Carruthers, Capt. Joseph N.

Catlett, Lt. (JG) George F., Jr. (Navy Medical Officer)

Clabaugh, 2nd Lt. John W., Jr.

Clem, Capt. William B.

Cushman, Maj. Thomas J., Jr.

Day, 1st Lt. Marvin E.

Dennis, Capt. Harrel J.

Dochterman, Maj. Lloyd B., Jr.

Durnford, Capt. Dewey F., Jr.

Euster, 1st Lt. Jerold P.

Fauchier, Capt. Clifford E.

Fournier, 1st Lt. Willard D.

Fox, Maj. James G.

Glenn, Maj. John H., Jr.

Hagans, Capt. Harold F.

Harrison, Maj. Patrick

Haping, 1st Lt. Donald G.

Hawkins, 1st Lt. Lawrence R.

Heiland, 2nd Lt. John F.

Helms, Capt. Jonee L.

Hendershot, Capt. Jerry N.

Heintz, 1st Lt. William H.

Himes, Capt. John W.

Hollenbeck, Maj. Marvin K.

Hollowell, Capt. Forris M.

Jablonski, 2nd Lt. Raymond C.

Janssen, 1st Lt. Paul G.

Keck, 1st Lt. Frank L., Jr.

Kurtz, Capt. Francis D.

Lovette, Capt. Lenhrew E.

Magill, Maj. James H.

McGraw, Capt. William C., Jr.

Massey, Capt. William W.

McPherson, 1st Lt. Robert W.

Mendes, Maj. Jonathan D.

Milt, Maj. Jack W.

Mitchell, Maj. Joseph A.

Miller, 1st Lt. Robert E.

Montague, Capt. Paul B.

Moret, Maj. Alfred T., Jr.

Murdoch, Capt. James G.

Nettleton, 1st Lt. Russell W.

Newendrop, Capt. Arthur W.

Nordell, Capt. Robert I.

Parrish, 1st Lt. Darold D.

Peine, Maj. Robert H.

Petersen, Capt. Conrad H.

Ritchie, Capt. John A.

Ross, Capt. Walter L., III

Rudy, 1st Lt. Rylen B.

Sabot, Maj. Robert

Sample, 1st Lt. Edward J.

Schuerman, Capt. Mervyn T.

Schlage, 1st Lt. Raymond P., Jr.

Scott, Capt. Lee L., Jr.

Smith, Capt. Floyd

Spencer, 1st Lt. Richard T.

Stephens, Capt. Glenn A.

Street, Capt. Charles E., Jr.

Traut, 1st Lt. Earl W.

Verdi, 1st Lt. John M.

Wade, Capt. Robert

Walley, Maj. James M.

Whitefield, Capt. Melvin L.

Whitney, 1st Lt. Robert L.

Williams, Capt. Theodore S.

Young, Capt. Robert J.

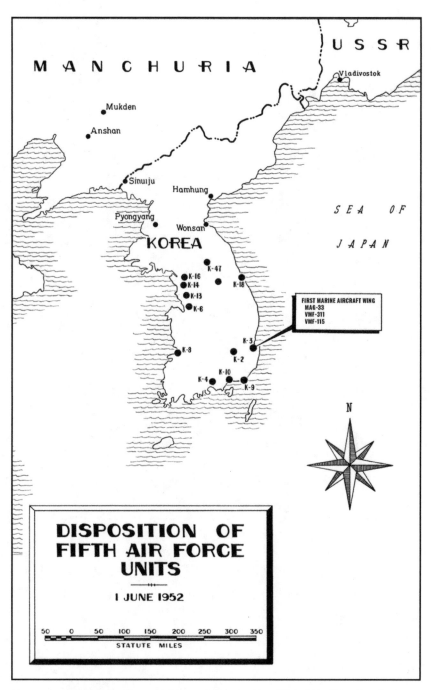

Map courtesy of the United States Air Force; edited by Lara Laughlin Tolchin, Ebb + Flow Design.

Acknowledgments

Someone in the publishing industry once told me, and I'm paraphrasing, that no one cares about your Acknowledgments section other than the people mentioned in it.

I'm sure that's true, but it totally misses the point. I believe the Acknowledgments section exists for that exact reason.

Nevertheless, there's wisdom in that largely cynical aforementioned statement so I'll keep this as brief as possible.

My wife, Sarah, and my parents, Dr. Hillard and Joan Lazarus, deserve top billing as always here. And this time around I'll add my two boys, Aaron and Benny, who showed great interest in this subject. Aaron especially enjoyed tales of the astronaut and cross-country-sound-barrier-breaking pilot; Benny, tales of the man who during one whole season got four hits for every ten at-bats.

But the rest of my thanks belong to this list of individuals, without whose generous efforts this story would never have made it to the page:

My dedicated agent at Aevitas Creative Management, Justin Brouck-aert, and esteemed political reporter at the *Atlanta Journal-Constitution* Greg Bluestein; my editor, Denise Silvestro, and the entire staff at Citadel Press; my Kenyon College Lords football teammates Kris Cheney, Tom Giberson, Mike Ferzoco, and especially Major Benjamin Van Horrick, USMCR; my brother Jeff Lazarus, my mother-in-law, Betsy Gard, and uncle James Siegelman; Alejandra Jaramillo Ariza; Carly Dearborn at Ohio State University, Alyson K. Mazzone at the Marine Corps History Division, Nicholas Herold at the National Archives and Records Administration, Hal and Ted Barker of the Korean War Project, and André Sobocinski at the U.S. Navy Bureau of Medicine and Surgery; Chris Conley, Dr. Richard P. Hallion, Major General Larry S. Taylor, USMCR (ret.), Fred Gaudelli, Bill Nowlin, and Ben Bradlee, Jr.; Lyn Glenn, Dr. David Glenn, Claudia Williams, Barbara Clem Alvarez, Kathy Moran Truitt,

Robin Campbell, Jay Campbell IV, Dr. Fred Miser, John I. Hense, Jr., Cindy Gregoire, Robin Merriman, and all the relatives of those who served at K-3 in the winter and spring of 1953.

Others certainly made great contributions to my research, interviewing, writing, editing, etc. But these men and women really went above and beyond, and for that I am forever grateful.

Notes

Epigraph

vii   ***"Fighter formation flying"*** "MARINE FIGHTING SQUADRON
      TWO HUNDRED EIGHTEEN: SQUADRON DOCTRINE,"
      courtesy of the John H. Glenn Archives at the Ohio State University,
      Box 14, Folder 20, Location 01-8-26-09-04-0-1, p. 5.

Author's Note

ix   ***"The word is particularly"*** "A Pocket Guide to Korea," 1 September
     1950, Armed Forces Information & Education Division, Office of
     the Secretary Defense, Courtesy of University of Illinois at Urbana-
     Champaign, p. 34–35

Prologue

1   ***"greatest team in 25"*** "Muskie Eleven Seen School's 'Greatest Team In
    25 Years,'" *East Liverpool (OH) Review*, November 18, 1939.

1   ***"got a little out of line"*** The John H. Glenn, Jr., Oral History Project,
    Oral History Interview 4, Brien R. Williams, December 12, 1996, p. 14.

1   ***"I didn't have to peek to"*** The John H. Glenn, Jr., Oral History Project,
    Oral History Interview 4, Brien R. Williams, December 12, 1996, p.
    14.

2   ***"I enjoyed it"*** The John H. Glenn, Jr., Oral History Project, Oral
    History Interview 4, Brien R. Williams, December 12, 1996, p. 4.

2   ***"Welcome to the War!"*** Correspondence with Chris Conley, November
    22, 2021.

3   ***"daring, skill, and fearless"*** Headquarters U.S. Marine Corps,
    Citation: Distinguished Flying Cross to Second Lieutenant Robert F.
    Conley, USMCR, Circa September 1943.

3   ***"About then my gunner"*** "Capt. Conley Back in States After 7 Months
    at Guadalcanal," *Daily Jeffersonian (OH)*, November 20, 1943.

3   ***"We are not at war"* . . . *"United Nations"*** "The President's News
         Conference, June 29, 1950," Courtesy of the Harry S. Truman
         Presidential Library and Museum.

3   ***"truce tents"*** "Still Panmunjom," *New York Times*, December 16, 1951.

4   ***"The Marine Corps for the"*** "55,000 Draft Call Set For February," *New
         York Times*, December 9, 1951.

4   ***"individuals that desired"*** Ernest H. Guisti, *Mobilization of the Marine
         Corps Reserve in the Korean Conflict 1950–1951* (1951), Historical
         Branch, G-3 Division, Headquarters, U.S. Marine Corps, Washington,
         D.C., 20380, p. 34.

5   ***"We called up a lot"*** Ed Leach, "Visiting Marine Made Honorary
         Texan," *Longview (TX) Morning Journal*, September 9, 1973.

5   ***"Assignment to extended active"*** Letter written by the Commandant
         of the Marine Corps to Captain Theodore S. Williams, April 9, 1952,
         Freedom of Information Act.

5   ***"What are you doing?"*** Chris Conley written memoirs of Robert F.
         Conley, Sr., received March 7, 2021.

CHAPTER ONE: From Fenway to Fighter Jets

7   ***"I don't care whether"*** "Williams Denies Spitting at Fans," *Fort Myers
         News-Press*, March 20, 1951.

7   ***"Breaking into a tantrum"*** Dick Farrington, "Fancy That," *St. Louis
         Post-Dispatch*, March 20, 1951.

8   ***"[Soon] a few critics began"*** Roger Birtwell, "Ted's Age an Obstacle to
         Sox Trading Effort," *Boston Globe*, December 11, 1951.

8   ***"As far as I'm concerned"*** "Open for Trades, Says New Leader," *New
         York Times*, October 23, 1951.

8   ***"We would be a sucker"*** "Yanks May Want Williams Now," *Boston
         Globe*, December 11, 1951.

9   ***"Fishing is how I relax"*** Joe Richler, "Ted Guards His Private Life,
         Loves Flycasting Audience," *Miami News*, June 23, 1950.

9   ***"fashionable"*** Jimmy Burns, "Spotlighting Sports," *Miami Herald*,
         January 10, 1952.

9   ***"Having spent my entire major"*** Arthur Simpson, "Ted Tickled He's
         Staying; Rolfe Sees Big '52 for Him," *Boston Herald*, December1 9,
         1951.

10 *"the field artillery"* Harold Kaese, "Teddy Rates Another Exam," *Boston Globe*, January 14, 1952,

10 *"slacker and draft dodger"* Ralph McGill, "One More Word," *Atlanta Constitution*, March 8, 1942.

10 *"I'm no slacker"* Bill Cunningham, "'I'm No Slacker,'"*Liberty*, April 25, 1942.

11 *"fresh and chesty"* George A. Barton, "Sport Graphs," *Minnesota Morning Tribune*, November 4, 1942.

11 *"He did not pull sufficient"* Bob Husted, "The Referee," *Dayton Herald*, November 4, 1942.

11 *"Why, if Ted had only hustled"* Burt Whitman, "Ted Williams Misses A.L. Award," *Boston Herald*, November 4, 1942.

11 *"I have to think the reason"* Ted Williams with John Underwood, *My Turn at Bat* (New York: A Fireside Book Published by Simon & Schuster, 1988), p. 96.

12 *"The ball players go"* Harold Kaese, "Neophyte Flyer Faces Big Grind Getting Wings,"*Boston Globe*, December 5, 1942.

12 *"Flying is the last thing"* Bill King, "Ted Williams Bats High as Navy Flier," *Philadelphia Inquirer*, December 2, 1942.

12 *"Yellow Peril"* Carl Leiter, "Williams: Player, Soldier," *Kokomo Tribune*, November 5, 1994.

12 *"You can tell from the way"* "Aviation Cadet Ted Williams Wins, Big Sendoff at Bunker Hill," *Indianapolis Star*, December 7, 1943.

13 *"He had a great touch"* Gail Rippey, "He Taught This Star to Soar," *Lancaster Sunday News*, July 7, 2002.

13 *"Once he came up to my right"* John Vellante, "Veteran Recalls Flying Days with Ted Williams," *Boston Globe*, July 28, 2002.

13 *"From what I heard"* Ed Linn, *Hitter: The Life and Turmoils of Ted Williams* (San Diego: Harcourt Brace, 1994), p. 247.

14 *"They told me when I"* Henry Berry, *Hey, Mac, Where Ya Been?* (New York: St. Martin's Press, 1988), p. 291.

15 *"As far as Uncle Sam"* Frank Eidge, Jr., "Ted Seems Unconcerned at Recall That Could End His Career," *Pensacola Journal*, January 11, 1952.

15 *"I resented the way they"* Austen Lake, "Ted's War Grows," *Boston Evening American*, April 2, 1957.

15   *"if you could tell me how I"* Letter written by Carol Leavitt to Mr. Harry S. Truman, April 9, 1952, Freedom of Information Act.

15   *"What earthly use can"* Austen Lake, "Whisper Grows the Marines Will '4-F' Ted," *Boston Evening American*, March 24, 1952.

16   *"With Williams out the Red"* Joe Levine, "7 Bone Chips Removed from Williams' Arm," *Miami News*, July 13, 1950.

17   *"With more temper than tact"* Joe Reichler, "The Williams I Know," *Sport*, February 1966.

17   *"no significant limitations"* Hy Hurwitz, "Williams Believes He Will Play When Service Ends," *Boston Globe*, April 3, 1952.

17   *"I'm 49, and I'm a pilot"* Hy Hurwitz, "Williams Believes He Will Play When Service Ends," *Boston Globe*, April 3, 1952.

17   *"negligible"* Hy Hurwitz, "Elbow 'Weather Ache' Considered Not Unusual," *Boston Globe*, April 1, 1952.

17   *"when they told Williams"* Author interview with David Fisher, November 29, 2021.

17   *"purely personal"* Letter written by General Lemuel C. Shepard, Jr., to Ted Williams, May 22, 1952, courtesy of the personal archives of Ben Bradlee, Jr.

18   *"Naturally I feel greatly"* "Wednesday 'Ted's Day' at Fenway," *Lowell Sun*, April 27, 1952.

18   *"a miracle"* "'Miracle' If Ted Returns," *Washington Daily*, January 10, 1952.

18   *"If the Marines want me"* Frank Eck, "Ted Williams Will Quit Baseball If Recalled by Marines," *Elizabethton (TN) Star*, March 30, 1952.

18   *"If I pass the examination"* Larry Claflin, "Calls Swamp Office; Fans Sorry for Ted," *Boston American*, April 2, 1952.

18   *"Why don't you write"* Arthur Simpson, "Teddy Passes Physical, Says He's All Through as Ball Player," *Boston Herald*, April 3, 1952.

18   *"I don't know whether"* "Ted Uncertain of Baseball Future on Eve of Departure for Marines," *Newport (RI) Daily News*, April 30, 1952.

19   *"I'm speaking for the guys"* Jack McCarthy, "Auld Lang Syne Affects Happy, Trembling Teddy," *Boston Herald*, May 1, 1952.

19   *"I might let some kids play"* "Ted Jokes About Ball Given by Writers," *Boston Globe*, May 1, 1952.

19   **"Some wagon!"** Pres Hobson, "He Planned the Hat," *Patriot Ledger*, May 1, 1952.

19   **"It's a day I'll long remember"** "Grand Farewell to Ted," *Cincinnati Enquirer*, May 1, 1952.

19   **"never acknowledge their"** Jerry Nason, "Most Dramatic Man Any of Us Will See on a Baseball Field," *Boston Globe*, May 1, 1952.

20   **"that lanky body twisted around"** *Baseball: A Film by Ken Burns*, "Inning 6: The National Pastime," Ken Burns, PBS Home Video, 2004.

20   **"Everyone in the stands"** "Fan Gives Williams Home Run Ball," *Boston Globe*, May 1, 1952.

20   **"They can talk all"** Mike Gillooly, "Ted Refuses to Say Career Ended," *Boston American*, May 1, 1952.

20   **"It seems that the fans"** George C. Carens, "Ted Tops Day Playing Host," *Boston Traveler*, May 1, 1952.

21   **"Ted, try to get into jets"** Henry Berry, *Hey, Mac, Where Ya Been?* (New York: St. Martin's Press, 1988), p. 292.

22   **"That made a lot of sense"** Henry Berry, *Hey, Mac, Where Ya Been?* (New York: St. Martin's Press, 1988), p. 292.

22   **"At first they couldn't find"** Henry Berry, *Hey, Mac, Where Ya Been?* (New York: St. Martin's Press, 1988), p. 293.

22   **"mock assault"** "Marines Plan Mock Assault," *Charlotte Observer*, November 7, 1952.

23   **"Flying right now is"** Bob Quincy, "Williams Is a Worker, but He Doesn't Study Flying All the Time," *Charlotte News*, July 23, 1952.

23   **"I didn't want that"** Bob Quincy, "Williams Is a Worker, But He Doesn't Study Flying All the Time," *Charlotte News*, July 23, 1952.

23   **"He came to us inadequately"** Arthur M. Moran, unpublished memoir, 1988.

23   **"shoot landings"** Bob Quincy, "He Takes Instruction Well, Say Those Who Watch Him in Action," *Charlotte News*, July 21, 1952.

23   **"navigational computor"** "The Captain Was the Kid (Caption)," *Charlotte News*, July 22, 1952.

23   **"Dilbert Dunker"** Bud Johns, "Capt. Ted Says 'Sox Have Stuff to Take It,'" *Sporting News*, July 16, 1952.

24   **"Sure, it was rough"** Bob Quincy, "Williams Is a Worker, but He Doesn't Study Flying All the Time," *Charlotte News*, July 23, 1952.

24   *"I'm losing two very important"* Whitey Martin, "Ted Williams Uncertain About Baseball Future," *Asheville Citizen Times*, September 12, 1952.

24   *"I can handle one"* Bob Quincy, "Ted Williams Says Baseball Helps in Switch to Jet Pilot," *Boston Herald*, July 29, 1952.

24   *"Outstanding" . . . "Endurance" . . . "Cooperation"* Official Fitness Reports, United States Marine Corps, Completed July 28, 1952, and August 31, 1952, Freedom of Information Act.

24   *"a fine young officer"* Official Fitness Report, United States Marine Corps, Completed July 28, 1952, Freedom of Information Act.

25   *"compared with the First World War"* Darrell Garwood, "Korean War Proving Costliest in United States History," *New Journal and Guide*, December 6, 1952.

26   *"I think I could play baseball"* Jeane Hoffman, "Korea-Bound Ted Quit for Sure if Sox Trade Him," *Los Angeles Times*, January 3, 1953.

26   *"no one can throw a fastball"* David Halberstam, *Summer of '49* (New York: First Perennial Classics, 2002), p. 191.

26   *"I'd jettison my tanks"* Bob Quincy, "He Takes Instruction Well, Say Those Who Watch Him in Action," *Charlotte News*, July 21, 1952.

26   *"sliding in"* "Ted May Rejoin Sox in April (Caption)," *Boston Globe*, August 28, 1952.

26   *"I really enjoy it"* Whitey Martin, "Ted Williams Uncertain About Baseball Future," *Asheville Citizen Times*, September 12, 1952.

26   *"Then he said—and this"* Frank Graham, "Graham's Corner," *New York Journal-American*, March 26, 1953.

CHAPTER TWO: My Life's Work

27   *"You could hear 'Bud'"* "'The John Glenn Story': A Redhead Named Bud . . . ," *Zanesville (OH) Times Recorder*, March 3, 1962.

27   *"the most curious little"* "Says Glenn 'Curious,'" *Mansfield (OH) News-Journal*, March 1, 1962.

28   *"Vultee Vibrator"* "Restoring Derelict Plane," *Corpus Christi Caller Times*, February 18, 1967.

28   *"flying boat"* NOAA National Marine Sanctuaries, "Rare Images Reveal Details of U.S. Navy Seaplane Lost in Pearl Harbor Attack," *Honolulu Star Advertiser*, December 18, 2015.

29   *"The Placid Plodder . . ."* Ev Hoskins, "Those Fabulous Gooney Birds," *Long Beach (CA) Independent*, October 4, 1970.

29   *"They had a very decided"* "WWII—'War Diary' of Marshall Islands, January-February 1945," courtesy of the John H. Glenn Archives at the Ohio State University, Box 14, Folder 8, Location 01-8-26-09-04-0-1, p. 5.

29   *"a small, fast ship that really gives"* "WWII—'War Diary' of Marshall Islands, January-February 1945," courtesy of the John H. Glenn Archives at the Ohio State University, Box 14, Folder 8, Location 01-8-26-09-04-0-1, p. 5.

29   *"unquestionably the best carrier"* "U.S. Lags in Fighter Planes, OWI Says, But Our Bombers Are Best in Their Fields," *St. Louis Post-Dispatch*, October 19, 1942.

29   *"Anytime John gets his sights"* Frank Van Riper, *Glenn: The Astronaut Who Would Be President* (New York: Empire Books, 1983), p. 94.

29   *"I've never been dressed down"* John Glenn with Nick Taylor, *John Glenn: A Memoir* (New York: Random House, 2000), pp. 110–111

30   *"Sniveling, among pilots"* "The Nation," *Time*, March 2, 1962, p. 16.

30   *"It is one of the finest"* "WWII—'War Diary' of Marshall Islands, January-February 1945," courtesy of the John H. Glenn Archives at the Ohio State University, Box 14, Folder 8, Location 01-8-26-09-04-0-1, p. 13–14.

31   *"[I] fed the fishes twice"* "WWII—'War Diary' of Marshall Islands, January-February 1945," courtesy of the John H. Glenn Archives at the Ohio State University, Box 14, Folder 8, Location 01-8-26-09-04-0-1, p. 21.

31   *"On strafing runs we generally"* Peter B. Germano, "Is Bombardier As Well as Pilot," *Zanesville (OH) Times Recorder*, January 23, 1945.

32   *"a rising young star"* Tom Shriver, "Medalist Advances by Keeping Scores Close to Even Four," *Harrisburg Telegraph*, July 19, 1941.

32   *"Red 2, are you aboard"* Frank Van Riper, *Glenn: The Astronaut Who Would Be President* (New York: Empire Books, 1983), p. 99.

32   *"I don't know if I've ever"* Frank Van Riper, *Glenn: The Astronaut Who Would Be President* (New York: Empire Books, 1983), p. 99.

33   *"a long, long flight"* The John H. Glenn, Jr., Oral History Project, "Oral History Interview 5," Brien R. Williams, January 16, 1997.

33   *"John was always stable"* Dr. Julian Craigmiles as told to Bill Knight, "The Man Inside the Space Suit," *Longview (TX) Daily News*, January 6, 1962.

34   *"I really got a kick out"* The John H. Glenn, Jr., Oral History Project, "Oral History Interview 15," Brien R. Williams, March 23, 1998.

34   *"So it was a time when"* The John H. Glenn, Jr., Oral History Project, "Oral History Interview 5," Brien R. Williams, January 16, 1997.

35   *"It was obvious that Glenn"* Bill Eaton, "Bay Flier Recalls Glenn as Gay, Carefree Marine," *Oakland Tribune*, March 7, 1962.

36   *"I didn't much want that"* The John H. Glenn, Jr., Oral History Project, "Oral History Interview 11," Brien R. Williams, May 12, 1997.

36   *"another assignment I didn't"* John Glenn with Nick Taylor, *John Glenn: A Memoir* (New York: Random House, 2000), p. 193.

36   *"It was the epitome of"* "Korean War—Speech 133 class, Quantico, VA, July 1952," courtesy of the John H. Glenn Archives at the Ohio State University, Box 16, Folder 34, Location 01-8-26-11-07-0-1.

36   *"The Korean war is two"* William C. Barnard, "Korea's Bitter 'Twilight War'" *Birmingham News*, June 22, 1952.

37   *"All the materials we had"* The John H. Glenn, Jr., Oral History Project, "Oral History Interview 14," Brien R. Williams, March 13, 1998.

37   *"Here"* ... *"I'm going to"* American History TV: C-SPAN3, "Remembering John Glenn," July 18, 2017, accessed February 1, 2022.

37   *"We didn't talk about how much"* John Glenn with Nick Taylor, *John Glenn: A Memoir* (New York: Random House, 2000), p. 198.

CHAPTER THREE: The Blow and Go Group

38   *"tactical aerial photographic"* VMJ-1 Type "B" Report (Command Diary), 1 to 28 February 1953.

39   *"Robertshaw impressed me so"* Jim Prime and Bill Nowlin, *Ted Williams: The Pursuit of Perfection* (Champaign, IL: Sports Publishing, LLC, 2002), Compact Disc insert, provided by Ted Patterson, Track 13.

39   *"So I get into K-3"* Richard Sisk, "The Right Stuff, 1998," *New York Daily News*, October 11, 1998.

40   *"sort of third in command"* The John H. Glenn, Jr. Oral History Project, "Oral History Interview 10," Brien R. Williams, April 28, 1997.

40   *"All the fellows are really"* Letter from John Glenn to Annie Glenn, February 27, 1953, courtesy of the John H. Glenn Archives at the Ohio State University, Box 118, Folder 23, Location 01-8-30-15-02-0-1.

40   *"Any guy who"* Letter from John Glenn to Annie Glenn, February 27, 1953. Courtesy of The John H. Glenn Archives at The Ohio State University, Box 118, Folder 23, Location 01-8-30-15-02-0-1.

40   *"Hate these weeks"* Letter from John Glenn to Annie Glenn, May 17, 1953, courtesy of the John H. Glenn Archives at the Ohio State University, Box 118, Folder 24, Location 01-8-30-15-02-0-1.

40   *"the time of my life"* Letter from John Glenn to Annie Glenn, March 9, 1953, courtesy of the John H. Glenn Archives at the Ohio State University, Box 118, Folder 23, Location 01-8-30-15-02-0-1.

40   *"I'm still praying for"* "Williams Joins Marines, Prays for Korean Truce," *Boston Globe*, May 3, 1952.

40   *"Looks like I'll beat the 15th"* Letter written by Ted Williams to Evelyn Turner, February 10, 1953, LiveAuctioneers.com, accessed January 7, 2021.

41   *"When Glenn joined the"* Interview with Major General Larry Taylor, "Veterans Day Tribute: An Interview with Ted Williams USMC Reservist, Baseball Legend," *Officer*, November 1999.

41   *"I didn't know what to expect"* Joe Hallett, "Glenn Remains Sky-High on Friendship with Ted Williams," *Columbus Dispatch*, July 14, 2002.

41   *"He is the greatest guy"* Arthur M. Moran unpublished memoir, 1988.

41   *"When we were going"* Dr. Julian Craigmiles as told to Bill Knight, "The Man Inside the Space Suit," *Longview (TX) Daily News*, January 6, 1962.

42   *"was just a nonentity"* Frank Van Riper, *Glenn: The Astronaut Who Would Be President* (New York: Empire Books, 1983), p. 103.

42   *"Let's see now, Bush"* Ted Williams as told to John M. Ross, "Where Do We Go from Here?" *American Weekly*, August 23, 1953.

42   *"dodging all those pop-bottles"* John Minturn Verdi, *First Hundred: A Memoir of the Korean War, 1952–1953* (Airdale & Chrünschi LLC, 2013), p. 392.

42   *"could get to first base"* "Here's What He Meant," Korean War—VMF-311 Policy from new commanding officer, (including policy created as a joke), February 1, 1953, courtesy of the John H. Glenn Archives at the Ohio State University, Box 16, Folder 45, Location 01-8-26-11-07-0-1.

42   *"just good friends"* Armand Archerd, "What's Marilyn's Success Secret,"
        Shreveport Times, January 4, 1953.

42   *"Ted Williams is in outfit"* Letter from John Glenn to Annie Glenn,
        February 15, 1953, courtesy of the John H. Glenn Archives at the Ohio
        State University, Box 118, Folder 23, Location 01-8-30-15-02-0-1.

43   *"Well, lieutenant colonels and"* Bill Nowlin, *Ted Williams at War*
        (Burlington, Massachusetts: Rounder Books, 2007), p. 216.

43   *"Pohang had a terrible"* William Miser personal diary, October 31,
        2000, courtesy of Dr. Fred Miser.

43   *"He didn't care for kimchi"* Author interview with David Glenn,
        March 6, 2021.

44   *"Nobody can fight in bitter"* Captain Ralph C. Wood, "Pickel
        Meadows," *Marine Corps Gazette*, October 1952.

44   *"everybody went out on"* Ted Williams with John Underwood, *My
        Turn at Bat* (New York: A Fireside Book Published by Simon &
        Schuster, 1988), p. 178.

44   *"These huts are like"* Letter written by Bill Clem to Marian Clem,
        February 8, 1953, courtesy of Barbara Clem Alvarez.

44   *"Korea is the coldest hole"* Author interview with Rylen B. Rudy,
        February 5, 2021

44   *"The Army was the one that"* Author interview with Rylen B. Rudy,
        December 21, 2021.

45   *"[The Panther] wouldn't go as"* The John H. Glenn, Jr., Oral History
        Project, Oral History Interview 14, Brien R. Williams, March 13, 1998,
        p. 4.

46   *"nape scrapes"* Letter from John Glenn to Annie Glenn, April 27,
        1953, courtesy of the John H. Glenn Archives at the Ohio State
        University, Box 118, Folder 24, Location 01-8-30-15-02-0-1.

46   *"Our job was to support"* Henry Berry, *Hey, Mac, Where Ya Been?* (New
        York: St. Martin's Press, 1988), p. 294.

46   *"What the hell good that"* Henry Berry, *Hey, Mac, Where Ya Been?*
        (New York: St. Martin's Press, 1988), p. 294.

47   *"cream puff hops"* Letter from John Glenn to Annie Glenn, February
        21, 1953, courtesy of the John H. Glenn Archives at the Ohio State
        University, Box 118, Folder 23, Location 01-8-30-15-02-0-1.

47   *"This is a really rough"* Letter from John Glenn to Annie Glenn,
        February 21, 1953, courtesy of the John H. Glenn Archives at the Ohio
        State University, Box 118, Folder 23, Location 01-8-30-15-02-0-1.

47   *"Indian Country"* . . . *"The Boot"* . . . *"Marilyn Monroe"* Letter from
          John Glenn to Annie Glenn, February 27, 1953, courtesy of the John
          H. Glenn Archives at the Ohio State University, Box 118, Folder 23,
          Location 01-8-30-15-02-0-1.

48   *"the guys"* Letter written by Bill Clem to Marian Clem, February 5,
          1953, courtesy of Barbara Clem Alvarez.

48   *"nervous, but not too"* Letter written by Bill Clem to Marian Clem,
          February 14, 1953, courtesy of Barbara Clem Alvarez.

48   *"Boy I really had my"* Letter written by Ted Williams to Evelyn Turner,
          February 14, 1953, LiveAuctioneers.com, accessed January 7, 2021.

49   *"One-Four, turning base"* "VMF-311 SOP for Tactical Flight
          Operations," courtesy of the John H. Glenn Archives at the Ohio State
          University, Box 16, Folder 47, Location 01-8-26-11-07-0-1.

49   *"Luck was with me"* Letter written by Bill Clem to Marian Clem,
          February 14, 1953, courtesy of Barbara Clem Alvarez.

49   *"I'm real mad at myself"* Letter written by Bill Clem to Marian Clem,
          February 14, 1953, courtesy of Barbara Clem Alvarez.

49   *"There is a big strike planned"* Letter written by Bill Clem to Marian
          Clem, February 14, 1953, courtesy of Barbara Clem Alvarez.

CHAPTER FOUR: Three Runs, Three Hits, Three Errors

50   *"I have never seen"* Letter from John Glenn to Annie Glenn, February
          21, 1953, courtesy of the John H. Glenn Archives at the Ohio State
          University, Box 118, Folder 23, Location 01-8-30-15-02-0-1.

50   *"One week since my"* Letter from John Glenn to Annie Glenn,
          February 21, 1953, courtesy of the John H. Glenn Archives at the Ohio
          State University, Box 118, Folder 23, Location 01-8-30-15-02-0-1.

50   *"Ingrid," "Hedy," and "Lara"* Letter from John Glenn to Annie
          Glenn, February 16, 1953, courtesy of the John H. Glenn Archives at
          the Ohio State University, Box 118, Folder 23, Location 01-8-30-15-
          02-0-1.

50   *"Hey, they got the Bush"* Glenn Infield, "The Day Ted Williams Almost
          Got It," in *Fighting Eagles: The Daring Exploits of America's Great Air
          Aces*, edited by Phil Hirsch (New York: Pyramid Willow Books, 1965),
          pp. 29–30.

51   *"Ted, I don't care whether"* Claire Trageser, "Military Aviator Survived
          Brushes with Death in World War II and Korea," *San Diego Daily
          Transcript*, June 8, 2011.

51   *"I can handle one"* Bob Quincy, "Ted Williams Says Baseball Helps in Switch to Jet Pilot," *Boston Herald*, July 29, 1952.

51   *"I felt the plane mush up"* Ed Hyde, "Ted Williams, Marine," *Sport*, July 1953.

52   *"John Glenn told me later"* Interview with Major General Larry Taylor, "Veterans Day Tribute: An Interview with Ted Williams USMC Reservist, Baseball Legend," *Officer*, November 1999.

52   *"I'm Captain T.S. Williams"* Henry Berry, *Hey, Mac, Where Ya Been?* (New York: St. Martin's Press, 1988), p. 294.

52   *"We actually had to physically"* J. David Truby, "Ted Williams' Almost Final Out," *Flight Journal*, August 2006.

52   *"Ted told me later the"* Smithsonian via YouTube, "John Glenn: Earning the Right Stuff as a Decorated Marine Aviator and Navy Test Pilot," May 25, 2012, accessed February 3, 2021.

53   *"You listen and here comes"* "Ted Williams: A Celebration of an American Hero," July 22, 2002, courtesy of New England Sports Network.

53   *"Would like to be a test"* 1948 Pine Grove High School Yearbook, p. 17.

53   *"If I had known then that"* Ted Williams as told to Joe Reichler and Joe Trimble, "This Is My Last Year," *Saturday Evening Post*, April 24, 1954.

54   *"The minute he hit the"* "ESPN SportsCentury: Ted Williams," October 8, 1999.

55   *"If I ever prayed in my"* John Underwood, *It's Only Me: The Ted Williams We Hardly Knew* (Chicago: Triumph Book, 2005), audio CD insert, track 3.

55   *"took off for high"* Author interview with Rylen B. Rudy, February 5, 2021.

55   *"a bit pale but"* Ed Hyde, "Ted Williams, Marine," *Sport*, July 1953.

55   *"Glad to meet you"* Frank Graham, "Graham's Corner," *New York Journal-American*, March 26, 1953.

55   *"We were ready to haul out"* Charles Harbin Jr., "Owensboro's Dan Moody Greets Ted Williams at Site of Crash," *Owensboro (KY) Messenger-Inquirer*, February 25, 1953.

56   *"Why'd the colonel hand you"* Leigh Montville, *Ted Williams: The Biography of an American Hero* (New York: Broadway Books, 2004), p. 166.

56   ***"I just got my ass blown"*** Leigh Montville, *Ted Williams: The Biography of an American Hero* (New York: Broadway Books, 2004), p. 166.

56   ***"Ted Williams had a deal"*** Letter from John Glenn to Annie Glenn, February 16, 1953, courtesy of the John H. Glenn Archives at the Ohio State University, Box 118, Folder 23, Location 01-8-30-15-02-0-1.

56   ***"Mommy, Mommy, there's"*** "Mrs. Williams Is Glad," *New York Daily News*, February 17, 1953.

57   ***"lost visual reference"*** Ted Williams with John Underwood, *My Turn at Bat* (New York: A Fireside Book Published by Simon & Schuster, 1988), p. 179.

57   ***"as we were going down"*** Henry Berry, *Hey, Mac, Where Ya Been?* (New York: St. Martin's Press, 1988), p. 296.

57   ***"I followed the guy in front"*** Ted Williams as told to John M. Ross, "Where Do We Go from Here?" *American Weekly*, August 23, 1953.

57   ***"for a comparatively green pilot"*** Ed Hymoff, "Williams Was 'Scared Stiff' During Crash," *Cedar Rapids Gazette*, February 17, 1953.

57   ***"Captain Ted Williams became the"*** MAG-33 Type-B Report (Command Diary), 1 to 28 February 1953.

58   ***"THIS IS TO CERTIFY THAT"*** MAG-33 Type-B Report (Command Diary), 1 to 28 February 1953.

58   ***"Pretty easy hop"*** Letter from John Glenn to Annie Glenn, February 27, 1953, courtesy of the John H. Glenn Archives at the Ohio State University, Box 118, Folder 23, Location 01-8-30-15-02-0-1.

58   ***"Just want to keep"*** Letter from John Glenn to Annie Glenn, March 3, 1953, courtesy of the John H. Glenn Archives at the Ohio State University, Box 118, Folder 23, Location 01-8-30-15-02-0-1.

59   ***"It gives me the biggest"*** Letter from John Glenn to Annie Glenn, March 15, 1953, courtesy of the John H. Glenn Archives at the Ohio State University, Box 118, Folder 23, Location 01-8-30-15-02-0-1.

59   ***"my first genuine People's"*** Letter from John Glenn to Annie Glenn, March 17, 1953, courtesy of the John H. Glenn Archives at the Ohio State University, Box 118, Folder 23, Location 01-8-30-15-02-0-1.

59   ***"more willing to take"*** Dr. Julian Craigmiles as told to Bill Knight, "The Man Inside the Space Suit," *Longview (TX) Daily News*, January 6, 1962.

60   ***"You didn't want to be on Glenn's"*** Author interviews with Rylen B. Rudy, February 5, 2021, and December 21, 2021.

60   *"was rather intent on"* The John H. Glenn, Jr., Oral History Project, "Oral History Interview 15," Brien R. Williams, March 23, 1998.

61   *"I told John that the"* Frank Van Riper, *Glenn: The Astronaut Who Would Be President* (New York: Empire Books, 1983), p. 105.

61   *"this no-rank-in-the"* Letter from John Glenn to Annie Glenn, March 3, 1953, courtesy of the John H. Glenn Archives at the Ohio State University, Box 118, Folder 23, Location 01-8-30-15-02-0-1.

61   *"The flight leader always"* Frank Van Riper, *Glenn: The Astronaut Who Would Be President* (New York: Empire Books, 1983), pp. 105–106.

61   *"I see that son of a"* Frank Van Riper, *Glenn: The Astronaut Who Would Be President* (New York: Empire Books, 1983), p. 106.

62   *"Boy, those anti-aircraft"* Michael Kramer, "John Glenn: The Right Stuff?," *New York*, January 31, 1983.

62   *"I'm going to ease out"* Jeffrey Kluger, "An American Icon, "*Time Commemorative Edition: John Glenn, A Hero's Life, 1921–2016.*

62   *"buying the farm"* Frank Van Riper, *Glenn: The Astronaut Who Would Be President* (New York: Empire Books, 1983), p. 106.

62   *"Took two hands to manhandle"* Letter from John Glenn to Annie Glenn, April 6, 1953, courtesy of the John H. Glenn Archives at the Ohio State University, Box 118, Folder 24, Location 01-8-30-15-02-0-1.

62   *"That's a small sweat until"* Letter from John Glenn to Annie Glenn, April 6, 1953, courtesy of the John H. Glenn Archives at the Ohio State University, Box 118, Folder 24, Location 01-8-30-15-02-0-1.

62   *"'Twas up Sinanju way"* "Korean War—Poetry written by John Glenn, circa 1950s," courtesy of the John H. Glenn Archives at the Ohio State University, Box 16.1, Folder 6, Location 01-8-23-06-05-0-1. (NOTE: Multiple typos in the original document have been corrected by the author.)

65   *"Lovely subject—know"* Letter from John Glenn to Annie Glenn, March 17, 1953, courtesy of the John H. Glenn Archives at the Ohio State University, Box 118, Folder 23, Location 01-8-30-15-02-0-1.

65   *"I've come to the conclusion"* Letter from John Glenn to Annie Glenn, April 6, 1953, courtesy of the John H. Glenn Archives at the Ohio State University, Box 118, Folder 24, Location 01-8-30-15-02-0-1.

66   *"I went under him to"* John Minturn Verdi, *First Hundred: A Memoir of the Korean War, 1952–1953*, (Airdale & Chrünschi LLC, 2013), p. 349.

66   *"Tell me, does John"* John Minturn Verdi, *First Hundred: A Memoir of the Korean War, 1952–1953* (Airdale & Chrünschi LLC, 2013), pp. 349–351.

66   *"he had seen something"* Arthur M. Moran, unpublished memoir, 1988.

66   *"I told him to be careful"* Arthur M. Moran, unpublished memoir, 1988.

66   *"You normally don't"* Arthur M. Moran, unpublished memoir, 1988.

67   *"I thought instantly he had"* John Minturn Verdi, *First Hundred: A Memoir of the Korean War, 1952–1953* (Airdale & Chrünschi LLC, 2013), p. 352.

67   *"You know, I sometimes"* Letter from John Glenn to Annie Glenn, April 10, 1953, courtesy of the John H. Glenn Archives at the Ohio State University, Box 118, Folder 24, Location 01-8-30-15-02-0-1.

67   *"[Glenn was] another of"* John Minturn Verdi, *First Hundred: A Memoir of the Korean War, 1952–1953*, (Airdale & Chrünschi LLC, 2013), p. 349.

67   *"He seemed to draw"* Sara W. Bock, "Sea Stories," *Leatherneck,* September 2015.

Chapter Five: Hospitality

68   *"Everyone just counts the"* Letter written by Bill Clem to Marian Clem, February 12, 1953, courtesy of Barbara Clem Alvarez.

68   *"I remember Ted Williams"* David Cataneo, *I Remember Ted Williams* (Nashville, Tennessee: Cumberland House, 2002), p. 180.

68   *"That is the right attitude"* Arthur M. Moran, unpublished memoir, 1988.

68   *"all right, I guess"* "Korean Flying Tough Work, Ted Reports," *Long Beach Independent*, February 20, 1953.

69   *"Moran, what in the hell"* Arthur M. Moran, unpublished memoir, 1988.

69   *"I was really sick"* Ted Williams with John Underwood, *My Turn at Bat* (New York: A Fireside Book Published by Simon & Schuster, 1988), p. 182.

70   *"He wasn't very happy"* Author interview with Nicholas A. Gandolfo, February 12, 2021.

70   *"the arrogant son of"* Oral history interview with John Breske, Jr,
          Wisconsin Veterans Museum, interview by Mik Derks, September 22,
          2004, p. 23.

70   *"We were all interested"* Author interview with Tony Ybarra, February
          14, 2021.

70   *"the most gracious fellow"* Jan K. Herman interview with Nancy
          "Bing" Crosby, Naval History Bureau of Medicine and Surgery,
          December 26, 2001, courtesy of United States Navy.

70   *"Capt. Williams, I used"* Dick Hill, *Battle Talk!: Memoirs of a Marine
          Radio Correspondent* (Edina, MN: Beaver Pond Press, 2006), p. 90.

71   *"Well, I really don't"* Dick Hill, *Battle Talk!: Memoirs of a Marine Radio
          Correspondent*, (Edina, Minnesota: Beaver Pond Press, 2006), audio CD
          insert, track 2.

71   *"weak as a cat"* Letter written by Ted Williams to Evelyn Turner,
          March 22, 1953, LiveAuctioneers.com, accessed January 7, 2021.

71   *"They took a piece about"* Letter written by Ted Williams to Evelyn
          Turner, March 27, 1953, LiveAuctioneers.com, accessed January 7,
          2021.

72   *"always wanted to finish"* "Williams Relates Ailment in Letter," *Los
          Angeles Times*, April 19, 1953.

72   *"I&I, which is Intercourse and Intoxication"* Author interview with
          Robert "Woody" Woodbury, May 28, 2021.

72   *"Good luck in opener"* "Luck from Ted," *Philadelphia Inquirer*, April
          17, 1953.

73   *"damn good steaks"* Letter written by Ted Williams to Evelyn Turner,
          April 21, 1953, LiveAuctioneers.com, accessed January 7, 2021.

73   *"an Indian prince or"* Letter written by Ted Williams to Evelyn Turner,
          June 4, 1953, LiveAuctioneers.com, accessed January 7, 2021.

73   *"I went on R&R to Japan"* Smithsonian via YouTube, "John Glenn:
          Earning the Right Stuff as a Decorated Marine Aviator and Navy Test
          Pilot," May 25, 2012, accessed February 3, 2021.

73   *"[a] 100% change from"* Letter from John Glenn to Annie Glenn,
          April 10, 1953, courtesy of the John H. Glenn Archives at the Ohio
          State University, Box 118, Folder 24, Location 01-8-30-15-02-0-1.

74   *"[The boy] swung with all"* "Ted Williams: A Celebration of an
          American Hero," July 22, 2002, courtesy of New England Sports
          Network.

75   *"Nothing gave him more pleasure"* "Ted Williams: A Celebration of an American Hero," July 22, 2002, courtesy of New England Sports Network.

Chapter Six: Bush and Old Magnet Ass

76   *"They had a policy that"* Smithsonian via Youtube, "John Glenn: Earning the Right Stuff as a Decorated Marine Aviator and Navy Test Pilot," May 25, 2012, accessed February 3, 2021.

76   *"road recce"* . . . *"road"* The John H. Glenn, Jr., Oral History Project, "Oral History Interview 14," Brien R. Williams, March 13, 1998.

76   *"early-early"* VHS Copy of "An Evening With #9," November 10, 1988, courtesy of the personal archives of Ben Bradlee, Jr.

76   *"a. Check the bombline"* VMF-311 SOP for Tactical Flight Operations, courtesy of the John H. Glenn Archives at the Ohio State University, Box 16, Folder 47, Location 01-8-26-11-07-0-1.

77   *"Some of our troops"* John Glenn with Nick Taylor, *John Glenn: A Memoir* (New York: Random House, 2000), p. 214.

77   *"We worked closer"* Smithsonian via YouTube, "John Glenn: Earning the Right Stuff as a Decorated Marine Aviator and Navy Test Pilot," May 25, 2012, accessed February 3, 2021.

78   *"I have an emergency"* VMF-115 *"Able Eagles" Standard Operating Procedures Manual, January 1953,* courtesy of the John H. Glenn Archives at the Ohio State University, Box 16, Folder 40, Location 01-8-26-11-07-0-1.

78   *"We got up before light"* VHS Copy of "An Evening With #9," November 10, 1988, courtesy of the personal archives of Ben Bradlee, Jr.

79   *"If dropping those with"* Letter from John Glenn to Annie Glenn, March 15, 1953, courtesy of the John H. Glenn Archives at the Ohio State University, Box 118, Folder 23, Location 01-8-30-15-02-0-1.

79   *"4 to 5 second delay"* MAG-33 Type-B Report (Command Diary), 1 to 30 April 1953.

79   *"There had been some proximity"* The John H. Glenn, Jr., Oral History Project, "Oral History Interview 14," Brien R. Williams, March 13, 1998.

80   *"On my chart I thought"* The John H. Glenn, Jr., Oral History Project, "Oral History Interview 14," Brien R. Williams, March 13, 1998.

80   *"I was calling him"* Joel Hallett, "Glenn Remains Sky-High on Friendship with Ted Williams," *Columbus Dispatch*, July 14, 2002.

80   *"You made that 180"* VHS Copy of "An Evening With #9," November 10, 1988, courtesy of the personal archives of Ben Bradlee, Jr.

80   *"two (2) 500 GPs were"* "VMF-311 Type 'B' Report (Command Diary), for the period 1 to April 1953 through 30 April 1953."

80   *"I never took off"* John Glenn with Nick Taylor, *John Glenn: A Memoir* (New York: Random House, 2000), p. 214.

80   *"I knew where I was"* Interview with Major General Larry Taylor, "Veterans Day Tribute: An Interview with Ted Williams USMC Reservist, Baseball Legend," *Officer*, November 1999.

81   *"You fly as a two-person"* Bill Nowlin, *Ted Williams at War* (Burlington, MA: Rounder Books, 2007), p. 312.

81   *"We were just better trained"* The John H. Glenn, Jr., Oral History Project, "Oral History Interview 14," Brien R. Williams, March 13, 1998.

82   *"He didn't like to fly"* Sweeny Murti interview of John Glenn, August 26, 2012, courtesy of CBS New York.

82   *"Been working some on"* Letter from John Glenn to Annie Glenn, May 17, 1953, courtesy of the John H. Glenn Archives at the Ohio State University, Box 118, Folder 24, Location 01-8-30-15-02-0-1.

83   *"Ted flew my wing this"* Letter from John Glenn to Annie Glenn, May 21, 1953, courtesy of the John H. Glenn Archives at the Ohio State University, Box 118, Folder 24, Location 01-8-30-15-02-0-1.

83   *"Heavy winds made"* "Sox Slugger Lands Safely After Raid," *Boston Globe*, April 28, 1953.

83   *"I watched the first three"* Jim Lucas, "Ted Williams Gets 2 Hits in 39 Times Up—in Korea," *Knoxville News-Sentinel*, June 28, 1953.

84   *"I knew I was hit"* Jim Lucas, "Ted Williams Gets 2 Hits in 39 Times Up—in Korea," *Knoxville News-Sentinel*, June 28, 1953.

84   *"His wingman in Korea"* C-SPAN, "John Glenn Funeral Service," December 17, 2016, accessed April 13, 2021.

84   *"It wasn't that important"* "Red Sox Slugger Has Close Call," *Japan Times*, April 29, 1953.

84   *"this was a little bit"* Bill Nowlin interview transcript, conducted October 1, 1996, courtesy of Bill Nowlin.

85   *"A big damn rock"* Jim Lucas, "Ted Williams Gets 2 Hits in 39 Times Up—in Korea," *Knoxville News-Sentinel*, June 28, 1953.

85   ***"pouring 100,000 pounds of"*** "United Nations," *New York Times*, April 29, 1953.

85   ***"secondary explosion"*** The John H. Glenn, Jr., Oral History Project, "Oral History Interview 14," Brien R. Williams, March 13, 1998.

85   ***"They tell me rocks"*** Jim Lucas, "Ted Williams Gets 2 Hits in 39 Times Up—in Korea," *Knoxville News-Sentinel*, June 28, 1953.

85   ***"all done up"*** Charles L. Whipple, "The Come-Back Kid: Life Story of Ted Williams, Chapter IX," *Boston Globe*, July 3, 1955.

85   ***"We always kidded him"*** Bill Nowlin interview transcript, conducted October 1, 1996, courtesy of Bill Nowlin.

Chapter Seven: Liberty

86   ***"Dimmitt's only complete fuel"*** "Classified," *Castro County (TX) News*, December 7, 1950.

86   ***"He worked for Phillips 66"*** David Cataneo, "On This Memorial Day Ted Williams Remembers Those Who Didn't Make It Home," *Boston Herald*, May 26, 1997.

86   ***"greatly loved and respected"*** "Capt. Bailes' Funeral Rites Slated Today," *Tyler Morning Telegraph*, July 8, 1953.

87   ***"And, God, there's his"*** David Cataneo, "On This Memorial Day Ted Williams Remembers Those Who Didn't Make It Home," *Boston Herald*, May 26, 1997.

87   ***"It's the first guy we've"*** Letter written by Ted Williams to Evelyn Turner, May 8, 1953, LiveAuctioneers.com, accessed January 7, 2021.

88   ***"stinkers"*** Letters written by John Hense to Mary Ann Hense, March 13, 1953, and April 18, 1953, courtesy of John Hense, Jr.

87   ***"Rice Paddie Bijou Theatre"*** First Marine Aircraft Wing, Command Diary, 1 to 28 February 1953.

88   ***"I never could've sat"*** "Conversation Piece: Subject: Ted Williams," *Sports Illustrated*, Joan Flynn Dreyspool, August 1, 1955.

89   ***"A flip of the wrist"*** Author interview with Rylen B. Rudy, February 5, 2021

89   ***"Rivalry was intense"*** Letter written by Senator John Glenn to Dr. Frank E. Romack, August 11, 1987, courtesy of Kathy Moran Truitt.

90   *"use of KROINDYKES"* "From: Commanding Officer . . . ," Korean
        War—VMF-311 Policy from new commanding officer (including
        policy created as a joke), February 1, 1953, courtesy of the John H.
        Glenn Archives at the Ohio State University, Box 16, Folder 45,
        Location 01-8-26-11-07-0-1.

90   *"supposed to spread"* Letter written by Ted Williams to Evelyn Turner,
        April 29, 1953, LiveAuctioneers.com, accessed January 7, 2021.

91   *"Ted and I have shot"* Ed Hyde, "Ted Williams, Marine," *Sport*, July
        1953.

91   *"Making me provost"* Ben Bradlee, Jr., interview of Edmund Buchser,
        Jr., April 28, 2004, courtesy of the personal archives of Ben Bradlee, Jr.

91   *"He could shoot a shotgun"* Steve Waters, "Duck Days in Korea," *South
        Florida Sun-Sentinel*, July 11, 2002.

92   *"We weren't there 10"* Steve Waters, "Duck Days in Korea," *South
        Florida Sun-Sentinel*, July 11, 2002.

92   *"hill-billy band"* Letter from John Glenn to Annie Glenn, February
        27, 1953. Courtesy of The John H. Glenn Archives at The Ohio State
        University, Box 118, Folder 23, Location 01-8-30-15-02-0-1.

93   *"they don't drink anything"* Letter written by Ted Williams to Evelyn
        Turner, April 11, 1953, LiveAuctioneers.com, accessed January 7, 2021.

93   *"It'll be done with"* "Ex-Cambridge Boy Commands Fighter Group
        That Is Knocking Out MIG's," *Daily Jeffersonian (OH)*, March 3, 1953.

94   *"So he goes up to Ted"* Author interview with Bob Massaro, November
        23, 2021.

94   *"Ted, do you know"* Author interview with Bob Massaro, November
        23, 2021.

94   *"I had to leave and"* Author interviews with Robert "Woody"
        Woodbury, December 10, 2020, and May 28, 2021.

95   *"The Commie's"* . . . *"I hope to raise a"* "Korean War—G.I. songs,
        no date," courtesy of the John H. Glenn Archives at the Ohio State
        University, Box 16.1, Folder 8, Location 01-8-23-06-05-0-1.

95   *"After the performance"* Letter written by Bill Clem to Marian Clem,
        April 11, 1953, courtesy of Barbara Clem Alvarez.

95   *"the authorized absence"* *Marine Corps Personnel Manual*, circa
        1961, https://www.hqmc.marines.mil/Portals/61/Docs/FOIA/
        MCPM%5B1%5D.pdf. Accessed February 15, 2022.

96   *"The old Pappa-san has"* Letter from John Glenn to Annie Glenn, February 27, 1953, courtesy of the John H. Glenn Archives at the Ohio State University, Box 118, Folder 23, Location 01-8-30-15-02-0-1.

96   *"immoral purposes"* First Marine Aircraft Wing Headquarters Squadron Type "B" Report (Command Diary), 1 to 31 May 1953.

96   *"venereal disease rate among"* First Marine Aircraft Wing Headquarters Squadron Type "B" Report (Command Diary), 1 to 31 May 1953.

96   *"lectures with visual aids"* "1st MAW General Order No. 131," First Marine Aircraft Wing General Orders, Memorandums, and the Modifications and Changes Thereof (Command Diary 3), 1 to 31 March 1953.

96   *"character and self-control"* "Chaplain's Report," MAG-33 Type -B Report (Command Diary), 1 to 31 March 1953.

97   *"He confided to a nurse"* Leigh Montville, *Ted Williams: The Biography of an American Hero* (New York: Broadway Books, 2004), p. 182.

97   *"All the nurses were there"* Bill Nowlin, *Ted Williams at War* (Burlington, MA: Rounder Books, 2007), p. 184.

97   *"spies"* Steve Waters, "Duck Days in Korea," *South Florida Sun-Sentinel,* July 11, 2002.

97   *"guerrillas"* Jack Kofoed, "Korean War Is a Nightmare," *Miami Herald,* March 6, 1953.

98   *"We always went by"* Don Moore interview with Lawrence R. Cote, conducted April 29, 2014, courtesy of Veterans History Project, Library of Congress.

98   *"They would take that"* Author interview with Lawrence R. Cote, January 27, 2022.

98   *"The buddy to this other"* Don Moore interview with Lawrence R. Cote, conducted April 29, 2014, courtesy of Veterans History Project, Library of Congress.

98   *"Korea in early 1953"* John Glenn with Nick Taylor, *John Glenn: A Memoir* (New York: Random House, 2000), p. 201.

99   *"Children like you and"* Letter from John Glenn to Lyn Glenn, February 5, 1953, courtesy of the John H. Glenn Archives at the Ohio State University, Box 118, Folder 23, Location 01-8-30-15-02-0-1.

99   *"You can't conceive"* Jack Kofoed, "Korean War Is a Nightmare," *Miami Herald,* March 6, 1953.

99   **"We keep our animals in"** "Korea—'Land of Lost Children,'"
         Portsmouth (NH) Herald, June 6, 1953.

100   **"Bought it plenty"** Letter from John Glenn to Annie Glenn, May
         29, 1953, courtesy of the John H. Glenn Archives at the Ohio State
         University, Box 118, Folder 24, Location 01-8-30-15-02-0-1.

100   **"adopted children"** First Marine Aircraft Wing, Command Diary, 1 to
         31 December 1952.

101   **"One of our young lieutenants"** Author interview with Rylen B. Rudy,
         February 5, 2021.

101   **"The little kids crowded"** Bill Nowlin, *Ted Williams at War* (Burlington,
         MA: Rounder Books, 2007), p. 212.

102   **"With one hand the Marine"** "Marine Orphanage Is Haven for
         Korea," *Johnson County Courier,* May 7, 1953.

102   **"December 22 . . . Dedicated to the"** Photographs provided by Colonel
         Dennis Lloyd Hager II, USMC, and Mrs. Ha Kyong Cha.

CHAPTER EIGHT: Every Man a Tiger

103   **"Glenn was such a prince"** Author interview with Rylen B. Rudy,
         February 5, 2021.

103   **"Makes me so darn"** Letter from John Glenn to Annie Glenn, May
         17, 1953, courtesy of the John H. Glenn Archives at the Ohio State
         University, Box 118, Folder 24, Location 01-8-30-15-02-0-1.

103   **"only one man who"** John Minturn Verdi, *First Hundred: A Memoir of
         the Korean War, 1952–1953* (Airdale & Chrünschi LLC, 2013), p. 362.

103   **"Glenn was acknowledged"** Jonathan D. Mendes, *A Marine's Journey:
         Semper Fi* (Lulu Press, 2018), p. 41.

104   **"John was"** Arthur M. Moran, unpublished memoir, 1988.

104   **"a cool cucumber"** "Ted Prayed for Glenn; Buddies in Korea," *Boston
         Globe,* February 22, 1962.

104   **"John Glenn?"** Jeffrey Kluger, "An American Icon," *Time
         Commemorative Edition: John Glenn, A Hero's Life, 1921–2016.*

104   **"the man is crazy"** Ronald D. Clark and Brian T. Usher, "Glenn's Done
         Almost Everything," *Akron Beacon-Journal,* July 4, 1976.

104   **"Any time he'd be"** Ed Linn, *Hitter: The Life and Turmoils of Ted
         Williams* (San Diego: Harcourt Brace, 1994), p. 249.

104   **"I never heard Ted"** "Ted Williams: A Celebration of an American
         Hero," July 22, 2002, courtesy of New England Sports Network.

104   ***"an honest man"*** John Minturn Verdi, *First Hundred: A Memoir of the Korean War, 1952–1953*, (Airdale & Chrünschi LLC, 2013), p. 400.

104   ***"Everybody tried to make"*** Ted Williams with John Underwood, *My Turn at Bat* (New York: A Fireside Book Published by Simon & Schuster, 1988), p. 182.

105   ***"Ted's [99-] percentile"*** John Minturn Verdi, *First Hundred: A Memoir of the Korean War, 1952–1953* (Airdale & Chrünschi LLC, 2013), p. 399.

105   ***"the fellows ahead of"*** Charles L. Whipple, "The Come-Back Kid: Life Story of Ted Williams, Chapter IX," *Boston Globe*, July 3, 1955.

105   ***"Those guys were all"*** Charles L. Whipple, "The Come-Back Kid: Life Story of Ted Williams, Chapter IX," *Boston Globe*, July 3, 1955.

105   ***"I hoped he fell"*** Mike Gillooly, "The Case for Ted Williams: Today's Witness: Lt. Col. Harrison, USMC Ted's Roommate in the Korean War," *Boston American*, January 7, 1958.

105   ***"If a few of those infuriated"*** Mike Gillooly, "The Case for Ted Williams: Today's Witness: Lt. Col. Harrison, USMC Ted's Roommate in the Korean War," *Boston American*, January 7, 1958.

105   ***"Not only has he done"*** "Ted's First 3 Weeks," *Boston Globe*, May 26, 1952.

106   ***"a spoiled brat-type"*** Ben Bradlee Jr., *The Kid: The Immortal Life of Ted Williams* (New York: Little, Brown and Company, 2013), p. 351.

106   ***"I can wrap up Ted"*** Author interview with Rylen B. Rudy, February 5, 2021.

106   ***"He could cuss like"*** Ben Bradlee, Jr., interview of Edmund Buchser, Jr., April 28, 2004, courtesy of the personal archives of Ben Bradlee, Jr.

106   ***"Williams wouldn't even"*** Author interview with Rylen B. Rudy, February 5, 2021.

107   ***"There were a couple"*** Author interview with Robert "Woody" Woodbury, December 10, 2020.

107   ***"team player"*** Mike Gillooly, "The Case for Ted Williams: Today's Witness: Lt. Col. Harrison, USMC Ted's Roommate in the Korean War," *Boston American*, January 7, 1958.

107   ***"All that stuff"*** Letter written by Bill Clem to Marian Clem, April 25, 1953, courtesy of Barbara Clem Alvarez.

108   ***"He taxied out to join"*** Author interview with Jonathan D. Mendes, December 21, 2021.

108   **"He had 'ear trouble"** Author interview with Rylen B. Rudy, February 5, 2021.

108   **"We were all mad"** Bill Nowlin, *Ted Williams at War* (Burlington, MA: Rounder Books, 2007), p. 112.

108   **"However, at times this officer"** Addendum to SF-88 dated 25 June 1953, on CAPT. Theodore Samuel WILLIAMS, 037773, USMCR, Courtesy of the National Personnel Records Center, National Archives.

108   **"From that point on"** Author interview with Rylen B. Rudy, February 5, 2021.

108   **"never heard anything"** Author interview with Jonathan D. Mendes, January 23, 2021.

108   **"He told me that war"** Ed Hyde, "Ted Williams, Marine," *Sport*, July 1953.

109   **"He wasn't afraid or"** Bill Nowlin, *Ted Williams at War* (Burlington, MA: Rounder Books, 2007), pp. 237–238.

110   **"forward area"** Addendum to SF-88 dated 25 June 1953, on CAPT. Theodore Samuel WILLIAMS, 037773, USMCR, Courtesy of the National Personnel Records Center, National Archives.

110   **"We've had the atom"** John J. Casserly, "Ted Williams Says U.S. 'Not Trying to Win' in Korea," *Morning Call (Allentown, PA)*, June 29, 1953, courtesy of United Press International.

110   **"guy with six kids"** . . . **"who can't"** John J. Casserly, "Ted Williams Says U.S. 'Not Trying to Win' in Korea," *Morning Call (Allentown, PA)*, June 29, 1953, courtesy of United Press International.

110   **"Many Americans have"** John J. Casserly, "Ted Williams Says U.S. 'Not Trying to Win' in Korea," *Morning Call (Allentown, PA)*, June 29, 1953, courtesy of United Press International.

110   **"one of the finest"** John J. Casserly, "Bosox' Williams Going Home— Possibly Back to Home Plate," *Pacific Stars and Stripes*, June 29, 1953, courtesy of United Press International.

110   **"Ted Williams—he"** John J. Casserly, "Bosox' Williams Going Home—Possibly Back to Home Plate," *Pacific Stars and Stripes*, June 29, 1953, courtesy of United Press International.

111   **"But I also hoped for"** John Glenn with Nick Taylor, *John Glenn: A Memoir* (New York: Random House, 2000), p. 217.

112   **"MiG Alley"** "MIG's Intercepted Flying South," *New York Times*, January 23, 1953.

112   *"This is fun compared"* Gordon Gammack, "'Glad' War in Korea, Not Home," *Des Moines Tribune*, June 9, 1953.

112   *"I loved the bird and"* Robert Miller interview with Harvey Jensen, conducted May 24, 2007, courtesy of Center for Oral and Public History, California State University, Fullerton, El Toro Marine Corps Air Station Oral History Project.

112   *"I've been waiting for ten"* Letter from John Glenn to Annie Glenn, June 4, 1953, courtesy of the John H. Glenn Archives at the Ohio State University, Box 118, Folder 25, Location 01-8-30-15-02-0-1.

112   *"Hope I have the orders"* Letter from John Glenn to Annie Glenn, May 29, 1953, courtesy of the John H. Glenn Archives at the Ohio State University, Box 118, Folder 24, Location 01-8-30-15-02-0-1.

113   *"The North Korean and"* Author interview with Rylen B. Rudy, February 5, 2021.

113   *"You son of a gun, they"* Ed Hyde, "Ted Williams, Marine," *Sport*, July 1953.

113   *"Just keep a good lookout"* Letter from John Glenn to Annie Glenn, June 10, 1953, courtesy of the John H. Glenn Archives at the Ohio State University, Box 118, Folder 25, Location 01-8-30-15-02-0-1.

114   *"Teamwork among the F-86"* "John Glenn's report Fighter Interceptor Flying in Korea," courtesy of the John H. Glenn Archives at the Ohio State University, Box 16.1, Folder 1, Location 01-8-23-06-05-0-1.

114   *"Aggressiveness is greatly"* "John Glenn's report Fighter Interceptor Flying in Korea," courtesy of the John H. Glenn Archives at the Ohio State University, Box 16.1, Folder 1, Location 01-8-23-06-05-0-1.

114   *"We better get out"* Nash Stublen, "Maj. Gen. Giraudo Was Pilot in Three Wars," *Tampa Tribune*, November 14, 1977.

114   *"Famous last words"* Nash Stublen, "Maj. Gen. Giraudo Was Pilot in Three Wars," *Tampa Tribune*, November 14, 1977.

115   *"This Giraudo is"* Letter from John Glenn to Annie Glenn, June 12, 1953, courtesy of the John H. Glenn Archives at the Ohio State University, Box 118, Folder 25, Location 01-8-30-15-02-0-1.

115   *"Never had anyone going"* Letter from John Glenn to Annie Glenn, August 2, 1953, courtesy of the John H. Glenn Archives at the Ohio State University, Box 118, Folder 27, Location 01-8-30-15-02-0-1.

115   *"You son of a bitch"* John Glenn with Nick Taylor, *John Glenn: A Memoir* (New York: Random House, 2000), pp. 231–232.

115   *"It hurt enough as"* John Glenn with Nick Taylor, *John Glenn: A Memoir* (New York: Random House, 2000), p. 232.

116   *"Glenn was not shy"* Frank Van Riper, *Glenn: The Astronaut Who Would Be President* (New York: Empire Books, 1983) p. 106.

116   *"The peace news today has"* Letter from John Glenn to Annie Glenn, June 8, 1953, courtesy of the John H. Glenn Archives at the Ohio State University, Box 118, Folder 25, Location 01-8-30-15-02-0-1.

116   *"MiG Mad Marine"* December 26, 1983, *Newsweek*, "Glenn: Don't Count Me Out."

117   *"It was very disappointing"* Major John H. Glenn, "New Concord Air Hero Describes Experiences in Korea Jet Combat," *Zanesville (OH) Sunday Times Signal*, January 24, 1954.

117   *"There was a lot of"* Sheree Scarborough interview with John Glenn, conducted August 25, 1997, courtesy of NASA Johnson Space Center Oral History Project, National Aeronautics and Space Administration.

117   *"So there were times"* The John H. Glenn, Jr., Oral History Project, "Oral History Interview 15," Brien R. Williams, March 23, 1998.

117   *"Dearest Annie, Dave"* "Letter from John Glenn to Annie Glenn, July 12, 1953, courtesy of the John H. Glenn Archives at the Ohio State University, Box 118, Folder 26, Location 01-8-30-15-02-0-1.

118   *"I really didn't"* Author interview with Captain Kent Ewing, January 25, 2021.

Chapter Nine: Big Shot

119   *"I'll always be able"* Jack McDonald, "Ted Returns Home, Plans to Rejoin Sox," *Sporting News*, July 15, 1953.

119   *"I was in a bad"* Will Connolly, "Ted: No Baseball Until '54—If Then," *San Francisco Chronicle*, July 10, 1953.

119   *"That sure sounds like"* "Williams Inquires About AL Pitchers," *Philadelphia Inquirer*, July 12, 1953.

120   *"It's possible I might"* Bob Holbrook, "Ted May Return to Sox This Year," *Boston Globe*, July 15, 1953.

120   *"The big deal now is"* Lin Raymond, "Ted Wants War Pals Home," *Patriot Ledger*, July 30, 1953.

120   *"Ted, I understand that your"* *Baseball: A Film by Ken Burns*, "Seventh Inning: The Capital of Baseball," Ken Burns, PBS Home Video, 2004.

121   *"It seemed as though a"* Clif Keane, "'As Though a Tragedy Had Struck'—Rosen: Ted May Return to Sox This Year," *Boston Globe*, August 10, 1953.

121   *"more like Albert Einstein"* William R. Manchester, "Navy Test Pilots Take Exams 8,000 Feet Up," *Baltimore Evening Sun*, December 15, 1948.

121   *"People think a test pilot"* William R. Manchester, "Navy Test Pilots Take Exams 8,000 Feet Up," *Baltimore Evening Sun*, December 15, 1948.

122   *"It was a very rigorous"* The John H. Glenn, Jr., Oral History Project, Oral History Interview 16, Brien R. Williams, March 27, 1998, p. 13.

123   *"I can do better"* "New Concord Pilot Cracks Record in Unofficial Try," *Zanesville (OH) Times Recorder*, September 7, 1954.

123   *"It was all paperwork"* The John H. Glenn, Jr., Oral History Project, Oral History Interview 17, Jeffrey W. Thomas, March 7, 2008, p. 13.

124   *"They were going to do"* The John H. Glenn, Jr., Oral History Project, Oral History Interview 2, Brien R. Williams, October 28, 1996, p. 18.

125   *"That was a high pressure"* Adam Condo, "Record Flight Was Just the Beginning," *Albuquerque Times*, July 16, 1987.

125   *"It was a beautiful trip"* Kim Clark, "'Johnny Dropped a Bomb!,'" *U.S. News & World Report*, August 13, 2007.

125   *"I couldn't find him"* Kim Clark, "'Johnny Dropped a Bomb!,'" *U.S. News & World Report*, August 13, 2007.

125   *"I guess Johnny must"* Clair Stebbins, "Jet Major Shakes Up Home Town," *Columbus Dispatch*, July 17, 1957.

125   *"mysterious blast"* "Jet Plane Cause of Blast Here," *Pittsburgh Press*, July 17, 1957.

126   *"all over again tomorrow"* "Record Jet Flight Was 'Lot of Fun,'" *Columbus Dispatch*, July 17, 1957.

126   *"I could do with a"* "Ted Williams Could Use Vacation," *Arizona Daily Star*, August 29, 1953.

126   *"indulged in a course"* "Ted Williams' Wife Files Suit for Separation," *Boston Globe*, January 24, 1954.

127   *"strictly friends"* "Airline Stewardess Denies She'll Wed Ted Williams," *Newport (RI) Daily News*, February 8, 1954.

127   *"hit, beaten, and struck"* J. L. (Dixie) Smith, "Baseball Star Sued by Wife," *Miami Herald*, January 24, 1954.

127   *"There's no question about"* "Ted Williams Reiterates Statement He's
       Quitting Baseball for Good," *Hartford Courant*, September 27, 1954.

127   *"If I had enough dough"* John J. Casserly, "Ted Cries Shame at
       U.S.," *Boston Daily Record*, June 29, 1953, courtesy of United Press
       International.

128   *"My arm is sore, my"* Harold Kaese, "Ted Finds It Hard to Shed 10
       Pounds," *Boston Globe*, May 23, 1955.

128   *"I'd spit again at"* Bob Holbrook, "'I'd Do It Again,' Says Seething
       Ted," *Boston Globe*, August 8, 1956.

129   *"[Williams] should quit baseball"* Harold Kaese, "Ted Should Quit—
       Kaese," *Boston Globe*, August 8, 1956.

129   *"Podres is paying the"* Bob Holbrook, "'I've Burned a Long Time,' Says
       Ted After Draft Blast," *Boston Globe*, March 14, 1956.

129   *"get Ted to say"* Hy Hurwitz, "What Ted Really Said," *Boston Globe*,
       April 2, 1957.

130   *"I used to admire Senator"* Hy Hurwitz, "What Ted Really Said,"
       Boston Globe, April 2, 1957.

130   *"I have too many friends"* Bob Holbrook, "What Ted Said Today,"
       Boston Globe, April 2, 1957.

130   *"drinking excessively"* Bob Holbrook, "What Ted Said Today," *Boston
       Globe*, April 2, 1957.

130   *"What I said about the"* "Ted Admits He Blasted Taft, Marines,"
       Boston Globe, April 2, 1957.

131   *"Theodore Samuel Williams"* Joe Cashman, "Ted Uses Hot Bat to
       Silence Critics," *Boston Daily Record*, July 16, 1957.

131   *"had begun husbanding"* Edwin Pope, *Ted Williams: The Golden Year,
       1957* (New York: Manor Books, 1970), p. 91.

131   *"CONGRATULATIONS ON"* "Test Pilot—Project Bullet—
       Correspondence and events about flight, July 1957–March 1958 and
       2003," courtesy of the John H. Glenn Archives at the Ohio State
       University, Box 18, Folder 27, Location 01-7-23-20-06-0-1.

Chapter Ten: Life Begins at 40

132   *"There's a man, who could"* "Case Eyes Astronaut—He's in Spot to
       Catch Fly Balls," *The Sporting News*, March 7, 1962.

132   *"At 36, Major Glenn is"* "Man in the News: Supersonic Champion,"
       New York Times, July 17, 1957.

132   ***"thinning red hair"*** "Leatherneck Salutes . . . Major John Glenn, Jr.," *Leatherneck*, September 1957.

132   ***"any bouquets around"*** "Marine in Trans-U.S. Jet Record," *Oakland Tribune*, July 16, 1957.

132   ***"Old Girl"*** Maj. John Glenn Jr., "'Going Like Scalded Duck' Record Smasher Says," *Pittsburgh Sun Telegraph*, July 17, 1957.

132   ***"a scalded duck"*** "Easier Than Driving," *Logansport Pharos Tribune*, July 17, 1957.

132   ***"Flying at 1,000 miles"*** "Record Jet Flight Was 'Lot of Fun,'" *Columbus Dispatch*, July 17, 1957.

134   ***"To say the least"*** Jeff Shesol, *Mercury Rising: John Glenn, John Kennedy, and the New Battleground of the Cold War* (New York: W. W. Norton & Company, 2021), pp. 36–37.

134   ***"rocket planes"*** "Veteran Test Pilot Named for Rocket Plane," *Redlands Daily Facts*, April 27, 1957.

134   ***"spaceships"*** Daniel Lang, "Von Braun's Romantic Explore Universe," *London (U.K.) Observer*, February 2, 1958.

135   ***"They gave us fictitious"*** The John H. Glenn, Jr., Oral History Project, Oral History Interview 18, Jeffrey W. Thomas, April 21, 2008, p. 7.

135   ***"do not discuss Project"*** Frank Van Riper, *Glenn: The Astronaut Who Would Be President* (New York: Empire Books, 1983), p. 127.

136   ***"TED WILLIAMS!!!"*** "Loyal Appreciation," *Berkshire (MA) Eagle*, August 15, 1957.

136   ***"Funny thing about"*** Eddie Storin, "Ted a 'Sleeper' as Bat King," *Baseball Digest*, February 2, 1958.

136   ***"Ted and I have it all"*** James Ellis, "Ted Calls Orioles First-Division Club," *Baltimore Evening Sun*, January 14, 1958.

137   ***"I felt ready to just die"*** Clif Keane, "'I Felt Ready to Die,'" *Boston Globe*, September 22, 1958.

137   ***"It doesn't make any"*** "Ted 'Through' With Writers,' *Tampa Bay Times*, November 24, 1957.

138   ***"He was writing to tell"*** Ted Williams with John Underwood, *My Turn at Bat* (New York: A Fireside Book Published by Simon & Schuster, 1988), pp. 205–206.

138   ***"I was careful"*** "John Glenn Says Closest Brush with Death Was In Indianapolis," *Palladium Item*, February 6, 1983.

138   ***"monkey business. . . . top banana"*** "No Monkey Business! These 2 are 'Top Bananas' on Space," *St. Cloud Times*, May 29, 1959.

138   ***"costly . . . highly publicized"*** "Astronauts: Too Risky?," *Newsweek*, February 8, 1960.

139   ***"If we didn't know"*** "Astronauts Ready, Without Qualm, for Space Trip," *Orlando Sentinel*, September 6, 1959.

139   ***"sidekick"*** Tom Wolfe, *The Right Stuff* (New York: Picador, 1979), p. 138.

139   ***"I cut out smoking"*** Roger Greene, "How Hard to Lick Is Heat Barrier Around World? Answer May Be Near," *Ogden (UT) Standard-Examiner*, July 29, 1960.

140   ***"regal, cold, on edge"*** Jeff Shesol, *Mercury Rising: John Glenn, John Kennedy, and the New Battleground of the Cold War* (New York: W. W. Norton & Company, 2021), p. 82.

140   ***"understanding"*** Jeff Shesol, *Mercury Rising: John Glenn, John Kennedy, and the New Battleground of the Cold War* (New York: W. W. Norton & Company, 2021), p. 85.

140   ***"I talked to both"*** Frank Van Riper, *Glenn: The Astronaut Who Would Be President* (New York: Empire Books, 1983), p. 152.

140   ***"an enigma"*** John Glenn with Nick Taylor, *John Glenn: A Memoir* (New York: Random House, 2000), p. 319.

140   ***"As time went by"*** Tom Wolfe, *The Right Stuff* (New York: Picador, 1979), p. 137.

140   ***"most articulate of"*** Jean Person, "7 Great Guys Train for 1st Trip in Space," *Detroit Free-Press*, December 7, 1959.

140   ***"the flying monk, or"*** Tom Wolfe, *The Right Stuff* (New York: Picador, 1979), p. 105.

141   ***"from a somewhat"*** Loudon S. Wainwright, "New Astronaut Team, Varied Men with One Goal Poise for the Violent Journey," *Life*, March 3, 1961.

141   ***"to keep their pants"*** Tom Wolfe, *The Right Stuff* (New York: Picador), 1979. p. 173.

141   ***"You're making everybody"*** Howell Raines, "John Glenn: The Private Man," *New York Times*, November 13, 1983.

141   ***"We're just afraid"*** Jean Person, "7 Great Guys Train for 1st Trip in Space," *Detroit Free Press*, December 7, 1959.

142   *"I know a lot of people are"* "'Don't Count Me Out Yet' Insists Sox' Ted Williams," *Newport (RI) Daily News*, June 24, 1959.

142   *"Ted Williams is coming"* "Ike in Sharp Opening Form," *Chicago Tribune*, April 19, 1960.

142   *"one of the longest home"* Whitney Shoemaker, "Pascual Fans 15, Sets New Club Record," *Berkshire Eagle*, April 19, 1960.

142   *"While both the President"* Letter written by Richard Nixon to Ted Williams, April 18, 1960, courtesy of the Richard Nixon Presidential Library and Museum.

143   *"He looked like he had"* "Ted Prayed for Glenn; Buddies in Korea War," *Boston Globe*, February 22, 1962.

143   *"I don't know what they"* Bob Dunbar, "John Glenn Trained Williams to Become Flyer in Marines," *Boston Herald*, February 21, 1962.

143   *"John came in the clubhouse"* Ben Bradlee, Jr., interview of Don Gile, August 11, 2003, courtesy of the personal archives of Ben Bradlee, Jr.

143   *"He was going through"* Tom Brokaw interview of Ted Williams on NBC News live coverage, October 29, 1998, courtesy of NBC News and NBC Universal.

143   *"at his age you more"* "Bad Cold Keeps Ted Williams in Hotel Room," *Berkshire Eagle*, May 27, 1960.

144   *"My mind is made up"* Joe Reichler, "Williams in Character Even to Dramatic End," *Newport (VT) Daily Express*, June 18, 1960.

144   *"I hit two balls that"* *Baseball: A Film by Ken Burns*, "Seventh Inning: The Capital of Baseball," Ken Burns, PBS Home Video, 2004.

144   *"I had a really warm"* Stephen Hanks, *150 Years of Baseball* (Lincolnwood, IL: Publications International, Ltd., 1989), p. 342.

145   *"I felt all through spring"* Len Harsh, "Baseball Great Ted Williams Makes Short Visit to City," *Fort Myers (FL) News-Press*, April 12, 1961.

146   *"He tested them too"* Leigh Montville, *Ted Williams: The Biography of an American Hero* (New York: Broadway Books, 2004), p. 240.

146   *"time of self-doubt and"* John Glenn with Nick Taylor, *John Glenn: A Memoir* (New York: Random House, 2000), p. 376.

146   *"We have a good many"* August 10, 1961, "News Conference 15," courtesy of the John F. Kennedy Presidential Library and Museum.

147   *"That's our ride?"* Gordon Cooper with Bruce Henderson, *Leap of Faith: An Astronaut's Journey into the Unknown* (New York: HarperCollins, 2000), p. 3.

147   *"The Atlas was a peculiar"* The John H. Glenn, Jr., Oral History Project, Oral History Interview 19, Jeffrey W. Thomas, May 23, 2008, p. 12.

147   *"As soon as I"* The John H. Glenn, Jr., Oral History Project, Oral History Interview 19, Jeffrey W. Thomas, May 23, 2008, pp. 4, 6.

148   *"My condition is good"* Transcript of the Friendship 7 Radio Communications, Cape Canaveral, Re-entry, "Celebrate the Friendship 7 Flight," courtesy of the Ohio State University.

149   *"space fireflies"* "Glenn Tells of 'Space Fireflies,' Orange Ball," *Cincinnati Enquirer*, February 22, 1962.

149   *"Man, this is beautiful"* Transcript of the Friendship 7 Radio Communications, Canton Island, First Orbit, "Celebrate the Friendship 7 Flight," courtesy of the Ohio State University.

149   *"If we're looking straight"* Roger Greene, "Test to Decide Whether Man Can Enter Space and Return," *Paducah (KY) Sun*, July 29, 1960.

149   *"I was rather surprised"* "Orbital Flight of John H. Glenn, Jr: Hearing Before the Senate Committee on Aeronautical and Space Sciences," February 28, 1962, National Archives Catalog, Archives.gov.

149   *"I looked around"* "Didn't Need to See Him," *Spokesman Review*, May 11, 1962.

150   *"The God I pray to"* "Didn't Need to See Him," *Spokesman Review*, May 11, 1962.

150   *"It was a community"* The John H. Glenn, Jr., Oral History Project, Oral History Interview 19, Brien R. Williams, October 25, 1996, p. 48.

150   *"Presbyterian Pilot"* Tom Wolfe, *The Right Stuff* (New York: Picador, 1979), pp. 265, 275, 277, 278.

150   *"The church I grew up"* The John H. Glenn, Jr., Oral History Project, Oral History Interview 19, Brien R. Williams, February 10, 1997, p. 6.

150   *"the idol and the hero"* "Orbital Flight of John H. Glenn, Jr: Hearing Before the Senate Committee on Aeronautical and Space Sciences," February 28, 1962, National Archives Catalog, Archives.gov.

151   *"his spirit of reverence and"* "Orbital Flight of John H. Glenn, Jr: Hearing Before the Senate Committee on Aeronautical and Space Sciences," February 28, 1962, National Archives Catalog, Archives.gov.

151   *"I can't say that while"* "Orbital Flight of John H. Glenn, Jr: Hearing Before the Senate Committee on Aeronautical and Space Sciences," February 28, 1962, National Archives Catalog, Archives.gov.

151   ***"our prayers were answered"*** "Glenn Sr.: 'We're Christians, Our Prayers Were Answered,'" *Minneapolis Morning Tribune*, February 21, 1962.

151   ***"thanking God or giving"*** Letters to John Glenn (Houston, TX: World Book Encyclopedia Science Service, Inc., 1964), p. 168.

151   ***"Glad you got back"*** Letters to John Glenn (Houston, TX: World Book Encyclopedia Science Service, Inc., 1964), p. 167.

152   ***"I think you are"*** Letters to John Glenn (Houston, TX: World Book Encyclopedia Science Service, Inc., 1964), p. 219.

152   ***"festering resentment"*** Ben Bradlee Jr., *The Kid: The Immortal Life of Ted Williams* (New York: Little, Brown and Company, 2013), p. 645.

152   ***"Protestant"*** ... ***"My religion is"*** "TFB Form #50, U.S. Naval Air Training Center, Pensacola Florida," Official Military Personnel File for Theodore Williams, Courtesy of National Archives Catalog, U.S. National Archives and Records Administration.

152   ***"Once, I remember him"*** Claudia Williams, *Ted Williams, My Father* (New York: Ecco, 2014), p. 195.

152   ***"I don't pray"*** "Ted Prayed for Glenn; Buddies in Korea War," *Boston Globe*, February 22, 1962.

153   ***"Williams hoped that Glenn"*** "Ted Prayed for Glenn; Buddies in Korea War," *Boston Globe*, February 22, 1962.

153   ***"Williams called Glenn"*** "Ted Prayed for Glenn; Buddies in Korea War," *Boston Globe*, February 22, 1962.

153   ***"intuitive feeling"*** Ted Williams, "When to Quit," *Boston Globe*, June 17, 1962.

153   ***"We've always heard the"*** June 17, 1962, *Boston Globe*, Ted Williams, "When to Quit"

Chapter Eleven: The Slow Boring of Hard Boards

155   ***"We had some great"*** Jeff Jacobs, "Friendship Heaven," *Hartford Courant*, July 23, 2002.

155   ***"struck mild terror into"*** Frank Van Riper, *Glenn: The Astronaut Who Would Be President* (New York: Empire Books, 1983), p. 75.

155   ***"somewhat of an independent"*** Brady Black, "Taft Faces Fight Because He Chose Apprenticeship," *Cincinnati Enquirer*, January 26, 1964.

155   ***"a conservative Democrat"*** David R. Jones, "Glenn Enters Senate Race in Ohio," *New York Times*, January 18, 1964.

155   **"I'm not registered"** "Hometown Welcome for Astronaut Glenn," *Staunton (VA) Daily News Leader*, March 4, 1962.

156   **"how Annie is getting"** "Glenn Pays Visit to the President," *New York Times*, February 6, 1962.

156   **"Where's the monkey"** "Caroline Kennedy Cuts Spacemen Down to Size by Asking About Monkey," *Tampa Tribune*, February 27, 1962.

156   **"remained dry, just"** "Kennedys at Play Still Make Big Splashes," *Hartford Courant*, June 21, 1962.

157   **"a fantastic drama"** "In the Nation: Glenn's a Movie Star," *New York Daily News*, July 13, 1962.

157   **"He's the head of state"** David Miller, "'Wonderful,' Glenn Says of His Day," *New York Herald Tribune*, March 2, 1962.

157   **"Why Sears signed Ted"** "Why Sears signed Ted Williams—as a playing manager,"*Life*, March 2, 1962, p. 6.

157   **"to add a cold, professional"** "Why Sears signed Ted Williams—as a playing manager," *Life*, March 2, 1962, p. 6.

157   **"Most sleeping bags"** "Why Sears signed Ted Williams—as a playing manager," *Life*, March 2, 1962, p. 6.

158   **"the former 'Splendid'"** "'Splendid Splinter' No Longer Splinter," *Eureka Humboldt Standard*, January 21, 1966.

158   **"I couldn't do anything"** Milt Sosin, "Ted Williams' Wife Wins Divorce Here," *Miami News*, October 13, 1966.

158   **"moody and indifferent"** Mort Lucoff, "Ted Williams, Wife Try Again," *Miami News*, August 12, 1965.

158   **"Who are you?"** Ted Williams with John Underwood, *My Turn at Bat* (New York: A Fireside Book Published by Simon & Schuster, 1988), p. 222.

158   **"resemblance to Jackie Kennedy"** "Transition," *Newsweek*, June 24, 1968.

158   **"old flames"** Shelby Whitfield, *Kiss It Goodbye* (New York: Abelard-Schuman Published by Simon & Schuster, 1988), p. 33.

159   **"Fact is, Ted doesn't"** Shelby Whitfield, *Kiss It Goodbye* (New York: Abelard-Schuman Published by Simon & Schuster, 1988), p. 33.

159   **"When are you going to"** Jeane Hoffman, "Ted Williams' First Love, but Too Expensive," *Los Angeles Times*, March 27, 1957.

159   **"Never"** Jeane Hoffman, "Williams, Almost 40, Says He Would Never Manage Ball Club," *Los Angeles Times*, July 11, 1958.

159   *"No, definitely not"* Will McDonough, "Ted Sounds Off on Red Sox, Baseball," *Boston Globe*, February 1, 1966.

160   *"He's head and"* "NLV 'Glenn for President,'" *Las Vegas Review-Journal*, February 27, 1962.

160   *"I think [Glenn's]"* "NLV 'Glenn for President,'" *Las Vegas Review-Journal*, February 27, 1962.

160   *"I still wanted to"* The John H. Glenn, Jr., Oral History Project, Oral History Interview 20, Jeffrey W. Thomas, October 20, 2008, p. 15.

161   *"I guess along with every"* The John H. Glenn, Jr., Oral History Project, Oral History Interview 20, Jeffrey W. Thomas, October 20, 2008, p. 16.

161   *"The average American"* "Astronaut Glenn Says He'll Shoot for Senate," *Fort Worth Star Telegram*, January 18, 1964.

161   *"He has chosen to enter"* John W. Finney, "Capital Critical of Glenn's Move," *New York Times*, January 18, 1964.

161   *"I'm not going to allow"* Robert Crater, "Astronaut Nixes Use Of Name, Photo in Soft Drink Advertising," *Pittsburgh Press*, October 20, 1964.

162   *"I thought you gave a"* "Robert Kennedy's speech at Vanderbilt's 1968 Impact Symposium," Vanderbilt University Special Collections and University Archives, posted to YouTube, November 19, 2018.

162   *"one of the hardest"* John Glenn with Nick Taylor, *John Glenn: A Memoir* (New York: Random House, 2000) p. 501.

162   *"John Glenn had great"* Bob Greene, "When RFK Died, John Glenn Faced His Toughest Duty," *Wall Street Journal*, June 5, 2018.

163   *"responsibility toward"* Shelby Whitfield, *Kiss It Goodbye* (New York: Abelard-Schuman Published by Simon & Schuster, 1988) p. 44.

163   *"You have always flatly"* Red Smith, "Another Republican Answers the Call," *Washington Post*, February 18, 1969.

164   *"As a young boy, my"* Jim Prime and Bill Nowlin, *The Pursuit of Perfection: Ted Williams* (Champaign, IL: Sports Publishing, LLC, 2002), compact disc insert, provided by Ted Patterson, track 13.

164   *"A college associate of"* Memorandum written by Colgate S. Prentice to Richard H. Finch and Herbert G. Klein, May 27, 1960, courtesy of the Richard Nixon Presidential Library and Museum.

165   *"glorified bootlegger who"* Ben Bradlee, Jr., *The Kid: The Immortal Life of Ted Williams* (New York: Little, Brown and Company, 2013), p. 488.

165   *"Tell him I'm a"* S. L. Price, "Rounding Third," *Sports Illustrated*, November 25, 1996.

165   *"If You Don't Like"* Shelby Whitfield, *Kiss It Goodbye* (New York: Abelard-Schuman Published by Simon & Schuster, 1988) p. 38.

165   *"championship qualities"* "Athletes for Nixon" pamphlet, circa 1968, courtesy of the Richard Nixon Presidential Library and Museum.

166   *"Why start a rookie"* "Athletes for Nixon" pamphlet, circa 1968, courtesy of the Richard Nixon Presidential Library and Museum.

166   *"The help you gave"* Letter written by President Richard M. Nixon to Ted Williams, November 5, 1969, courtesy of the Richard Nixon Presidential Library and Museum.

166   *"one of the biggest"* "John Glenn: Fame No Fancy," *Washington Post*, March 5, 1972.

166   *"And then I had to make"* The John H. Glenn, Jr., Oral History Project, Oral History Interview 23, Jeffrey W. Thomas, June 19, 2009, p. 30.

167   *"the Colonel"* David Hess, "Metzenbaum Brawls Back in Late Start," *Akron Beacon Journal*, April 28, 1974.

167   *"never held a job"* Brad Tillson, "Metzenbaum Has Gilligan Boost," *Dayton Daily News*, April 19, 1974.

167   *"Howard, I can't believe"* Excerpt from John Glenn-Howard Metzenbaum Debate, May 4, 1974, courtesy of the Ohio State University Library.

168   *"Something is out of"* Tom Morganthau with Richard Manning and Howard Fineman, "Glenn Meets the Dream Machine," *Newsweek*, October 3, 1983.

168   *"I think most people"* The John H. Glenn, Jr., Oral History Project, Oral History Interview 23, Jeffrey W. Thomas, June 19, 2009, p. 21.

168   *"more than just about"* Michael Kramer, "John Glenn: The Right Stuff?," *New York*, January 31, 1983.

169   *"The room we were in"* Michael Kramer, "John Glenn: The Right Stuff?," *New York*, January 31, 1983.

169   *"exercised poor judgement"* Helen Dewar, "Panel Finds 'Credible Evidence' Cranston Violated Ethics Rules," *Washington Post*, February 28, 1991.

169   *"I think when the Keating"* Author interview with Scott Miller, February 3, 2021.

169   *"We made so many"* "Glenn Still Has the Right Stuff," *Cleveland Plain Dealer*, March 15, 2015.

169   *"He isn't just a man"* Dan Balz, "Methodical Hero With a Zest for Duty," *Washington Post*, January 15, 1984.

169   *"Everybody was getting"* Dan Balz, "Methodical Hero With a Zest for Duty, " *Washington Post*, January 15, 1984.

170   *"His thinking is not"* Dan Balz, "Methodical Hero With a Zest for Duty," *Washington Post*, January 15, 1984.

170   *"started to remind people"* David S. Broder, "Mondale reply wins important praise," *The Columbian (Vancouver, WA)*, September 29, 1983.

170   *"I wasn't doing* Hellcats *"* Steve Neal, "Glenn: Ex-Astronaut Finds Entering Presidential Orbit Is Tricky," *Chicago Tribune*, January 25, 1984.

170   *"During his 1980"* Howell Raines, "Glenn Joins the Race for Presidential Nomination," *New York Times*, April 22, 1983.

170   *"If I were you, I'd"* John Glenn: A Life of Service, John Glenn: 1984 Presidential Bid, PBS.org, Original airdate, July 17, 2013.

171   *"Why does John Glenn"* Microcassette recording- New Hampshire presidential campaign speeches and press conferences - circa 1983–1984, Courtesy of The John H. Glenn Archives at The Ohio State University, Box 8, Item 89, Location 01-7-32-02-07–1-1.

171   *"I think he felt"* Author interview with Scott Miller, February 3, 2021.

172   *"speaking style was"* Bill Sternberg, "John Glenn, the Last Hero," *USA Today*, December 8, 2016.

172   *"he puts people to sleep"* Bill Sternberg, "John Glenn, the Last Hero," *USA Today*, December 8, 2016.

172   *"Mr. Checklist"* David S. Broder, "Mr. Checklist, " *Washington Post*, October 18, 1982.

172   *"He's a technocrat"* David S. Broder, "Mr. Checklist," *Washington Post*, October 18, 1982.

172   *"new technologies"* Barbara Janesh, "Glenn Launches Presidential Campaign," *Zanesville (OH) Times-Recorder*, April 22, 1983.

172   *"We must have leadership"* Robert Shogan, "Sky Not Limit, Glenn Says as He Announces," *Los Angeles Times*, April 22, 1983.

172   *"He did not think"* Author interview with Greg Schneiders, January 27, 2021.

172   ***"Better electrical energy"*** Curtis Wilkie, "Glenn's Tendency to Ramble on the Stump," *Boston Globe*, January 11, 1984.

172   ***"Now, it turns out"*** Author interview with Greg Schneiders, January 27, 2021.

174   ***"portrait of an"*** John Leonard, "Books of the Times: The Splendid Splinter Sox It to 'Em," *New York Times*, July 8, 1969.

174   ***"the biggest signing"*** Merrell Whittlesey, "Senators' Collapse Gets No Sympathy," *Washington (D.C.) Evening Star*, September 6, 1969.

175   ***"He knows the slant of"*** Mike Gillooly, "The Case for Ted Williams: Surgeon Amazed Every Time Sox Slugger Hits Home Run," *Boston Herald*, January 16, 1958.

175   ***"It's as professorial"*** Jim Murray, "Ted's Book a Big Hit," *Los Angeles Times*, June 29, 1971.

175   ***"To the young baseball"*** Ted Williams with John Underwood, *The Science of Hitting* (New York: Simon and Schuster), p. 5.

176   ***"read the book cover"*** Philip Hersh, "America bids 'Kid' adieu," *Chicago Tribune*, July 6, 2002.

176   ***"there are certain good"*** Tom Jackson, "Plant's Wade Boggs-baby ruthless is ready for the pros," *Tampa Times*, April 24, 1976.

176   ***"chicks dig the"*** "Cy Youngs are looking old," Chuck Johnson, *The Courier-News* (Bridgewater, New Jersey), May 19, 1999.

176   ***"personal reasons"*** Harold McKinney, "Williams Resigns as Field Boss of Texas Rangers," *Fort Worth Star-Telegram*, October 1, 1972.

176   ***"Nixon had to do"*** George Minot, Jr., "Pundit Ted Williams Splinters Nixon's Critics," *Washington Post*, May 10, 1972.

177   ***"the greatest president"*** George Minot, Jr., "Pundit Ted Williams Splinters Nixon's Critics," *Washington Post*, May 10, 1972.

177   ***"those four guys make"*** George Minot, Jr., "Pundit Ted Williams Splinters Nixon's Critics," *Washington Post*, May 10, 1972.

177   ***"Good God, I think"*** Katherine Switzer, "Ted Williams Lays It on the Line," *Argosy*, July 1973.

178   ***"constantly swinging his bat"*** Peter Pascarelli, "Hitting It Off," *Philadelphia Inquirer*, March 10, 1984.

178   ***"one of the most natural"*** Peter Gammons, "Detroit Pondering Who's First at Third," *Boston Globe*, March 11, 1984.

178   ***"I can't vote for him"*** Glenn Schwarz, "Kingsman's Future Rides on Beating Out Lopes," *San Francisco Chronicle*, March 11, 1984.

178   ***"God it killed me that"*** Bob Costas interview with Ted Williams, *Costas Coast to Coast*, March 13, 1988, courtesy of the National Baseball Hall of Fame and Museum.

178   ***"He was momentarily crushed"*** Author interview with Steve Avakian, February 15, 2021.

Chapter Twelve: My Greatest Regret

179   ***"There is always something"*** "Ted's Speech," *Boston Globe*, August 18, 1953.

179   ***"I feel awful good up"*** "Williams Feels Good at Bat, But Says Legs Aren't Ready," *Berkshire Evening Eagle*, August 17, 1953.

180   ***"They weren't out to see"*** "15,000 Applaud Ted During Parade," *Boston Globe*, August 18, 1953.

180   ***"Ted is not a new friend"*** Red McQueen "Hoomalimali: Cancer Fund Gets $125,000 from Williams Dinner," *Honolulu Advertiser*, August 26, 1953.

181   ***"I'd heard this Williams"*** "Ted and Tommy Talk Some Baseball; Slugger Homers for a Sick Little Boy," *Chattanooga Times*, April 8, 1947.

181   ***"burned at the stake"*** "Glenny Fights Back Tears; Learns His Legs Are Gone," *Boston Globe*, May 14, 1947.

181   ***"He's very, very good"*** Bob Holbrook, "Children, Veterans Cheer Ted's Return," *Boston Globe*, May 13, 1955.

182   ***"In closing, I only wish"*** "Ted's Speech,"*Boston Globe*, August 18, 1953.

182   ***"It was like heaven when"*** Ian Thomsen, "Williams Goes to Bat for the Jimmy Fund," *Boston Globe*, November 11, 1988.

183   ***"I'd do anything asked"*** "Williams Gets Rousing Boston Ovation, Then 'Parks' Homer," *Fort Worth Star Telegram*, August 26, 1972.

183   ***"Every year we wanted"*** Tim Horgan, "A New Ball Game for Teddy," *Boston Herald*, November 4, 1988.

184   ***"I've gotten 10,000"*** Ian Thomsen, "Williams Goes to Bat for the Jimmy Fund," *Boston Globe*, November 11, 1988.

184   ***"I plan to win"*** "Glenn Predicts Three Southern Victories," *Kenosha (WI) Sunday News*, March 4, 1984.

184   ***"is very much alive"*** "Glenn Stays in Race," *Daily Hampshire Gazette*, March 14, 1984.

184   *"a poor way to"* Microcassette recording – presidential campaign interview on miscellaneous issues – circa 1983–1984, Courtesy of The John H. Glenn Archives at The Ohio State University, Box 8, Item 88, Location 01-7-32-02-07–1-1.

184   *"I know that we're not"* Microcassette recording – presidential campaign interview on miscellaneous issues – circa 1983–1984, Courtesy of The John H. Glenn Archives at The Ohio State University, Box 8, Item 88, Location 01-7-32-02-07–1-1.

185   *"the nature of the campaign"* Microcassette recording – presidential campaign interview on miscellaneous issues – circa 1983–1984, Courtesy of The John H. Glenn Archives at The Ohio State University, Box 8, Item 88, Location 01-7-32-02-07–1-1.

185   *"staring out the window"* Tom Price, "Glenn set for another 'blastoff,'" *Dayton Daily News*, February 15, 1987.

185   *"I guess in my whole"* Tom Price, "Glenn Set for Another 'Blastoff,'" *Dayton Daily News*, February 15, 1987.

186   *"ought to be ashamed"* John J. Casserly, "Ted Williams Says U.S. 'Not Trying to Win' in Korea," *Morning Call Allentown (PA)*, June 29, 1953, courtesy of United Press International.

186   *"Too often, I think"* July 10, 1985, Congressional Record, Task Force on Libraries and Memorials, Hearing on H.R. 2205.

186   *"cleanup hitter"* Korean War Memorial testimony - July 10, 1985, Courtesy of The John H. Glenn Archives at The Ohio State University, Box 2, Item 8, Location 01-7-07-12-04–1-2.

186   *"I guess I already have"* Korean War Memorial testimony - July 10, 1985, Courtesy of The John H. Glenn Archives at The Ohio State University, Box 2, Item 8, Location 01-7-07-12-04–1-2.

186   *"While he was standing"* Korean War Memorial testimony - July 10, 1985, Courtesy of The John H. Glenn Archives at The Ohio State University, Box 2, Item 8, Location 01-7-07-12-04–1-2.

187   *"I can't pass along those"* Korean War Memorial testimony - July 10, 1985, Courtesy of The John H. Glenn Archives at The Ohio State University, Box 2, Item 8, Location 01-7-07-12-04–1-2.

187   *"He's on everybody's"* "Will John Glenn Fly as Democrats' VP Nominee?," *San Luis Obispo, (CA) Country Telegram Tribune*, June 10, 1988

188   *"We tried to take advantage"* Ben Bradlee, Jr., interview of John H. Sununu, February 2, 2006, courtesy of the personal archives of Ben Bradlee, Jr.

188   ***"Tip, if Glenn's on"*** Mike Barnicle, "Musings from the Last Liberal," *Boston Globe*, July 19, 1988.

189   ***"Senator, you're no Jack"*** Jon Schwantes, "Ecstatic Texas Democrats Score It 'Lloyd 1, Duck 0,'" *Indianapolis News*, October 6, 1988.

189   ***"This is the Marine"*** VHS Copy of "An Evening with #9," November 10, 1988, courtesy of the personal archives of Ben Bradlee, Jr.

190   ***"As far as I'm concerned"*** VHS Copy of "An Evening with #9," November 10, 1988, courtesy of the personal archives of Ben Bradlee, Jr.

191   ***"ability to be strong"*** VHS Copy of "An Evening with #9," November 10, 1988, courtesy of the personal archives of Ben Bradlee, Jr.

191   ***"It's hard to beat that"*** VHS Copy of "An Evening with #9," November 10, 1988, courtesy of the personal archives of Ben Bradlee, Jr.

191   ***"And all I could see"*** VHS Copy of "An Evening with #9," November 10, 1988, courtesy of the personal archives of Ben Bradlee, Jr.

191   ***"That man right there"*** VHS Copy of "An Evening with #9," November 10, 1988, courtesy of the personal archives of Ben Bradlee, Jr.

Chapter Thirteen: No Cure for the Common Birthday

192   ***"Gee, I'm so fuckin'"*** Richard Ben Cramer, "What Do You Think of Ted Williams Now?," *Esquire*, June 1986.

193   ***"The last thing we need"*** Claudia Williams, *Ted Williams, My Father* (New York: Ecco, 2014), p. 196.

193   ***"I love this old guy"*** Joe Falls, "Williams Savors Dog Days of Life," *Fort Myers (FL) News-Press*, February 25, 1995.

193   ***"Since I've become"*** "Slugger's Best Friend," *Boston Globe*, July 22, 1994.

193   ***"not unlike a presidential"*** Dan Shaughnessy, "Museum of Hitting Artistry," *Boston Globe*, February 9, 1994.

194   ***"mobile condo"*** Keith C. Epstein and Tom Diemer, "Lost VP Bid May Cost Glenn More Than Pride," *Cleveland Plain Dealer*, July 18, 1988.

195   ***"Dad asked Ted about"*** Author interview with Lyn Glenn, March 6, 2021.

195   ***"When you fly in combat"*** Jeff Jacobs, "Friendship Heaven," *Hartford Courant*, July 23, 2002.

195   *"Now, Theodore, stop"* Ohio State University's John Glenn College of Public Affairs. Remarks by Secretary of Defense Jim Mattis, National Press Club, Washington, D.C.," June 20, 2017, courtesy of U.S. Department of Defense Information.

195   *"the most profane man"* David M. Shribman, "Astronaut Who Defined a Historic Era Hits Another Milestone," *Pittsburgh Post-Gazette*, July 17, 2011.

196   *"Here it was two weeks"* Richard Sisk, "The Right Stuff, 1998," *New York Daily News*, October 11, 1998.

196   *"For all the advances"* Patrick Jackson, "An Era Ends," *Zanesville (OH) Times Recorder*, February 21, 1997.

197   *"I think some of the romance"* Marjie Lambert, "Cost Brings Space Race to a Crawl," *Fresno Bee*, December 5, 1993.

197   *"The mind set of a few people"* Paul Wiseman, "NASA Cut Safety by Cutting Costs," *Cincinnati Enquirer*, June 10, 1986.

197   *"I'd like to go up"* "Glenn Flew 30 Years Ago Today," *Mansfield (OH) News Journal*, February 20, 1992.

198   *"I believed that America"* Author interview with Dan Goldin, May 16, 2022.

198   *"[They] put me through"* Joe Hoover, "John Glenn: 'This research is important to a lot of people,'" *Newark Advocate*, February 3, 1998.

198   *"I was really, really angry"* Author interview with David Glenn, February 24, 2021.

199   *"He came down for"* Author interview with Scott Parazynski, July 15, 2022.

199   *"Hell, he's in excellent"* Richard Sisk, "The Right Stuff, 1998," *New York Daily News*, October 11, 1998.

199   *"You bet I'll be there"* Richard Sisk, "The Right Stuff, 1998," *New York Daily News*, October 11, 1998.

199   *"I stepped on him"* Gordon Edes, "He's Still Big Hit," *Boston Globe*, March 25, 1998.

199   *"Bring the damned"* Claudia Williams, *Ted Williams, My Father* (New York: Ecco, 2014), p. 235.

200   *"He was only 10 feet"* Author interviews with Larry Taylor, January 22, 2021 and June 16, 2022.

200   ***"I am privileged beyond"*** Tom Brokaw interview of Ted Williams
on NBC News live coverage, October 29, 1998, courtesy
of NBC News and NBC Universal.

201   ***"a great senator"*** Tom Brokaw interview of Ted Williams
on NBC News live coverage, October 29, 1998, courtesy
of NBC News and NBC Universal.

201   ***"Ted was great"*** Tom Brokaw interview of Ted Williams
on NBC News live coverage, October 29, 1998, courtesy
of NBC News and NBC Universal.

201   ***"Those were dangerous"*** Tom Brokaw interview of Ted Williams
on NBC News live coverage, October 29, 1998, courtesy
of NBC News and NBC Universal.

201   ***"That's my friend!"*** Jeff Jacobs, "Friendship Heaven," *Hartford Courant,*
July 23, 2002.

201   ***"I never admired anybody"*** Mitchell Zuckoff, "Earthbound Stars,
Regular Folk Join Festivities for a VIP Sendoff," *Boston Globe*, October
30, 1998.

201   ***"When he got up into"*** Author interview with Scott Parazynski, July
15, 2022.

202   ***"Count Dracula"*** Michael Cabbage, "'I Wish There Were Words to
Describe What It's Like,'" *Orlando Sentinel*, November 2, 1998.

202   ***"bloodlettings"*** Michael Cabbage, "'I Wish There Were Words to
Describe What It's Like,'" *Orlando Sentinel*, November 2, 1998.

202   ***"I pray every day"*** Michael Cabbage, "'I Wish There Were Words to
Describe What It's Like,'" *Orlando Sentinel*, November 2, 1998.

203   ***"He grabbed me by"*** Greg Pearson, *Fenway Fanatics: 50 Boston Red Sox
Fans Tell Their Stories* (New York: Ecco, 2014), p. 185.

204   ***"We hit it off"*** Author interview with Larry Taylor, January 22, 2021.

204   ***"As I told John Glenn"*** Bob Broeg, "Museum Shows Teddy Ballgame
in Top Form," *St. Louis Post-Dispatch*, March 16, 1997.

205   ***"Normally you have to"*** Antonya English, "Slugging Great a Hit at
Baseball Ceremony," *Tampa Bay Times*, February 16, 1999.

205   ***I had never in my life even"*** Joseph White, "The Splendid Splinter at
80: A Baseball Mind Forever Sharp," *Corvallis Gazette Times*, November
11, 1998.

205   ***"What a man he"*** Jeff Schweers, "Splendid Splinter Views Dawn
Launch," *Florida Today*, May 28, 1999.

205   *"recruited"* Furman Bisher, "Heavy Hitters Go to Bat for Jackson," *Atlanta Journal*, November 25, 1998.

205   *"He wasn't sure if"* Ben Bradlee, Jr., *The Kid: The Immortal Life of Ted Williams* (New York: Little, Brown and Company, 2013), p. 691.

206   *"We were all in"* Author interview with Sean McDonough, April 1, 2022.

207   *"The Marine Corps was"* Mike Barnicle, "Ted Williams, the Real John Wayne," *New York Daily News*, July 7, 2002.

207   *"For months afterward"* Claudia Williams, *Ted Williams, My Father* (New York: Ecco, 2014), p. 241.

207   *"Gentlemen, start your"* Allen Lessels, "Williams Becomes a Starter," *Boston Globe*, July 12, 1999.

207   *"I've watched them on"* Yuri Pride, "Craven Finally Has a Reason to Smile," *Concord Monitor*, July 12, 1999.

208   *"His eyes lit up"* Author interview with Saul Wisnia, June 14, 2022.

208   *"I just remember feeling"* Author interview with Saul Wisnia, June 14, 2022.

Chapter Fourteen: Losing a Great Friend

209   *"[Williams] was very stoic"* Ben Bradlee, Jr., *The Kid: The Immortal Life of Ted Williams* (New York: Little, Brown and Company, 2013), pp. 696–697.

209   *"we're gonna be together"* Notes, entitled "Videotape, Ted Williams, 1999 and 2000 N.H. Baseball Dinner, Manchester, N.H.," courtesy of the personal archives of Ben Bradlee, Jr.

209   *"ashes mixed with Slugger's"* Peter Kersotis, "Ted Williams' Ordeal Drags On," *Florida Today*, July 5, 2003.

209   *"Ted loved Slugger so"* Ben Bradlee, Jr., *The Kid: The Immortal Life of Ted Williams* (New York: Little, Brown and Company, 2013), p. 697.

210   *"John-Henry would come"* Author interviews with Rick Ruoff, February 6, 2022, and June 21, 2002.

210   *"It's almost a bittersweet"* Paul Doyle, "The Kid's Kid Takes Some Hits," *Hartford Courant*, November 5, 2000.

210   *"His son would come"* Author interview with Robert Hogerheide, January 31, 2022,

210   *"Sign, sign, sign. They"* "Son Tough on Williams, Friends Say," *Palm Beach Post*, July 13, 2002.

211   ***"Dad wanted to get"*** Author interview with Lyn Glenn, February 24, 2021.

211   ***"Ted Williams is a"*** Tom Brokaw interview of Ted Williams on NBC News live coverage, October 29, 1998, courtesy of NBC News and NBC Universal.

212   ***"It was disgusting"*** Ben Bradlee, Jr., *The Kid: The Immortal Life of Ted Williams* (New York: Little, Brown and Company, 2013), p. 694.

212   ***"demanding that his father"*** Ben Bradlee, Jr., *The Kid: The Immortal Life of Ted Williams* (New York: Little, Brown and Company, 2013), p. 691.

213   ***"I've never been very"*** Ira Berkow, "Ted Williams Still Living on His Terms," *New York Times*, November 9, 2000.

213   ***"How is he?"*** Larry Tye, "Words Speak Volumes in Williams's Recovery," *Boston Globe*, March 16, 2001.

213   ***"It meant that right"*** Larry Tye, "Words Speak Volumes in Williams's Recovery," *Boston Globe*, March 16, 2001.

214   ***"He had some salty"*** Ben Bradlee, Jr., interview of John Glenn, October 25, 2004, courtesy of the personal archives of Ben Bradlee, Jr.

214   ***"I had a lot of nightmares"*** Author interview with Glenn Koocher, June 22, 2022.

214   ***"John Glenn only"*** "Is There a Meffid to Their Madness?," *Patriot Ledger*, April 7, 2001.

214   ***"I'm feeling pretty"*** Dan Shaughnessy, "Spirit Won't Be Muted," *Boston Globe*, September 30, 2001.

214   ***"The first thing he wanted"*** Jeff Jacobs, "Friendship Heaven," *Hartford Courant*, July 23, 2002.

215   ***"I was very encouraged"*** Jules Crittenden and Franci Richardson, "Pals: Williams Was Unable to Write in Final 18 Months," *Boston Herald*, July 13, 2002.

215   ***"celebration of his life"*** Dan Shaughnessy, "Son Abides: No Funeral Services," *Boston Globe*, July 6, 2002.

216   ***"I got to know Ted very"*** "Ted Williams: A Celebration of an American Hero," July 22, 2002, courtesy of New England Sports Network.

216   ***"Baseball may have lost"*** "Ted Williams: A Celebration of an American Hero," July 22, 2002, courtesy of New England Sports Network.

216   ***"She was both upset about"*** Author interview with Beth Daley, June 23, 2022.

217   *"sprinkled at sea"* Letter written by Ted Williams to Robert E. McWalter, Esquire, December 19, 1991, courtesy of the personal archives of Ben Bradlee, Jr.

217   *"put in bio-statis after"* Richard Sandomir, "Note Dated 2000 Says Williams Wanted His Remains Frozen," *New York Times*, July 26, 2002.

217   *"There's no way"* Peter Kerasotis, "Ted Williams' Ordeal Drags On," *Florida Today*, July 5, 2003.

217   *"John-Henry had just"* Author interview with Larry Taylor, January 22, 2021.

218   *"told me we could sell"* Beth Daley, "Williams Daughter: Body Being Frozen," *Boston Globe*, July 6, 2002.

218   *"They thought John-Henry"* Author interview with John Heer, June 22, 2022.

218   *"John-Henry could be difficult"* Author interview with Richard Kerensky, February 7, 2022 and March 30, 2023.

219   *"The aftershock was"* Author interview with Beth Daley, June 23, 2022.

219   *"Tedsicles"* Leigh Montville, *Ted Williams: The Biography of an American Hero* (New York: Broadway Books, 2004), p. 470.

219   *"Top Ten Good Things"* "Morning Buzz," *Sports Business Journal*, July 10, 2002.

219   *"secret weapon"* John Danziger, *Morning Call Allentown (PA)*, July 14, 2002, p. A18.

219   *"It's Ted Williams, who's"* John Danziger, *Morning Call Allentown (PA)*, July 14, 2002, p. A18.

219   *"Defrost Ted"* Author personal recollection.

219   *"knowledge about my"* Statement by Bobby-Jo Williams Ferrell, July 10, 2002, courtesy of John Heer.

219   *"John Glenn appreciated"* Statement by Bobby-Jo Williams Ferrell, July 10, 2002, courtesy of John Heer.

220   *"In my visits and conversations"* Untitled document from folder labeled "Williams Ted, tribute to, July 22, 2002," Courtesy of The John H. Glenn Archives at The Ohio State University, Box 106, Folder 41, Location 01-7-09–07-05-0-1.

220   *"I'm sure they're"* Joe Burris, "Glenn Pays Respect to Proud Fighter Pilot," *Boston Globe*, July 23, 2002.

220   *"I was surprised at"* Ben Bradlee, Jr., interview of John Glenn, October 25, 2004, courtesy of the personal archives of Ben Bradlee, Jr.

220   *"is not resting upside"* Tom Verducci, "What Really Happened to Ted," *Sports Illustrated*, August 18, 2003.

221   *"neuroseparation"* CNN Transcript, *American Morning*, "Battle Over a Legend," August 14, 2003.

221   *"joked about 'throwing"* Tom Verducci, "What Really Happened to Ted," *Sports Illustrated*, August 18, 2003.

221   *"batting practice"* Nathaniel Vinton, "Cold, Cruel Truth About Ted's Head," *New York Daily News*, October 2, 2009.

222   *"I've made a mistake"* Bill Madden, "Sends Chills Up His Spine," *New York Daily News*, February 19, 2003.

222   *"All I could think"* Bill Madden, "Sends Chills Up His Spine," *New York Daily News*, February 19, 2003.

222   *"I think you're talking"* CNN Transcript, *American Morning*, "Battle Over a Legend," August 14, 2003.

Chapter Fifteen: Fighter Pilot, Astronaut, US Senator

223   *"I'd rather burn out"* David M. Shribman, "Astronaut Who Defined a Historic Era Hits Another Milestone," *Pittsburgh Post-Gazette*, July 17, 2011.

223   *"There were a number of"* Author interview with Sweeny Murti, June 24, 2022.

224   *"Ted was a good friend"* Sweeny Murti interview of John Glenn, August 26, 2012, courtesy of CBS New York.

224   *"That was a thrill"* Marla Ridenour, "Space Legend Electrifies Tribe Game," *Akron Beacon Journal*, August 27, 2012.

224   *"a Republican college"* Julie Carr Smyth, "Former Astronaut: Evolution Should Be Taught in Schools," *Dayton Daily News*, May 22, 2015.

224   *"People intend to believe"* Joshua Chaney, "John Glenn Donates $50,000 to Museum," *Coshocton Tribune*, October 21, 2006.

225   *"It's not every day"* Mark McCarty, "Springsteen Raises His Voice for a Cause," *Dayton Daily News*, October 7, 2008.

225   *"He said he was probably"* Author interview with Captain Kent Ewing, January 25, 2021.

226   *"Annie was a severe"* Julie Carr Smyth, "Astronaut John Glenn, 93, Weathers Health Difficulties," *Fort Collins Coloradoan*, May 15, 2015.

226   ***"It's quite a thing"*** Marla Matzer Rose, "Taking Flight," *Columbus Dispatch*, June 29, 2016.

226   ***"He was a hero long"*** Jessica Wehrman, "Burial of John Glenn – Among the heroes," *Columbus Dispatch*, April 7, 2017.

227   ***"[That was] so like John"*** Jessica Wehrman, "Burial of John Glenn – Among the heroes," *Columbus Dispatch*, April 7, 2017.

Epilogue

228   ***"He liked him, he"*** Author interview with David Glenn, February 24, 2021.

229   ***"Williams called Glenn"*** "Ted Prayed for Glenn; Buddies in Korea War," *Boston Globe*, February 22, 1962.

229   ***"He put family life aside"*** Dave Davies interview with Ben Bradlee, Jr., *Fresh Air*, National Public Radio, December 3, 2013.

230   ***"All I want out of life"*** Arthur Daley, "Sports of the Times: Hail and Farewell," *New York Times*, September 30, 1960.

231   ***"an excellent combat"*** "Glenn: 'Ted Stood for Excellence,'" *Tampa Bay Tribune*, July 6, 2002.

231   ***"Ted only batted"*** VHS Copy of "An Evening with #9," November 10, 1988, courtesy of the personal archives of Ben Bradlee, Jr.

231   ***"Godspeed, John Glenn"*** "Godspeed, John Glenn,'" *Chicago Tribune*, December 9, 2016.

231   ***"[I] don't if it's"*** Joe Posnanski, "A Bleeping American Hero," https://joeposnanski.substack.com, December 9, 2016.

231   ***"Supposedly they were"*** Joe Posnanski, "A Bleeping American Hero," https://joeposnanski.substack.com, December 9, 2016.

Index